D0731813

VISUAL C#® 2005 DEMYSTIFIED

JEFF KENT

McGraw-Hill

New York Chicago San Francisco Lisbon London
Madrid Mexico City Milan New Delhi San Juan
Seoul Singapore Sydney Toronto

The McGraw·Hill Companies

McGraw-Hill
2100 Powell Street, 10th Floor
Emeryville, California 94608
U.S.A.

To arrange bulk purchase discounts for sales promotions, premiums, or fund-raisers, please contact **McGraw-Hill** at the above address.

Visual C#® 2005 Demystified

1234567890 CUS CUS 0198765

ISBN 0-07-226170-6

Acquisitions Editor
Wendy Rinaldi

Project Editor
Samik Roy Chowdhury (Sam)

Acquisitions Coordinator
Alexander McDonald

Technical Editor
Ron Petrusha

Copy Editor
Bart Reed

Proofreader
Debbie Liehs

Indexer
WordCo Indexing Services

Composition
International Typesetting
and Composition

Illustration
International Typesetting
and Composition

Cover Series Design
Margaret Webster-Shapiro

Cover Illustration
Lance Lekander

This book was composed with Adobe® InDesign® CS Mac.

I would like to dedicate this book to the two most important women in my life, my mom, Beatrice Baumgarten Kent, who gave up her career as a chemist for the even more important career of a mom; and my wife, Devvie Schneider Kent, who, in addition to being my best friend and lover, also is the #1 expert in C# at our home.

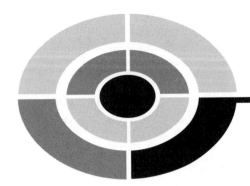

ABOUT THE AUTHOR

Jeff Kent is an Associate Professor of Computer Science at Los Angeles Valley College in Valley Glen, California. He teaches a number of programming languages, including C#, Visual Basic, C++, Java, and—when he's feeling masochistic—Assembler. He also manages a network for a Los Angeles law firm whose employees are guinea pigs for his applications, and as an attorney gives advice to young attorneys whether they want to hear it or not. He also has written several books on computer programming, recently *Visual Basic.NET: A Beginner's Guide and C++ Demystified* for McGraw-Hill, and wrote *Visual Basic 2005 Demystified* concurrently with this book.

Jeff has had a varied career—or careers. He graduated from UCLA with a Bachelor of Science degree in economics and then went on to obtain a Juris Doctor degree from Loyola (Los Angeles) School of Law and to practice law. During this time, when personal computers were still a gleam in Bill Gates's eye, Jeff was also a professional chess master, earning a third place finish in the United States Under-21 Championship and, later, an international title.

Jeff does find time to spend with his wife, Devvie, which is not difficult since she is also a computer science professor at Valley College. In addition to his other career pursuits, he has a part-time job as personal chauffeur for his teenage daughter Emily (his older daughter Elise now has her own driver's license), and what little spare time he has, he enjoys watching international chess tournaments on the Internet. His goal is to resume running marathons, since otherwise, given his losing battle to lose weight, his next book may be *Sumo Wrestling Demystified*.

CONTENTS

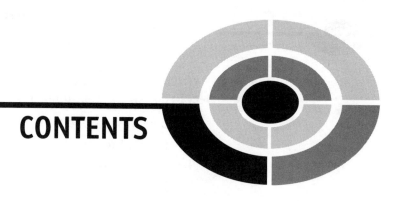

ACKNOWLEDGMENTS

It seems obligatory in acknowledgments for authors to thank their publishers (especially if they want to write for them again), but I really mean it. This is my sixth book for McGraw-Hill, and I hope there will be many more. It truly is a pleasure to work with professionals who are nice people as well as very good at what they do (even when what they are very good at is keeping accurate track of the deadlines I miss).

I first want to thank Wendy Rinaldi, who got me started with McGraw-Hill back in 1998 (has it been that long?). Wendy was also my first acquisitions editor. She has since received several well-deserved promotions, but is still my acquisitions editor. Indeed, this book was launched through a telephone call with Wendy at the end of a vacation with my wife Devvie, who, being in earshot, and with an are-you-insane tone in her voice, asked incredulously "You're writing another book?" I replied, "Of course not, honey ..." She interjected, "That's a relief!" I then continued, "... I'm writing two books." (I wrote *Visual Basic 2005 Demystified* concurrently with this book).

I must also thank my Acquisitions Coordinator, Alexander McDonald, and my Project Editor, Samik Roy Chowdhury (Sam). Both were unfailingly helpful and patient, while still keeping me on track in this deadline sensitive business (e.g., I'm so sorry you broke both your arms and legs; you'll still have the next chapter turned in by this Friday, right?").

Bart Reed did the copyediting. He was kind about my obvious failure during my school days to pay attention to my grammar lessons. He improved what I wrote while still keeping it in my words (that way if something is wrong it is still my fault).

Ron Petrusha was my technical editor. Ron's suggestions were quite helpful and added a lot of value to this book.

There were many other talented people working behind the scenes who also helped get this book out to press, and as in an Academy Award speech, I can't list them all. That doesn't mean I don't appreciate all their hard work, because I do.

I truly thank my wife Devvie, who in addition to being my wife, best friend (maybe my only one), and partner (I'm leaving out lover because computer programmers aren't supposed to be interested in such things), tolerated my incessant muttering about unreasonable chapter deadlines and merciless editors (sorry, Alex) while excusing myself from what she wanted to do (or wanted me to do). Similarly, I would like to give thanks to my daughters Elise and Emily and my mom, Bea Kent, for tolerating my absent-mindedness while I was preoccupied with unreasonable chapter deadlines and merciless editors (starting to notice a pattern here?). I also should thank my family in advance for not having me committed when I talk about writing my next book.

INTRODUCTION

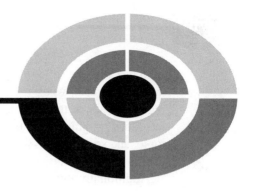

One of my favorite movie lines is in *Rocky III* when Mr. T (playing a boxer called Clubber Lang), who had beaten up Rocky badly in their first fight, says before their rematch, "Fool, you never should have come back."

Visual Studio must be saying this to me. A few years ago I wrote a book, *Visual Basic .NET: A Beginner's Guide*, timed to be on the bookshelves for the release of Visual Basic .NET, a component of Visual Studio .NET. Writing such a "day and date" book is added pressure, especially given that Microsoft is famous (or infamous) for last-minute changes from their most recent beta.

I must have a short memory or be a slow learner. With the next major change in Visual Studio, version 2005, here I go again writing another "day and date" book (actually two of them, as mentioned later).

Why Did I Write This Book?

Given my griping about writing another "day and date" book, you may legitimately wonder why I wrote this book. I assure you that the reason was not because I thought it would get me riches, fame, or beautiful women. I may be misguided, but I'm not completely delusional or, in the case of my wife's reaction to the beautiful women part, suicidal.

To be sure, there likely will be many introductory-level books on Visual C# 2005. Nevertheless, I wrote this book because I believe I bring a different and, I hope, valuable perspective.

As you may know from my author biography, I teach computer science at Los Angeles Valley College, a community college in the San Fernando Valley area of Los Angeles, where I grew up and have lived most of my life. I also write computer programs, but teaching programming has provided me with insights into how students learn that I could never obtain from just writing programs. These insights are gained not just from answering student questions during lectures. I spend hours each week in our college's computer lab helping students with their programs, and more hours each week reviewing and grading their assignments. Patterns emerge regarding which teaching methods work and which don't, the order in which to introduce programming topics, the level of difficulty at which to introduce a new topic, and so on. I joke with my students that they are my beta testers in my never-ending attempt to become a better teacher, but there is much truth in that joke.

Additionally, my beta testers... err, students, seem to complain about the textbook no matter which book I adopt. Many ask me why I don't write a book they could use to learn C#. They may be saying this to flatter me (I'm not saying it doesn't work), or for the more sinister reason that they will be able to blame the teacher for a poor book as well as poor instruction. Nevertheless, having written other books, these questions planted in my mind the idea of writing a book that, in addition to being sold to the general public, also could be used as a supplement to a textbook.

Who Should Read This Book

Anyone who will pay for it! Just kidding, although no buyers will be turned away.

It is hardly news that publishers and authors want the largest possible audience for their books. Therefore, this section of the introduction usually tells you this book is for you, whoever you may be and whatever you do. However, no programming book is for everyone. For example, if you exclusively create game programs using Java, this book may not be for you (though being a community college teacher I may be your next customer if you create a space beasts vs. community college administrators game).

Although this book of course is not for everyone, it very well may be for you. Many people need or want to learn C#, either as part of a degree program, job training, or even a hobby. Unfortunately, many books don't make learning C# any easier, throwing at you a veritable telephone book of complexity and jargon. By contrast, this book, as its title suggests, is designed to "demystify" C#. Therefore, it goes straight to the core concepts and explains them in logical order and in plain English.

What This Book Covers

I strongly believe that the best way to learn programming is to write programs. The concepts covered by the chapters in this book are illustrated by programs you can write using tested and thoroughly explained code. You can run this code yourself and also use it as the basis for writing further programs that expand on the covered concepts.

Because, in my opinion, the best way to learn programming is to write programs, the first part of this book is designed to get you up and running with Visual C# 2005. Chapter 1 is titled "Getting Started with Your First Windows Program." The first step in programming in Visual C# 2005 is to obtain and install it. This chapter advises you how. The chapter then shows you how you can create your first Visual C# 2005 project. This chapter concludes by explaining core concepts such as what a computer program is, what a programming language is, and how your code is translated for the computer.

Chapter 1 shows you how to create a working Windows application without having to write any code. However, you will need to write code for even the simplest program. Therefore, Chapter 2, "Writing Your First Code," is about just that. This chapter explains key programming concepts, such as classes, objects, and properties, as well as gives you a tour of the Visual C# 2005 Integrated Development Environment (IDE). The chapter then describes the event-driven nature of a Windows application. The chapter finally shows you how to put this theory into practice by creating an event procedure.

Chapters 1 and 2 focus on the form, perhaps the most important part of a Windows application's graphical user interface (GUI). However, a form cannot possibly meet all the requirements of a Windows application. For example, the form does not have the functionality to permit the typing of text, listing of data, selecting of choices, and so forth. You need other, specialized controls for that additional functionality. Indeed, the form's primary role is to serve as a host, or container, for other controls that enrich the GUI of Windows applications, such as menus, toolbars, buttons, text boxes, and list boxes. Chapter 3, titled "Controls," explains how to add controls to your form and manipulate their properties. This chapter then uses a project to demonstrate how you can use a control's events in an application.

Now that you are up and running with Visual C# 2005, the next part of this book covers the building blocks of your programs—variables, data types and operators—starting with Chapter 4, "Storing Information—Data Types and Variables." Most computer programs store information, or *data*. Data comes in different varieties, such as numeric or text. The type of information, whether numeric, text, or Boolean, is referred to as the data type, and often is stored in a variable, which not only reserves the amount of memory necessary to store information, but also provides you with a name by which that information later may be retrieved. Finally, this chapter covers constants, which are similar to variables, but differ in that their initial value never changes while the program is running.

As a former professional chess player, I have marveled at the ability of chess computers to play world champions on even terms. The reason the chess computers have this ability is because they can calculate far more quickly and accurately than we can. Chapter 5, "Letting the Program Do the Math—Arithmetic Operators," covers arithmetic operators, which we use in code to harness the computer's calculating capabilities.

Now that we have covered the programming building blocks, it is time to use them in the next part of this book, which concerns controlling the flow of your program. As programs become more sophisticated, they often branch in two or more directions based on whether a condition is true or false. For example, although a calculator program would use the arithmetic operators you learn about in Chapter 5, your program first needs to determine whether the user has chosen addition, subtraction, multiplication, or division before performing the indicated arithmetic operation. Chapters 6, "Making Comparisons—Comparison and Logical Operators," introduces comparison and logical operators, which are useful in determining a user's choice. Chapter 7, "Making Choices—if and switch Case Control Structures," introduces the if and switch statements, which are used to direct the path the code will follow based on the user's choice.

When you were a child, your parents may have told you not to repeat yourself. However, sometimes your code needs to repeat itself. For example, if an application user enters invalid data, your code may continue to ask the user whether they want to retry or quit until the user either enters valid data or quits. Chapter 8, "Repeating Yourself—Loops and Arrays," introduces loops, which are used to repeat code execution until a condition is no longer true. This chapter then discusses arrays. Unlike the variables we had covered thus far in the book, which may hold only one value at a time, arrays may hold multiple values at one time. Additionally, arrays work very well with loops.

This book is a few hundred pages long. Imagine how much harder this book would be to understand if it consisted of only one, very long chapter, rather than being divided into multiple chapters, with each one divided into sections? Chapter 9, "Organizing Your Code with Methods," shows you how you similarly can divide up your code into separate methods. This has advantages in addition to making your code easier to understand. For example, if a method performs a specific task, such as sending output to a printer, which is performed several times in a program, you only need to write once in a method the code necessary to send output to the printer. Then you can call that method each time you need to perform that task. Otherwise, the code necessary to send output to the printer would have to be repeated each time that task was to be performed. Further, if you later have to fix a bug in how you perform that task, or simply find a better way to perform the task, you only have to change the code in one place rather than many.

The next part of this book focuses on the graphical user interface (GUI), starting with Chapter 10, "Helper Forms." Up until now, our applications have had one form that serves as the main application window. This one form may be sufficient for a simple application, but as your applications become more sophisticated, the main application form will become unable to perform all the tasks required by the application and need help from other forms. This chapter shows you how to create and use two dialog forms that will be workhorses in your applications—a built-in dialog form, the message box, and programmer-designed dialog forms. Although these dialog forms are helpful, they also present programming challenges involving communication between the main form and the dialog form. For example, the main form needs to know which button was clicked on the dialog form, and should execute different code depending on which button was clicked. Additionally, because the dialog form contains controls, the main form needs to know and take actions based on what the application user typed, checked, or selected in the controls in the dialog form. This chapter will show you how to solve these programming challenges.

Application users give commands to an application, such as to open, save, or close a file, print a document, and so on, through the GUI of the application. Chapter 11, "Menus," and Chapter 12, "Toolbars," cover the three most common GUI elements through which application users give commands to an application: the menu, shortcut or context menus, and toolbars. Additionally, commands such as Cut, Copy, and Paste often may be duplicated in a menu, a context menu, and a toolbar, providing the application user with the convenience of three different ways to perform the same command. However, you don't want to write the same code three times, so these chapters show you how to connect corresponding items in menus, context menus, and toolbars so they each execute the same code.

When I was finished writing this book for the evening, I closed Microsoft Word, and maybe even shut down my computer. Of course, the next evening I did not have to start over; what I had written the previous evening had been saved. However, up until now the programs in this book don't save data so that it will be available even after the applications exit. The next part of this book shows you how to save data. Chapter 13, "Accessing Text Files," explains how to write code that reads from and writes to a text file. This chapter also shows you how to add to your program Open and Save dialog boxes, such as those used in sophisticated programs like Microsoft Word, so you can open a text file to read from it, and save to a text file to write to it. Chapter 14, "Databases," explains how to write programs that access information stored in a database.

Throughout this book we have been writing Windows applications, which to be sure are heavily used. However, many of us are interacting ever more frequently with the subject of Chapter 15, "Web Applications." This chapter shows you how to create a web application that displays information from a database, similar to the Windows application you created in Chapter 14.

How to Read This Book

I have organized this book to be read from beginning to end. Although this may seem patently obvious, my students often express legitimate frustration about books (or teachers) that, in discussing a programming concept, mention other concepts that are covered several chapters later or, even worse, not at all. Therefore, I have endeavored to present the material in a linear, logical progression. This not only avoids the frustration of material that is out of order, but also enables you in each succeeding chapter to build on the skills you learned in the preceding chapters.

Special Features

Each chapter has detailed code listings so you can put into practice what you have learned. My overall objective is to get you up to speed quickly, without a lot of dry theory or unnecessary detail. So let's get started. It's easy and fun to write C# programs.

Contacting the Author

Hmmm! I guess it depends why. Just kidding. Although I always welcome gushing praise and shameless flattery, comments, suggestions, and, yes, even criticism also can be valuable. The best way to contact me is via e-mail; you can use jkent@genghiskhent.com. The domain name is based on my students' fond (?) nickname for me, Genghis Khent. Alternatively, you can visit my website: http://www.genghiskhent.com. Don't be thrown off by the entry page; I use this site primarily to support the online classes and online components of other classes that I teach at the college, but there will be a link to the section that supports this book.

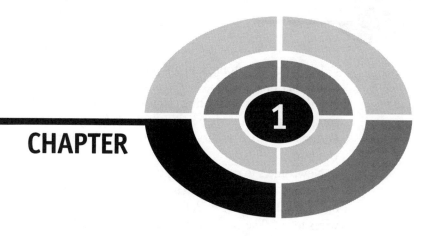

CHAPTER

Getting Started with Your First Windows Program

You probably have seen on television an interviewer ask a victorious athletes for the secret of their success. Can you imagine the athletes replying that they never trained but instead just read about their sport a lot? I doubt it. The only way to become a good swimmer, runner, or weightlifter is to swim, run, or lift weights. Of course, good coaching helps, but a good swimmer must swim, a good runner must run, and a good weightlifter must lift weights.

Although computer programming is mental rather than physical exercise, similarly you cannot become a good computer programmer only by reading about computer programming. Instead, you have to write computer programs—lots of them.

Don't get me wrong, I'm not trying to discourage you from buying a book, especially this one! A good book is like a good coach, making your learning more efficient and less frustrating. However, even with the best book, if you don't write computer programs, it will be difficult for you to learn computer programming. Fortunately, it is easy to start writing computer programs; this chapter will show you how.

Newcomers to programming sometimes shy away from writing programs because something may go wrong. They may think of scenes in action movies where someone has only seconds to defuse a bomb and they have to guess which one of several wires to cut. The consequences in those circumstances of making a mistake are life and death.

However, you are not defusing a bomb. You are writing a computer program. If you do make a mistake in your program, neither you nor your computer will disappear in a fireball. You just correct the mistake. Indeed, you learn best from your mistakes.

Since I have given you this speech on the importance of your writing programs, it is only fair that I help you get started writing programs. The first step is for you to obtain and install Visual C# 2005. In this chapter, I first will help you choose the edition of Visual C# 2005 that is best for you, and assist you in ensuring that your computer meets the hardware requirements of Visual C# 2005. After you install Visual C# 2005, I will show you how to use it to create a Windows application. Finally, you will learn just what a computer program is.

Obtaining and Installing Visual C# 2005

Visual C# 2005 comes in several editions. This section will help you choose the one right for you. However, before you buy any edition of Visual C# 2005, you should confirm that the computer on which you will install Visual C# 2005 meets the hardware requirements of Visual C# 2005.

Once you have purchased Visual C# 2005 and verified that the installation computer meets the hardware requirements, you are ready to install Visual C# 2005. This section will give you tips on the installation.

System Requirements

Installing Visual C# 2005 requires not only the right software, but hardware sufficient to run the software. Therefore, you should first confirm that the computer on which you are going to install Visual C# 2005 meets the system requirements, such as the operating system, processor, RAM, and available hard disk space.

NOTE *I will be referring in this chapter to Visual C# 2005, but my comments apply whether you are buying Visual C# 2005 alone or one of the editions of Visual Studio 2005, as discussed in the next section, "Choosing the Right Version."*

Here are my recommendations on the key requirements. Keep in mind these system requirements are truly the minimum requirements; therefore, Visual C# 2005 may run quite slowly if your computer only meets these bare-minimum requirements.

- **Operating system**   You must have Windows 2003, XP, or 2000; Windows NT, 95, 98, or Me will not work. If you have not yet purchased an operating system and are considering XP, I would recommend the Professional over the Home Edition, especially if you are developing web applications, which are discussed in Chapter 15.

- **Available hard drive space**   The requirement varies with the edition and type of installation and whether other components such as Internet Explorer (IE) already are installed on your computer. You should plan on the total installation taking between 2GB (gigabytes) and 5GB. A large (at least 80GB) hard drive is relatively inexpensive and easy to install, so if remaining space on your existing hard drive is scarce, you may wish to consider upgrading before installing Visual C# 2005.

- **Processor**   According to Microsoft, a processor speed of 600MHz (megahertz) is the minimum and 1GHz (gigahertz) is recommended. If you are on the borderline, given that upgrading a processor by replacing the motherboard is not so inexpensive or easy, another alternative is boosting your system RAM, next discussed.

- **RAM**   According to Microsoft, 128MB (megabytes) is the minimum, and 256MB is recommended. I would recommend 512MB, especially if you are running other programs at the same time.

Additionally, Visual C# 2005, in order to work properly, needs other software to be on your computer, in particular IE. If you are installing Visual C# 2005 at work and your company restricts browsers to Netscape or other non-IE browsers, you should check first with your system administrator before attempting to install Visual C# 2005 there.

Choosing the Right Version

You can buy Visual C# 2005 either by itself or as part of Visual Studio 2005, which includes, in addition to Visual C#, support for other programming languages such as C++ and Visual Basic. I recommend Visual Studio 2005 if your budget allows.

The additional cost usually is not that substantial, and you will have a program that works with other commonly used languages if your education, employment, or interests prompt you to work with other programming languages. This is more likely than you may think. Once you learn one programming language, learning additional ones becomes much easier because the concepts are essentially the same. Indeed, most programmers don't learn just one language.

If you buy Visual C# 2005 by itself, you have one choice: the Express Edition. If you instead buy Visual C# 2005 as part of Visual Studio 2005, you have three choices: Standard, Professional, and Team System Editions.

If you already have a copy of Visual C# 2005 through your school or job, any of the preceding choices should work fine for this book. If you do not already have a copy of Visual C# 2005, I recommend that you obtain the Academic version of the Professional Edition. The Academic version represents a substantial discount for students and teachers.

Microsoft's website on Visual Studio 2005, http://lab.msdn.microsoft.com/vs2005/ at the time this book was written (Microsoft does reorganize its website from time to time, so this location may change), has a product matrix that lists the differences between the editions.

Installing Visual C# 2005

Now you are ready to install Visual C# 2005! You will find it easy. The Visual C# 2005 installation may consist of more than one CD, depending on the edition. It is a large program, so it takes some time to install. However, Visual C# 2005 is not difficult to install. Installation is simply a matter of following directions and being patient. Patience is important in programming, and so it is with the installation of Visual C# 2005.

One unusual feature is that the help for Visual C# 2005 is not built into the program but instead is a separate program, MSDN Library. MSDN is an acronym for Microsoft Developer Network. This help also comes on one or more CDs, depending on the edition.

Starting Your First Visual C# 2005 Project

Now you're going to create your first Visual C# 2005 project. You not only will use this project for this chapter, but you also will use it as the starting point for the project in the next chapter.

NOTE   The following instructions assume you purchased Visual Studio 2005. However, the same basic information applies if you purchased Visual C# 2005 Express Edition, though some of the screenshots may look slightly different.

Starting the Program

Although you use Visual C# 2005 to create programs, it is itself a program. You start Visual C# 2005 by choosing All Programs from the Start menu, selecting the folder called Microsoft Visual Studio 2005, and then clicking the icon of the same name that appears in the submenu.

When you first start Visual Studio 2005, a form will display, asking you to choose your default environment settings (see Figure 1-1).

I chose General Development Settings, but you can choose the Development Settings for Visual C# or one of the other programming languages. I don't consider this choice an important issue because the various settings are not that different. I chose General Development Settings because that setting is the most generic and would work equally well if you are also programming in another language supported by Visual Studio 2005, such as Visual Basic.

The Start Page will display next, as shown in Figure 1-2.

Now you are ready to begin. So let's get started!

Figure 1-1   Choosing your default environment settings.

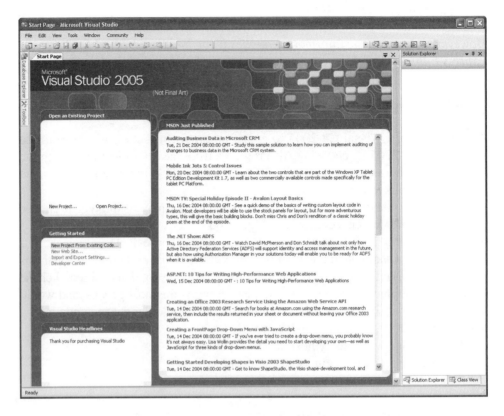

Figure 1-2   Start Page.

Specifying the Type of New Project

Because we want to create a new project, choose New from the File menu and then choose Project from the New submenu. This will display the New Project dialog box shown in Figure 1-3.

The left pane of the New Project dialog box lists project types. Project types are included for each of the languages in Visual Studio 2005. In addition to Visual C#, these are Visual Basic, Visual C++, and Visual J#. Because this book is about Visual C# 2005, choose Visual C#.

The right pane of the New Project dialog box lists templates for the various types of Visual C# applications you can create. A project template helps you get started by creating the initial files, code, and other settings for the selected project.

You certainly have a lot of templates to choose from. The ones starting with Windows CE or Pocket PC can be run on handheld computers, and the ones starting

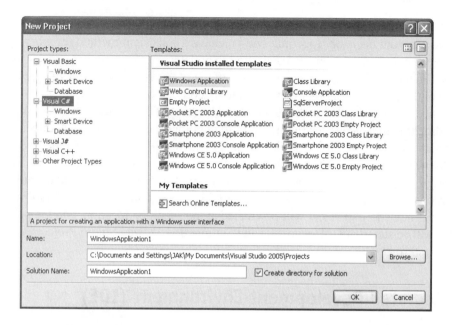

Figure 1-3 New Project dialog box.

with Smartphone can be run from phones. However, for most of this book, we will be creating Windows applications, so select Windows Application from the right pane. I will be discussing in Chapter 2 what a Windows application is. For now, just know that Microsoft Word and Excel are examples of Windows applications. Each has a window (or windows) in which you work, with a menu, toolbar, and other visual components with which you can interact.

As shown in Figure 1-3, when you choose the Windows Application project template, the description beneath the Project Types frame becomes, "A project for creating an application with a Windows user interface."

Specifying the Name and Location of the Project

The lower part of the New Project dialog box lists the name of and location for your project. The default name for your first project is WindowsApplication1, for the second WindowsApplication2, and so on. You should change this default name to one that will help you identify this project later. Otherwise, after you have created many projects, you may not recall what WindowsApplication52 did as opposed to WindowsApplication53.

The location for your project is up to you; the default location should work fine. Whatever your decision, I recommend you have a consistent method for where you store your projects so you can easily find them later.

In Figure 1-4, I have changed the name of the project to FirstProject and the location of the project to another drive, D, on my computer.

Once you are satisfied with the name and location of the project, click OK. Visual Studio 2005 then generates the files and folders for your first project. A folder with the same name as the project is also created in the location displayed in the Location field, which contains the parent folder where your project files will be located. Thus, in Figure 1-4, because the project will be located in D:\Documents and Settings\ JAK\Visual Studio Projects\Visual C# and the name of the project is FirstProject, a folder named FirstProject will be created at the specified location, and the project files will be stored at D:\Documents and Settings\JAK\Visual Studio Projects\Visual C#\FirstProject.

Integrated Development Environment (IDE)

Figure 1-5 shows a view of the Windows application FirstProject that is created after you click the OK button in the New Project dialog box.

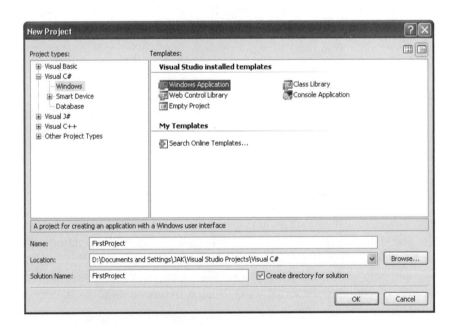

Figure 1-4   Changing the default name of and location for the project.

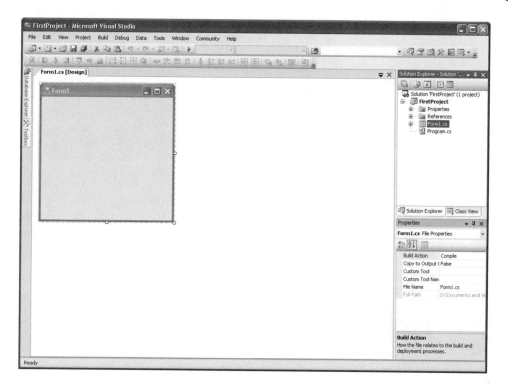

Figure 1-5 Newly created project.

Figure 1-5 displays what is called an Integrated Development Environment (IDE). The term "development environment" refers to Visual Studio 2005's role as an application to assist you in developing applications. The term "integrated" means that the tools to design your application, and the environment for writing, testing, and running your code, are all together under one (software) roof.

The IDE is complex, with many windows that perform many different functions. Don't worry; you don't need to know right away what they all do. Various components of the IDE will be introduced, described, and explained in this and succeeding chapters.

Run the Project!

We now will use the IDE to run the project. To run this project as an application, you must build additional files. You do so, naturally enough, from the Build menu,

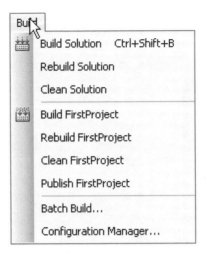

Figure 1-6 Build menu.

shown in Figure 1-6. From the Build menu, you choose one of the following four options:

- Build Solution
- Rebuild Solution
- Build FirstProject
- Rebuild FirstProject

NOTE *The name following "Build" in the third choice and "Rebuild" in the fourth choice is FirstProject because we changed the name of the project to FirstProject. If we had kept the default project name of WindowsApplication1, these menu items instead would be Build WindowsApplication1 and Rebuild WindowsApplication1.*

As will be explained later in this chapter, *building* means using the compiler to translate your code into machine language the computer can understand.

The difference between the Build menu items Build Solution and Build FirstProject is that the first concerns a solution and the second a project. A project contains all the files and links necessary for your application. A solution may contain multiple projects. Because the current application is simple and concerns only one project, there is no practical difference in this instance between the two menu commands.

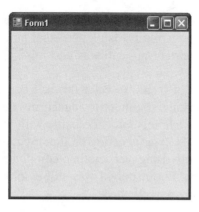

Figure 1-7   Windows application running.

The difference between Build and Rebuild is that if you previously have built your program, Build just builds the changes you made from the previous build, whereas Rebuild starts over and rebuilds the whole program. Rebuild consequently takes longer, so it is used when there have been extensive changes since the last build.

As a practical matter, there is little difference between the two commands. If you choose Build and the changes since the last build have been too extensive to avoid a rebuild, Visual C# 2005 will perform a rebuild instead. The additional time a re-build requires over a build is very minor, especially if you have a fast processor and ample RAM.

You now have a working Windows program without writing a single line of code! From the Debug menu, choose either Start or Start Without Debugging. The result is a window named Form 1, shown below in Figure 1-7.

The state of your project while it is running is referred to as *run time*. The state of your project before you run it, and after it stops running (such as when you click the close button of the form) is referred to as *design time*.

You now have created a working computer program. However, just what exactly is a computer program, and how does a programming language such as Visual C# 2005 fit in? The next sections answer those questions.

What Is a Computer Program?

You probably interact with computer programs many times during an average day. I certainly do. The other day, I arrived at the community college where I teach and found that my computer didn't work, so I called tech support. At the other end of the telephone line, a computer program forced me to navigate a voicemail menu maze and then tortured me while I was on perpetual hold with repeated insincere messages about how important my call was and false promises about how soon I would get through.

Finally my computer got fixed. To calm down, I decided to take a break and logged onto my now-working computer to launch my favorite game program, in which community college administrators do battle with hideous alien insects from the planet Megazoid. While I was cheering on the insects, the network administrator caught me goofing off using yet another computer program that monitors employee computer usage. Fortunately, I was still employed, so an accounts payable program generated my payroll check.

On my way home I decided I needed some cash and stopped at an ATM, where a computer program confirmed (hopefully) I have enough money in my bank account and then instructed the machine to dispense the requested cash and (unfortunately) deduct that same amount from my account.

Computers are so widespread in our society because they have three advantages over us humans. First, computers can store huge amounts of information. Second, computers can recall that information quickly and accurately. Third, computers can perform calculations with lightning speed and perfect accuracy.

The advantages that computers have over us even extend to thinking sports such as chess. I used to be a professional chess player. Although I have not played seriously for many years and am out of practice, I still was surprised that the chess program on my little Pocket PC handheld computer defeated me with ease. Even worse, the program, Pocket Fritz, taunted me in a German accent: "Dumpkopf, you have blundered again. You will now be liquidated!" My one victory was finding the mute button to silence this insolent program.

At least I have good company in defeat. In 1997, the computer Deep Blue beat the world chess champion, Garry Kasparov, in a chess match. In 2003, Kasparov was out for revenge against another computer, Deep Junior, but only drew the match. Kasparov, although perhaps the best chess player ever, is only human and therefore no match for the computer's ability to calculate and to remember prior games.

However, we have one very significant advantage over computers. We think on our own, whereas computers don't, at least not yet anyway. Indeed, computers fundamentally are far more brawn than brain. A computer cannot do anything without step-by-step instructions from us telling it what to do. These instructions are called a *computer program*, and of course are written by a human, namely a computer programmer. Computer programs enable us to harness the computer's tremendous power.

What Is a Programming Language?

When you enter a darkened room and want to see what is inside, you turn on a light switch. When you leave the room, you turn the light switch off.

The first computers were not too different from that light switch. These early computers consisted of wires and switches in which the electrical current followed a path dependent on which switches were in the on (one) or off (zero) position. Indeed, I built such a simple computer when I was a kid (which according to my kids was when dinosaurs still ruled the earth).

Each switch's position could be expressed as a number, 1 for the on position and 0 for the off position. Thus, the instructions given to these first computers, in the form of positions on switches, essentially were a series of ones and zeroes.

Today's computers of course are far more powerful and sophisticated than these early computers. However, the language computers understand, called *machine language*, remains the same, essentially ones and zeroes.

Although computers think in ones and zeroes, the humans who write computer programs usually don't. Additionally, a complex program may consist of thousands or even millions of step-by-step machine language instructions, which would require an inordinately long amount of time to write. This is an important consideration because, due to competitive market forces, the amount of time within which a program has to be written is becoming increasingly less and less.

Fortunately, we do not have to write instructions to computers in machine language. Instead, we can write instructions in a "higher-level" programming language such as Visual C# 2005. The term "higher level" means Visual C# 2005 (and other languages such as C++, Java, Visual Basic, and so forth) are far closer to the structure and syntax of human language than to the ones and zeroes understood by a computer. By contrast, machine language, although a programming language, is "low level" because it is far closer to the ones and zeroes understood by a computer than it is to the structure and syntax of human language. Additionally, code can be written much faster with programming languages than machine language because of programming languages abstract instructions; one programming language instruction can cover many machine language instructions.

Visual C# is but one of many programming languages. Other popular programming languages include Java, Visual Basic, and C++, and there are many more. Indeed, new languages are being created all the time. However, all programming languages have essentially the same purpose, which is to enable a human programmer to give instructions to a computer.

There really is no one "best" programming language, but Visual C# is an excellent choice. Although Visual C# is a relatively new language, it is increasingly used in the industry.

You may be wondering how this discussion of programming language applies given that you didn't have to write any code to achieve a working application. Although you didn't have to write any code, that doesn't mean code wasn't written. Remember when you chose the project template? Visual C# 2005 wrote code for you to create a basic Windows application.

Translating the Code for the Computer

Although you will understand the Visual C# code you will write, the computer won't. Computers don't understand Visual C# or any other programming language. They understand only machine language.

Visual C# 2005 includes a compiler. In general, a compiler translates the code you write into corresponding machine language instructions. There are different compilers for different programming languages, but the purpose of the compiler is essentially the same—the translation of a programming language into machine language—no matter which programming language is involved.

NOTE As discussed in more detail in Chapter 2, the compiler in Visual C# 2005 translates the code into an intermediate language that then is translated into machine language.

A compiler translates the code you write into corresponding machine language instructions, or into instructions that an operating system can understand and act on. However, the compiler can perform this translation only if your code is in the proper syntax for that programming language. Visual C# 2005, like other programming languages, and indeed most human languages, has rules for the spelling of words and for the grammar of statements. If there is a syntax error, the compiler cannot translate your code into machine language instructions and instead will call your attention to the syntax errors. Thus, in a sense, the compiler acts as a spell checker and grammar checker.

Conclusion

The way to become a good computer programmer is to write programs. To get started, you need to obtain and install Visual C# 2005. In this chapter, you learned about the different editions of Visual C# 2005 that are available, and how to ensure that your computer meets the hardware requirements of Visual C# 2005. After you installed Visual C# 2005, you learned how to use Visual C# 2005 to create a Windows application.

This chapter then discussed what a computer program is. Computers can store huge amounts of information, recall that information quickly and accurately, and perform calculations with lightning speed and perfect accuracy. However, computers cannot think on their own; they need step-by-step instructions from us telling them what to do. These instructions are called a *computer program*, written be a human computer programmer in a programming language such as Visual C# 2005. A compiler translates the computer program into machine language that a computer understands.

The computer program in this chapter simply displayed an empty form, or window. In the next chapter, you will examine that form further, and in the process learn what a Windows application is and then write your first code!

Quiz

1. What is the difference between Visual C# 2005 and Visual Studio 2005?

2. Which operating system do you need to install and run Visual C# 2005?

3. Which project template should you use to start creating a Windows application?

4. What is an IDE?

5. What is a computer program?

6. What is a programming language?

7. What is machine language?

8. What does "higher level" mean in the context of a programming language?

9. What does "lower level" mean in the context of a programming language?

10. What is the purpose of a compiler?

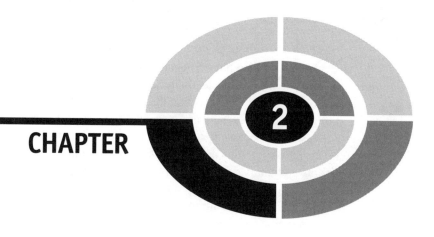

Writing Your First Code

When I was an elementary school student (back when dinosaurs roamed the earth, as far as my daughters are concerned), I learned through countless teacher-imposed exercises to multiply and divide several-digit numbers in my mind. Fast-forwarding more decades than I care to count, when I ask my daughters to compute the answers to less complex math homework problems, they whip out their calculators and tell me the answer—quite quickly and accurately, to be sure. When I then ask them instead to calculate the answer in their heads, they look at me as a prehistoric relic and tell me, "Aw, Dad, no one does that anymore."

Calculators do make our lives easier. Imagine the long line at your local fast food outlet if orders had to be calculated by pencil and paper rather than with the calculators built into cash registers. In business, software programs such as Microsoft Excel enable you to perform spreadsheet calculations in minutes that might take you hours with pencil and paper.

Calculators also have a negative side effect, however. Human nature being what it is, if we don't *need* to learn something, we may decide it is not worth the time and trouble. Research suggests that the availability of calculators has contributed substantially to a decline in students' computational skills. Despite calculators, computational skills still are necessary, not just in everyday situations in which a calculator may not be available, but also as a foundation for students to develop skills in creating algorithms and analyzing problems—skills essential in, among other areas, computer programming.

Just as calculators automate computation, Visual C# 2005 automates the creation of applications. For example, creating a Windows application strictly through code is difficult. By contrast, Chapter 1 shows that Visual C# 2005 enables you to create a Windows application without writing a single line of code! Granted, the resulting Windows application was basic, being no more than a window with default functionality. Nevertheless, even creating such a basic Windows application strictly through code would be no small undertaking.

There is a danger of Visual C# 2005 doing too much for beginning programmers. They may be seduced by how easy Visual C# 2005 makes creating a Windows application. Consequently, they may just plunge in and start writing programs without really understanding the code they are writing or how the different parts of the program fit together. I have witnessed this with my programming students. They try to write more complex programs, are unable to do so because they don't understand the necessary foundation, become frustrated, and quit.

Therefore, to make a long story short ("too late," as my daughters would say), this chapter will explain what an event-driven Windows application is all about, including how and why the code you write executes when the user takes an action such as a mouse click. But don't worry, this chapter is not all theory. You also will put in practice what you learned and write your first code!

Starting an Existing Project

Because you learn programming best by writing programs, start Visual C# 2005. In Chapter 1 you created a new Windows application project. In this chapter, we will use that existing project instead of creating a new one. Of course, we could create a new project, but you already learned in Chapter 1 how to do that. By instead using an existing project, you will learn something new.

To open an existing project, choose Open from the File menu and then Project/ Solution from the Open submenu, as shown in Figure 2-1. This will display the Open Project dialog box shown in Figure 2-2.

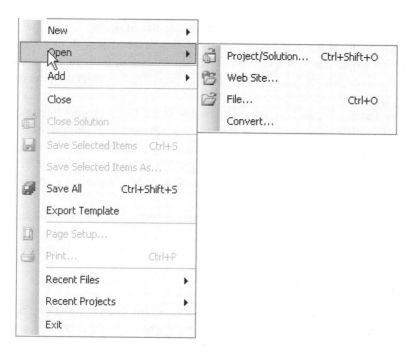

Figure 2-1   Opening an existing project.

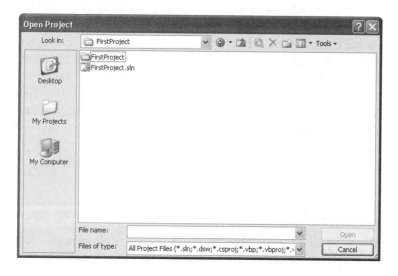

Figure 2-2   Open Project dialog box.

Using the Look In drop-down box, navigate to the folder where you saved First-Project when you created it in Chapter 1. You then will see a file with an .sln extension, named FirstProject.sln in Figure 2-2. The .sln extension indicates a solution file. As explained in Chapter 1, a solution contains one or more projects (here, one) used for your application.

Choose the .sln file and click the OK button in the Open Project dialog box. The Open Project dialog box will close and your FirstProject then should open, appearing as it did when you first created it in Chapter 1.

One of the windows in the project is called Solution Explorer, shown in Figure 2-3. If you don't see it, you can display it by choosing Solution Explorer from the View menu, as shown in Figure 2-4.

We will use Solution Explorer and the View menu to further examine features of this project.

Design View and Code View

You learned in Chapter 1 that the state of your program when it is running is referred to as *run time*, whereas the state of your program when it is not running is referred to as *design time*. In this section, we will be working in design time.

You can view your application two different ways during design time: designer view and code view. You choose designer view when you want to design your form, such as by resizing it, or adding to it controls such as buttons, labels, and text boxes. You choose code view when you want to view or write the code of your application.

You implement designer view by first selecting Form1.cs (the name of your form file) in Solution Explorer and then choosing Design from the View menu. An alternative is to right-click the form and choose View Designer from the shortcut menu. Either way, you will see the form, as shown in Figure 2-5.

You implement code view by first selecting Form1.cs in Solution Explorer and then by choosing Code from the View menu. Again, the alternative is to right-click the form and choose View Code from the shortcut menu. Either way, you will see code, as shown in Figure 2-6.

We will be working in both designer and code views in this chapter.

Object Browser

While in designer view, display the Object Browser by choosing Object Browser from the View menu. The Object Browser should appear as shown in Figure 2-7.

Figure 2-3 Solution Explorer.

Click the expander (plus sign) next to FirstProject and then highlight Form1. The Object Browser then should appear as shown in Figure 2-8.

The Object Browser, as its name suggests, permits you to browse or examine objects in your project, including the form. As Figure 2-8 shows, the lower-right pane of the Object Browser refers to "public class Form1." A similar reference to

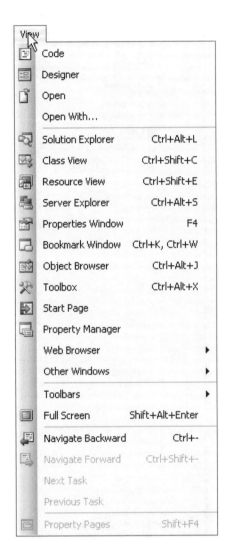

Figure 2-4 View menu.

"public partial class Form1" is in the code shown in Figure 2-6. Additionally, the lower-right pane of the Object Browser indicates the following: "public class Form1 : System.Windows.Forms.Form." This means that a "class" named Form1 "inherits" from System.Windows.Forms.Form.

What this terminology means is important in understanding how your first project and your future Windows application projects work. Therefore, let's now discuss this terminology.

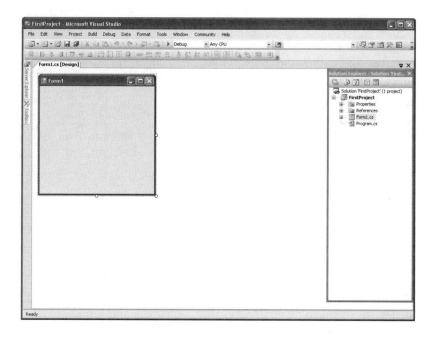

Figure 2-5   Form in designer view.

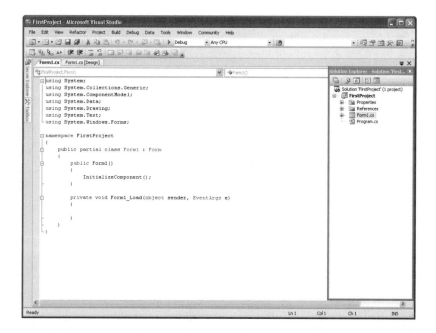

Figure 2-6   Code view.

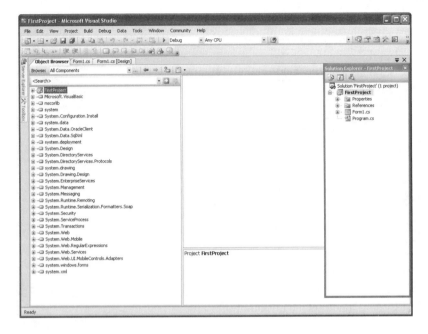

Figure 2-7   Object Browser.

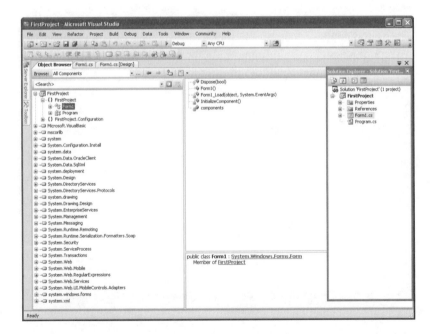

Figure 2-8   Object Browser showing information on Form1.

Classes and Objects

Most programs keep track of information that relates to persons, places, or things in the real world. Such information often is complex, consisting of numerous items. For example, each of my readers is a person, and as such share certain characteristics common to all persons, such as a name, height, weight, gender, age, and so forth.

Programming languages, including Visual C#, use classes to represent a person, place, thing, or concept. Thus, in programming parlance, each of us is an object of the Person class. A *class* is a pattern or template for an object, and an object is an instance of a class.

To illustrate, if my classroom contains 29 students and me as the teacher, there would be 30 objects of the Person class. Once again, each person's name, height, weight, gender, and age may differ from another's, but each of us in the room, being an object of the same class, Person, has certain common characteristics, such as a name, height, weight, gender, and age. The values of these characteristics are likely to vary—two persons are likely to have different names and heights, for example, but they share the characteristics themselves (that is, having a name, a height, and so forth).

As another example, the form in our first project originated from the Form class. The Form class represents, not surprisingly, a form. A form has a number of characteristics, such as height, width, background color, text on its title bar, and so forth. Although all forms have these characteristics in common, the values of these characteristics may differ from form to form. Just as persons in a room may look different, so can forms. Some forms may be short and wide and have a blue background, and others may be tall and thin and have a yellow background. However, each of these different-looking Form objects is created from the same Form class.

Inherits

The actual name of the class of the form in our application is not Form, but Form1. The Form1 class inherits, or starts out with, all the characteristics of the Form class. However, we can customize the Form1 class, even adding characteristics. We won't do that now, but we could.

Namespaces

As the lower-right pane of the Object Browser in Figure 2-8 indicates, the actual name of the Form class is System.Windows.Forms.Form. This means that the Form class is part of the System.Windows.Forms namespace.

To explain a namespace, let's make an analogy to the taxonomy of life you may have learned about in a biology class. All life is organized into separate kingdoms, the most commonly known being Animalia for animals and Plantae for plants. The animal kingdom is organized into several phylums, including Chordata for vertebrates. The vertebrates in the phylum Chordata are organized into several kingdoms, including Mammalia for mammals. The mammals in Mammalia belong to different orders, including Primates for primates. Primates are subdivided into different families, including Hominidae, which in turn are subdivided into different genera, including Homo, which finally are subdivided into species, including Homo sapiens. Thus, although in biology humans generally are referred to just by their species name, Homo sapiens, that species belongs to the Animalia.Chordota.Mammalia. Hominidae.Homo namespace.

Similarly, the Form class is part of the System.Windows.Forms namespace. The "Windows" in the namespace name stands for Windows applications. One purpose of using namespaces is to organize code in a hierarchal manner. Another purpose is the ability to use the same class name, but in another namespace. For example, there is another Form class in the System.Web.UI.MobileControls namespace. This namespace is used for forms in web applications accessed by mobile devices, such as Pocket PCs. By contrast, the Form class in the System.Windows.Forms namespace is used for Windows applications that run from desktop or laptop computers. Both classes have the same name, Form, but may do so because each belongs to a different namespace.

.NET Framework

The Form class and the System.Windows.Forms namespace are defined in the .NET Framework. You will see references to the .NET Framework and .NET throughout this book, so this would be a good time to briefly explain what these terms mean.

.NET is the name for Microsoft's strategy of software that is independent of a particular operating system or hardware. With respect to hardware, .NET projects are not limited to the traditional desktop computer. Instead, as you may recall from Chapter 1, the available templates for a Visual C# project include ones that can be run on handheld computers or phones. Visual Studio is a tool for the development of .NET applications.

The .NET Framework consists of the Common Language Runtime (CLR) and Class Libraries. As discussed in Chapter 1, a compiler translates the code you write into machine language instructions that an operating system can understand and act on. To make a long story short, the CLR acts as a middleman between the compiler and the ultimate machine language instructions, translating intermediate language created by the compiler into the instructions. The Class Libraries include the Form class and the System.Windows.Forms namespace, as well as many other classes that we will be using in this book.

Properties

A class generally has properties. For example, the Form class has properties such as Height for its height, BackColor for its background color, and Text for text on its title bar. Thus, objects created from the Form class have these properties. Similarly, objects created by classes that inherit from the Form class, such as the Form1 class, also have these properties.

Different classes may have some properties in common. For example, the Form class has a Height property, as would a Person class. However, often one class will have a property another does not. For example, a Person class may have an Eye-Color property, which the Form class does not have, whereas the Form class has a MinimizeBox property (pertaining to the minimize button at the upper right), which a Person class would not have. At least I have never seen a Person class with a minimize box!

Properties Window

While in designer view, choose Properties Window from the View menu. This will display the Properties window, as shown in Figure 2-9.

The Properties window lists various attributes or characteristics of the form, such as its height and width, background color, the text that appears in its title bar, and so forth. These attributes or characteristics, also referred to as *properties*, are listed in the left column. The values of these properties are listed in the right column. For example, in Figure 2-9, the value of the Text property is Form1, which is the text that appears in the title bar of the form in Figure 2-5.

The first button sorts the properties by category. This is the view in Figure 2-9. The second button sorts the properties in alphabetical order. This is the view in Figure 2-10. Don't worry about the other three buttons for now. We'll discuss the fourth icon from the left, which looks like a lightning bolt, later in this chapter in the section "Creating an Event Procedure Stub."

Many of the properties in Figures 2-9 and 2-10 have values. You did not assign those values to those properties. Rather, the IDE assigned those values because the form needs some background color, size, and so forth when you first create the application. These IDE-assigned values are referred to as default values. "Default" in this context refers to a property's value if you do nothing to change that value.

However, as the next section discusses, you may change default values.

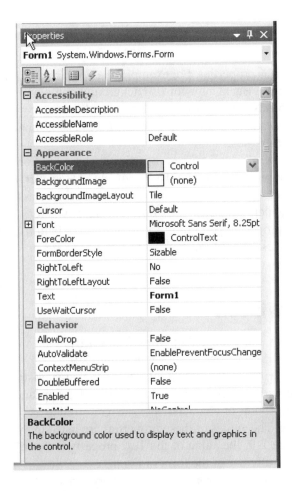

Figure 2-9   Properties window.

Changing Properties at Design Time

You can use the Properties window to view the properties of the form object in your first project. You also can use the Properties window to change the value of properties of that form object at design time. For example, in the Properties window, change the value of the Text property to MyForm or some other name and then press ENTER. The text in the form's title bar will change to MyForm or whatever other text you typed.

However, you cannot use the Properties window to change the value of properties of the form object at run time. Instead, you need to write code to change the value of properties of the form object at run time. You will learn in this chapter how

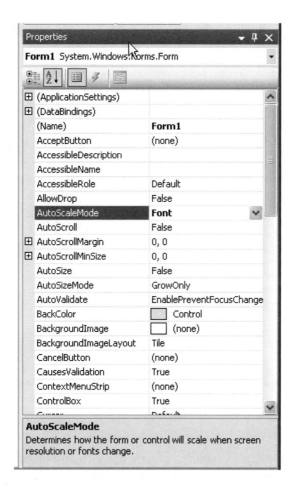

Figure 2-10   Properties listed in alphabetical order.

to do that. However, before we get there, let's first discuss what a Windows application is, because the answer will help you understand the code you will be writing.

What Is a Windows Application?

Nowadays the majority of applications are written for at least one if not more of the Windows operating systems, which include Windows 9x, NT, 2000, XP, and 2003. Figure 2-11 shows a familiar Windows application, Notepad, which is included by default in the installation of all Windows operating systems.

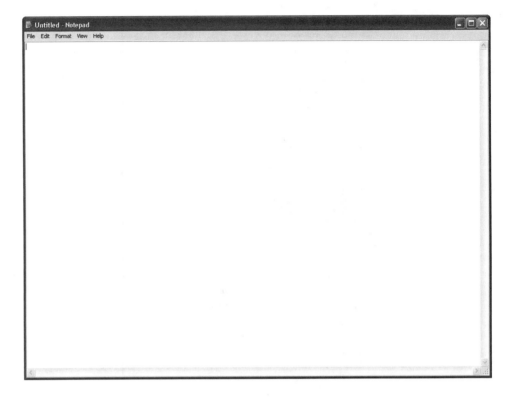

Figure 2-11 Notepad, a Windows application.

Although the Windows operating system has virtually taken over the computer world, it has not been with us that long. Windows was not introduced until 1985, and did not catch on until the introduction of Windows 3.0 in the early 1990s. Prior to the 1990s, applications often ran in the DOS operating system. Figure 2-12 shows a DOS text editor, the DOS equivalent of Notepad in the Windows operating system. A comparison of the DOS text editor in Figure 2-12 and Notepad in Figure 2-11 show that DOS applications have a decidedly different and less rich appearance than Windows applications.

The difference between DOS and Windows applications is more than skin deep. They also behave very differently. Let's now look at both differences.

Windows Applications Are "Gooey"

The hallmark of a Windows application is that the application is displayed in ... you guessed it, a window. However, there is more to a Windows application than a window.

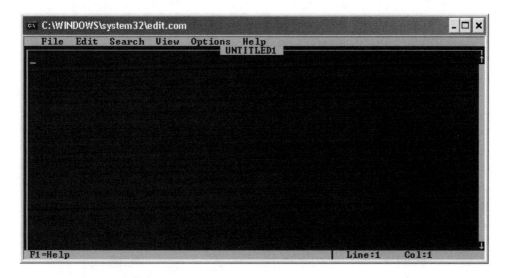

Figure 2-12   A console.

A Windows application has a graphical user interface, which is often referred to by the acronym GUI, pronounced "gooey."

A GUI usually includes a menu, such as the File, Edit, Format, View, and Help menus in Notepad, as shown in Figure 2-11. The DOS text editor in Figure 2-12 also includes a menu. However, a GUI is not limited to a menu, and normally includes other visual components, such as buttons to click, edit boxes in which to type text, and so on. DOS applications have few of these other visual components.

The GUI makes Windows applications prettier than console applications, but it serves a more important purpose, which is to make Windows applications easier to use. For example, the menu in Notepad makes it easy for you to open a file. Clicking the File menu and then the Open submenu displays another visual component, the Open dialog box (shown in Figure 2-13), from which you simply pick the file you want to open.

Figure 2-14 shows the Open dialog box in the DOS text editor. This Open dialog box is far clumsier to use than the Windows counterpart in Figure 2-13.

Of course, nothing is free in this world. The pretty GUI of a Windows application comes at a programming price. Code, lots of it, some of it rather complex, is required to create a window, not to mention to create the menu and other controls in the window.

Figure 2-13   Open dialog box in Notepad.

This is where Visual C# once again eases your task. You do not need to write copious, complex code to create a window. Instead, Visual C# creates the window for you when you start a new Windows application project, and it also writes the code necessary to make that window work. This spares you substantial grunt work.

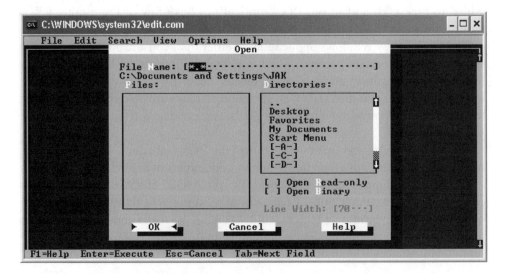

Figure 2-14   Open dialog box in DOS text editor.

Windows Applications Are Event-Driven

Windows applications behave differently, as well as look different, from their predecessors. Before Windows, applications often told the user what to do. For example, an application may tell the operating system to print to the screen the text message "Enter your name." The user would then input their name and press the ENTER key. The user could not have entered their name before this point, and they had to enter data at this point or the program would not continue. The program then may tell the operating system to print to the screen "Enter your age." The user would then input their age and press the ENTER key. Once again, the user could not have entered their age before this point, and had to enter data at this point or the program would not continue. Finally, the program may tell the operating system to output to the screen a sentence that includes the name and age entered, followed by whether the user is a minor, adult, or senior citizen, based on the age that was entered. The program input and output may look like this:

```
Enter your name: Jeff
Enter your age: 53
Jeff, age 53, you are an adult.
```

In this type of program, often called *procedural programming*, the application, not the user, determines the order in which things happen. However, Windows applications are just the opposite; the user tells the application what to do. What happens next after you open Notepad? The answer is, it depends. Specifically, it depends on what you, as the user, do next. If you click the File | Open menu item, the Open dialog box will display as shown previously in Figure 2-13. If instead you click the Help | Help Topics menu item, Notepad Help will display. Of course, you may decide you're tired of Notepad and close it by using the File | Exit menu item or the close button. Thus, in a Windows application, the user's actions, not the application, determine the order in which things happen.

A procedural program can be analogized to a recipe. The program follows the instructions step by step. By contrast, a Windows application can be analogized to a paramedic. The paramedic waits for a call. When a call comes, the paramedic takes the equipment warranted by the call and goes to the location. When finished, the paramedic returns to their station and waits for the next call, and when it comes, takes the equipment warranted by that call and goes to the next location.

In the parlance of Windows programming, the user's actions create *events* that cause the operating system to send messages to the application. For example, the user's act of clicking Notepad's File | Open menu item is an event that causes the operating system to send a message to the Notepad window that the File | Open menu command has been clicked. When Notepad receives that message, code in Notepad displays the Open dialog box. Because the events resulting from the user's actions drive the application, Windows programming often is referred to as being *event-driven*.

Classes Have Events

An event does not exist by itself. Rather, an event is something that happens to an object, usually as the result of user interaction with the object, such as its being clicked. For example, when the user clicks Notepad's File | Open menu item, the event is a click, and the object of the event is the File | Open menu item.

The File | Open menu item is an object that is created from a class. That Menu-Item class, and classes generally, have events in addition to having properties. For example, a Form object has a Click event that occurs when the user clicks the mouse on the form.

As with properties, different classes may have some events in common, but usually would not share the exact same set of events.

Creating an Event Procedure

As discussed in the section "Windows Applications Are Event-Driven," you write code so the user's action in clicking the File | Open menu item in Notepad will display an Open dialog box that permits the user to choose and open a file. You want this code to execute when, and only when, your application's user clicks the File | Open menu item. You use an event procedure to solve this problem, by associating the code that displays the Open dialog box with the Click event of the File | Open menu item object. The event procedure connects the mouse click of the File | Open menu item to the code you want to run when the menu item is clicked.

When the .NET Framework that underlies Visual C# 2005 detects an event such as a mouse click that happens to an object such as the menu item, it searches for an event procedure that matches the object and event. If the .NET Framework finds such an event procedure, it calls that event procedure, and the code inside the event procedure executes.

In this section, we will write code that will change the text displayed in the form's title bar when you click the form. To accomplish this, we need to write code for the Click event procedure of the form.

Writing code for an event procedure involves two steps. The first step is to create the event procedure stub. As will be illustrated in the next section, an event procedure stub is how the event procedure appears before you write any code. Your writing code inside that event procedure code is the second step.

Creating an Event Procedure Stub

To start creating an event procedure stub, go to designer view, as shown in Figure 2-5, and display the Properties window, as shown in Figure 2-9 or 2-10. Click on the fourth icon from the left, which looks like a lightning bolt. As shown in Figure 2-15, the Properties window then will display categories such as Action, Appearance, Behavior, and so forth.

Expand the plus sign next to Action. As shown in Figure 2-16, this will display various events, including Click and DoubleClick.

Figure 2-15   Categories of the Form1 class's events.

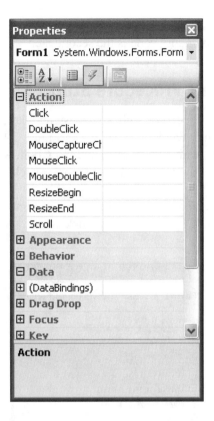

Figure 2-16   Listing of the Form1 class's Action events.

Double-click on Click. As shown in Figure 2-17, this creates an event procedure stub for the Click event of the Form1 class.

The event procedure stub is shown here:

```
private void Form1_Click(Object sender, EventArgs e)
{

}
```

The first line of code begins the event procedure and is the title of the event procedure. It includes the name of the class object (Form1) and the name of the event (Click) separated by an underscore (Form1_Click). Don't worry about the rest of the first line of code for now; we'll cover more later in this book.

The title of the event procedure is immediately followed by a left curly brace ({). The code you will write goes between this left curly brace and the right curly brace (}),

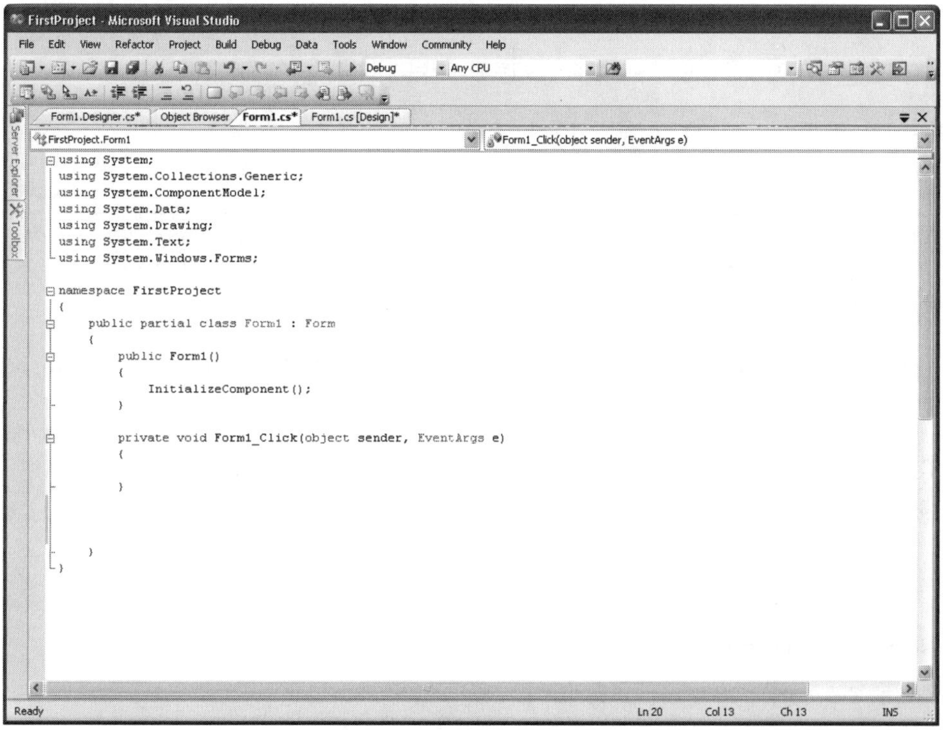

Figure 2-17   Event procedure stub.

which marks the end of the event procedure. The next section discusses writing that code.

Writing Code Inside the Event Procedure

The second step is to write code inside the event procedure that will change the text displayed in the form's title bar when you click the form. Type the following code inside the event procedure, between the two curly braces:

```
this.Text = "Eat at Joe's";
```

This code will be explained in the following sections on the semicolon and the assignment operator.

Now your event procedure should read like so:

```
private void Form1_Click(Object sender, EventArgs e)
{
    this.Text = "Eat at Joe's";
}
```

NOTE *I indented the code. This is not necessary, but it's a good habit, for reasons that will become more apparent as your code becomes more complex. Often the IDE will indent the code for you.*

Run the project by choosing Start Without Debugging from the Debug menu, as shown in Figure 2-18.

When the form first appears, the text in its title bar is the same as the value of the Text property shown in its Properties window. Now click on the form. The text in the form's title bar now should change to "Eat at Joe's."

The Semicolon

Notice that the code ends in a semicolon:

```
this.Text = "Eat at Joe's";
```

As discussed in Chapter 1, a computer program consists of step-by-step instructions from the programmer telling the computer what to do. Each instruction statement in C# ends in a semicolon. It does not matter if the instruction is on one

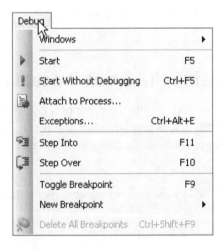

Figure 2-18 Running the Project from the Debug menu.

or more than one line, because in C# the end of a statement is not the end of a line, but the semicolon. For example, the code we just wrote could be placed on more than one line, with no change:

```
this.Text =
    "Eat at Joe's";
```

Not all the code in C# ends in a semicolon. For example, the title of an event procedure does not, and should not. Rather, instructions or statements end in a semicolon.

Assignment Operator

The code also contains what looks like an equals sign (=):

```
this.Text = "Eat at Joe's";
```

However, this is not an equals sign at all. Instead, it is called an assignment operator.

To the right of the assignment operator are words inside double quotation marks. This is called a string. A string usually consists of two or more characters, which may include a letter, a digit, a punctuation mark, or a space. The double quotation marks indicate a string; numeric values are not placed inside double quotation marks.

To the left of the assignment operator is the "this" keyword (a reference to the current Form1 object) and Text (a property of that object) separated by a dot, or period. The code this.Text thus refers to the Text property of the current Form1 object.

The purpose of the assignment operator is to assign the value to its right to the property to its left. Thus, the string "Eat at Joe's" is assigned to the Text property of the current Form1 object.

This code, being inside the Click event procedure of the form object, executes (or runs) when, and only when, the form is clicked. When the form is clicked, the string "Eat at Joe's" is assigned to the Text property of the current Form1 object, and therefore appears in the title bar of the form.

Comments

Change the line of code

```
this.Text = "Eat at Joe's";
```

to instead read as follows:

```
this.Text = "Eat at Joe's";   //Changes text in title bar
```

The program will run exactly the same. In fact, the code has not changed at all. The portion of the line beginning with the two forward slashes (//) followed by "Changes text in title bar" is a comment. The two forward slashes indicate that they, and what follows them on the line, are not part of the code, but rather are a comment.

A comment is for the benefit of a programmer reading the code. The purpose usually is an explanation of the code. An explanation may not be necessary for a line of code changing the value of the text shown in a form's title bar. However, as your applications become more complex, explanations may be helpful to fellow programmers who need to review your code. Indeed, you may find your own explanation of your own code helpful to refresh your memory if you have to return to your code months after you wrote it, either to enhance the code or to fix a problem.

If your comment spans more than one line, you have two alternatives. One is to precede each commented line with two forward slashes:

```
// first line of comments
// second line of comments
// third line of comments
```

The other option, which is preferable if you have many consecutive lines of comments, is to precede the first line with a forward slash and an asterisk (/*) and then end the last line with an asterisk and a forward slash (*/), as shown here:

```
/* first line of comments
second line of comments
third line of comments */
```

Conclusion

Visual C#, like other programming languages, represents each of the persons, things, and concepts that are the subject of an application as a class. Objects are created, or instantiated, from classes.

A class, and therefore the objects created from the class, usually have properties and events. A property is an attribute of an object, such as its height. An event is something that happens to an object, such as its being clicked.

A Windows application is displayed in a window that has a graphical user interface, referred to by the acronym GUI. Additionally, Windows applications are event-driven in that the user's actions, such as clicking a mouse, create events that cause the operating system to send messages to the application. You can write code that will run when those messages are received. That code is written inside an event procedure, which executes, or runs, when a specified event happens to an object.

Quiz

1. What is designer view?
2. What is code view?
3. What is a class in a programming language?
4. What is an object of a class?
5. What are namespaces used for?
6. What is a property of a class?
7. What are characteristics of a Windows application?
8. What is an event of a class?
9. What is an event procedure?
10. What is the purpose of the assignment operator?

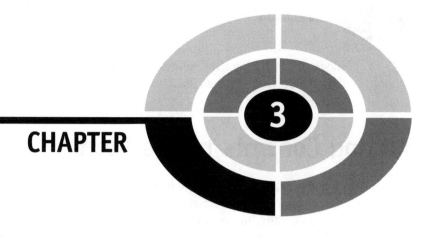

CHAPTER

Controls

Thus far we have focused on the Form class. The form is an important part of your application's GUI, perhaps the most important one. However, a form cannot possibly meet all the requirements of a Windows application. For example, the form does not have the functionality to permit the typing of text, listing of data, selecting of choices, and so forth. You need other, specialized controls for that additional functionality. Indeed, the form's primary role is to serve as a host, or container, for other controls that enrich the GUI of Windows applications, such as menus, toolbars, buttons, text boxes, and list boxes.

You will learn in this chapter how to add controls to your form using the Toolbox. You then will learn how to use the Forms Designer to change the size or location of the controls on the form.

These controls, like the form itself, have their own properties, which can be changed both at design time and at run time. This chapter will provide you with guidelines on whether to assign values at design time or run time in a given situation.

This chapter culminates with a project that uses a particular control, the Label control, for two purposes: first, to display data that does not change during the running of the application and, second, using event procedures, to display data that

does change during the running of the application. This project also shows you how to use information called *parameters* that's available to an event procedure.

Adding Controls to the Form

I, and perhaps you, too, have been requested when first visiting a website to fill out a registration form. Such forms may use many specialized controls. I may type my name in a TextBox control. I also may choose my state or country from a list supplied by a ListBox control. The purposes of the TextBox and ListBox controls are identified by Label controls displaying "Name" and "Country," respectively. When I am finished filling in the required information, I click a Button control often labeled "Submit."

Visual C# 2005 supports many specialized controls. However, the TextBox, Label, ListBox, and Button controls are perhaps the most commonly used.

The TextBox, Label, ListBox, Button, and other specialized controls cannot exist on their own. They must be contained, or hosted, in another specialized type of control—a container control. The form is the usual choice for a container control. Indeed, the form's primary purpose is to serve as a container or host for other controls.

Adding controls to a form through code is no easy task. Fortunately, Visual C# 2005 enables you to easily add available controls to a form through the Toolbox.

Toolbox

Visual C# uses a Toolbox to display controls that you can add to your form. Figure 3-1 shows the Toolbox, which you can display by choosing Toolbox from the View menu.

NOTE *In following along, you can either start a new project as you did in Chapter 1 or open an existing project as you did in Chapter 2.*

As Figure 3-1 shows, the Toolbox has a number of categories, each preceded by an expander (the + sign), to organize related items. If you see only the General category, the reason probably is that you are in code view rather than designer view. If so, simply switch to designer view.

The All Windows Forms category includes the controls used, naturally enough, in Windows forms. The Common Controls category includes, as its name suggests, commonly used controls. Figure 3-2 shows the Toolbox with both categories expanded. The Label control, which we will use in the next section, appears in both categories.

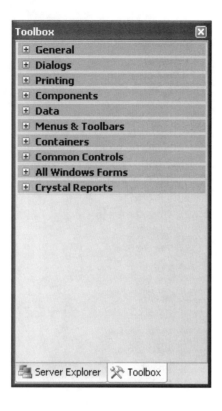

Figure 3-1   Toolbox.

NOTE   *The Toolbox may seem to disappear if you shift focus to Solution Explorer or another part of the Integrated Development Environment (IDE). This is a behavior known as* auto-hide. *To make the Toolbox reappear, click on the Toolbox icon on the left border of the IDE. The idea of auto-hide behavior is to maximize screen space by hiding visual elements not currently in use. If you don't want the auto-hide behavior, click the pushpin button at the top of the Toolbox. Clicking the pushpin button toggles between auto-hide and no auto-hide.*

Copying a Control from the Toolbox to the Form

You have several methods of adding a control from the Toolbox to your form. One way is to double-click the control in the Toolbox. The control will appear somewhere in the form, such as the top-left corner. Another alternative is to click on the control in the Toolbox, drag the control over the form, and then drop the control onto the form, where the control will appear where you dropped it. Thus, with the

Figure 3-2 Expanding of Toolbox categories.

double-click method, the IDE positions the control, whereas with the drag-and-drop method, you position the control.

Expand either the All Windows Forms or the Common Controls category to show the Label control; then use either the double-click or drag-and-drop method to add the

Label control to the form. Figure 3-3 shows the Label control after it is added to the form.

Changing the Control's Location

As mentioned earlier, the double-click method situates the Label control somewhere in the form, whereas the drag-and-drop method situates the Label control wherever you dragged and dropped it onto the form. Either way, you can reposition the Label control.

Put your mouse over the Label control. The mouse pointer should change to four arrows, as shown in Figure 3-4.

Next, click down on the left mouse button (but don't release it) and drag the Label control to another location. Release the mouse button when the control is at the desired location.

You can also change the position of the Label control relative to the form by selecting it and then choosing either the Format | Center in Form | Horizontally menu

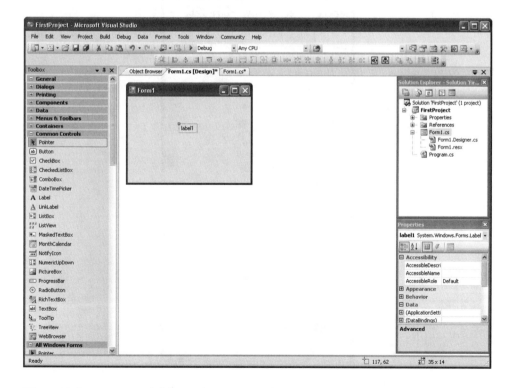

Figure 3-3   Label control inserted on the form.

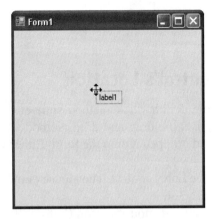

Figure 3-4   Mouse pointer before relocating control.

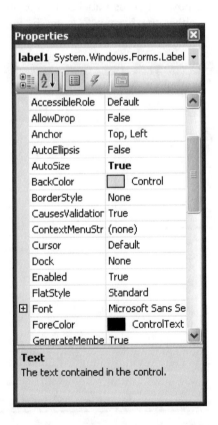

Figure 3-5   AutoSize property in the Label control's Properties window.

command or the Format | Center in Form | Vertically menu command, depending on whether you want to center the control on the form horizontally or vertically (or both).

If you have multiple labels, you can align the top, bottom, or sides of the controls by selecting all labels involved (click each label while holding down the SHIFT or CTRL key) and then choosing the Format | Align | Tops (or Middles, Bottoms, Lefts, Centers, or Rights) menu command. The label selected first (and shown with a darker highlight) will be the guide for the new alignment of all labels selected.

Changing the Control's Size

Resizing the Label control involves an extra step. The Label control has an Auto-Size property. This property, when set to True (the default), automatically resizes the label so it can display its text. Figure 3-5 shows the Label control's Properties window and the AutoSize property.

If you want to manually change the Label control's size, you first need to set the AutoSize property to False, using the drop-down box for the value of the AutoSize property. Next, select the Label control you want to resize. As Figure 3-6 depicts,

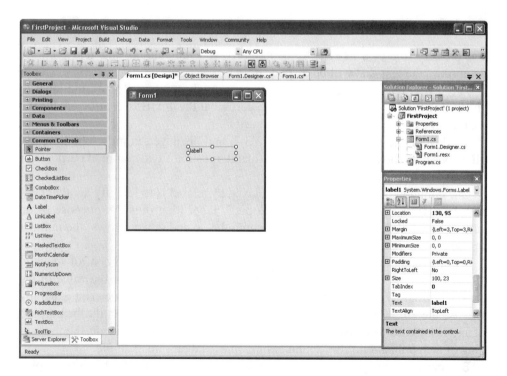

Figure 3-6   Resizing the Label control.

when you select the Label control, eight small squares appear on a box surrounding the Label control—four at the corners and four halfway between the corners.

You can resize the label by holding the mouse over one of these small boxes. The cursor should change to a two-headed arrow. Hold the mouse down and drag it to resize the label.

If you have multiple labels, and their AutoSize properties are all set to False, you can make them the same width, height, or size by selecting all the labels involved (click each label while holding down the SHIFT or CTRL key) and then choosing Width, Height, or Both from the Format | Make Same Size submenu. The size of the label selected first will become the new width, height, or size of all the labels selected.

Important Label Properties

The Label class has many properties, but the Text and the Name properties likely are the most important.

Text Property

The primary role of a label is to display text, and the value of the Text property determines the text that will be displayed.

The text is read-only to the application user, who cannot type on the label to change the label's text. Other controls, in particular the TextBox control, enable the user to type on the control to change the text.

The Print dialog box shown in Figure 3-7, and displayed in most Windows applications with the File | Print menu command, illustrates two common purposes of the text in a Label control.

One common purpose of the text displayed by a label is to identify another control. In Figure 3-7, the "Number of Copies" label identifies the purpose of an adjacent control that enables you to set (with the up and down arrows) the number of copies you want to print.

Another common purpose is to display data, such as the Label control showing "Ready" next to Status. As with the Form object, you can change the value of the Label control's Text property either at design time or through code. You generally will use the Properties window if the purpose of the label is to identify the purpose of another control because that information usually will not change during the running of the application. The "Number of Copies" label is an example.

By contrast, you generally will use code if the purpose of the label is to display data that may change during the running of the application. For example, the Text property of the label next to Status should be set through code because, during the

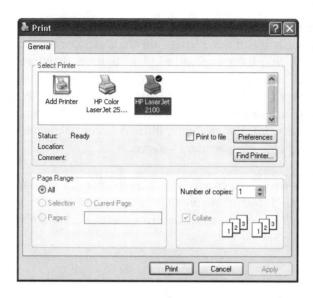

Figure 3-7   Print dialog box.

running of the application, the printer's status may change between being ready and going offline.

Name Property

The Name property is important because its value is how the label is referred to in code. By default, the first label you add to your form is named label1, the second label2, the third label3, and so forth. The default name is fine if you will not be referring to the label in your code. This would be the case if the purpose of the label simply is to identify the purpose of another control.

However, using a default name can cause you difficulty if you are referring to the label in code, such as if the purpose of the label is to display information that may change when the application is running. The difficulties you may encounter increase as the number of the labels in your application increase. For example, you may have difficulty remembering if label53 is the one that displays weather information or the one that displays your bank account balance.

I recommend you use a naming convention when naming your controls. A naming convention simply is a consistent method of naming controls. There are a number of naming conventions. It is not particularly important which one you use. What is important is that you use one and stick to it.

One often-used naming convention is to name a control with a prefix, usually all lowercase and consisting of three letters, that indicates the type of control it is, followed by a word, first letter capitalized, that suggests its purpose. For example, lblWeather would indicate a label that displays weather information. If you need more than one word to describe the control's purpose, you should combine the words into one (because a name cannot have embedded spaces) and capitalize the first letter of each word. For example, lblBankAccountBalance would indicate a label that displays your bank account balance.

TIP Be careful when you use prefixes such as lbl that you use a lowercase letter l and not the number 1. Interchanging the two can cause typos that are hard for you to see and also will result in a compiler error because control names cannot start with a number.

The Label Control in Action

In this section you will create a project (or reuse an existing project) to display the X and Y coordinates of the mouse pointer while the mouse is moving over the form. Figure 3-8 shows what the application looks like when it is running. Of course, the X and Y coordinates displayed will vary depending on where the mouse is located over the form.

Mouse Coordinates

A brief explanation of how mouse coordinates work may be helpful before explaining how the code works. Similar to the concept of coordinates in graphing, mouse coordinates are expressed in two numbers. The first is usually referred to as X and measures a horizontal distance from a reference point. The second is usually referred to as Y and measures a vertical distance from a reference point. In the context of a mouse moving over a form, the reference point is the top-left corner of the form. Therefore, the X coordinate measures the horizontal distance from the left side of the form, and the Y coordinate measures the vertical distance from the top of the form.

Coordinates by convention are expressed with the following syntax: X,Y. Therefore, the top-left corner of the form would be the coordinates 0,0. If a coordinate is 60,77, the mouse is 60 units to the right of the left edge of the form and 77 units below the top edge of the form.

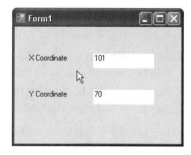

Figure 3-8   Application displaying mouse coordinates.

The unit of measure is a pixel, a shortened term for "picture element," a dot representing the smallest graphic unit of measure on a screen. Screen resolutions such as 1024 × 768 are expressed in pixels.

Creating the Application

Implement the following steps to create the application:

1. Either open an existing project or create a new one.

2. Using the Toolbox, add four labels to the form, one label at a time.

3. Using the Properties window, change the AutoSize property of all four labels from the default (True) to False. This step will make easier the customization of the labels in the following steps.

4. Size and align the four labels as shown in Figure 3-8. The preceding sections "Changing the Control's Location" and "Changing the Control's Size" explain how to align and size multiple labels.

5. Using the Properties window, change the Text properties of the two labels on the left to X coordinate and Y coordinate, respectively, because the purpose of these labels is to identify the two labels on the right. You are changing the value of the Text property of these labels at design time because the text on these labels will not change while the project is running.

6. Using the Properties window, change the Name properties of the two labels on the right to lblX and lblY, respectively. As discussed in the preceding section on the Name property, the prefix lbl (lowercase letter *l*, not the number 1) identifies these controls as labels to programmers reading the code, and the suffixes X and Y note the purpose of the controls (to display the X and Y

coordinates, respectively). It is not so important to rename the two labels on the left because it is unlikely you will need to refer to them in code.

7. Again using the Properties window, change the BackColor property of lblX and lblY to White (so they will be more visible after we delete their text in the next step). When you click the value of the BackColor property, a tabbed dialog box appears. Choose the Custom tab and then click on a box that is white.

8. Also using the Properties window, delete any value in the Text properties of lblX and lblY so both are blank. We don't want these labels' names to display as their text when the project first starts up.

9. Create an event procedure stub for the MouseMove event of the form. The process is similar to the one in Chapter 2, when you created a Click event procedure for the form. In designer view, display the Properties window for the form and then click on the fourth icon from the left, which looks like a lightning bolt. Next, expand (by clicking the plus sign) the Action category and then double-click on MouseMove to create an event procedure stub for the MouseMove event. The event procedure stub is shown in Figure 3-9.

10. Write the following code inside the event procedure stub:

```
lblX.Text = e.X.ToString();
lblY.Text = e.Y.ToString();
```

The completed event procedure now is shown in Figure 3-10 and reads as follows:

```
private void Form1_MouseMove
    (object sender, MouseEventArgs e)
{
    lblX.Text = e.X.ToString();
    lblY.Text = e.Y.ToString();
}
```

11. Compile the project from the Build menu and then run the project from the Debug menu. Move your mouse over the form. The two labels on the right should display numeric values, as shown in Figure 3-8, that change as you move the mouse.

How the Code Works

Although you know that the code works, you also need to know *how* the code works.

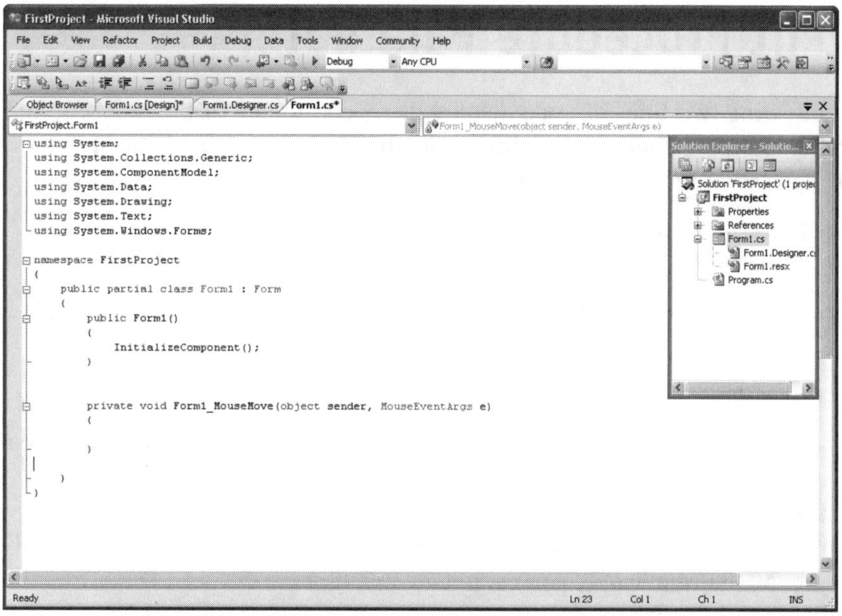

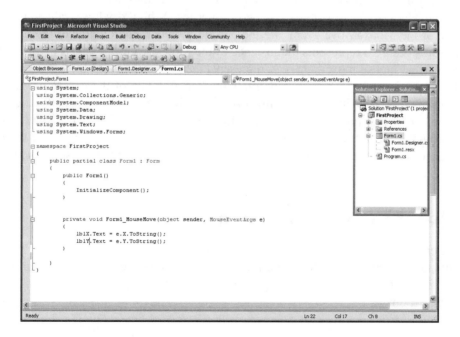

Figure 3-9   Event procedure stub for the MouseMove event of the form.

Figure 3-10   Completed MouseMove event procedure.

Using Event Procedure Parameters

The following two lines of code display the X coordinate of the mouse in the Text property of the Label control lblX and the Y coordinate of the mouse in the Text property of the Label control lblY:

```
lblX.Text = e.X.ToString();
lblY.Text = e.Y.ToString();
```

The "e" on the right side of the assignment operator also appears in the parentheses of the event procedure:

```
(object sender, MouseEventArgs e)
```

The parentheses of the event procedures contain its parameters. A parameter represents information that is available to a procedure.

An event procedure may have no parameters, one parameter, or two or more parameters. An event procedure's parameters are defined by Visual C# and the underlying .NET Framework; you cannot change them.

When a procedure has two or more parameters, the parameters are separated by a comma. The MouseMove event procedure of the Form class has two parameters.

The second parameter, represented by e, is an object of the MouseEventArgs class, which belongs to the System.Windows.Forms namespace.

The MouseEventArgs class has two properties, X and Y, whose values, in the case of the MouseMove event, are the current X and Y coordinates of the mouse cursor. Because e represents the instance of the MouseEventArgs class involved in the current mouse movement, e.X represents the X coordinate of the mouse when the mouse is moved, and e.Y represents the Y coordinate of the mouse when the mouse is moved. With the assignment operator, these X and Y coordinates are assigned to the Text properties of lblX and lblY, respectively, which then display these coordinates. Each time the mouse moves, the MouseMove event occurs, and therefore the code inside the event procedure executes, updating the text displayed in the two labels.

What If You Type the Wrong Code?

The code on the right side of the assignment operator is not just e.X and e.Y. It also calls the ToString method. Before I explain that method, let's examine what happens if you typed the wrong code, leaving out the ToString method, so your code read as follows:

```
private void Form1_MouseMove
    (object sender, MouseEventArgs e)
{
    lblX.Text = e.X;
    lblY.Text = e.Y;
}
```

Visual C# 2005 tries to warn you even before you attempt to compile your code. As Figure 3-11 shows, e.X and e.Y both will be underlined with a squiggly line similar to how Microsoft Word highlights misspellings.

If you hold your mouse over the underline code, a ToolTip shows with the following warning: "Cannot implicitly convert type 'int' to 'string.'" This warning appears because e.X and e.Y are both integers, whereas the Text properties of the two Label controls are strings. Visual C# does not permit you to assign an integer to a string.

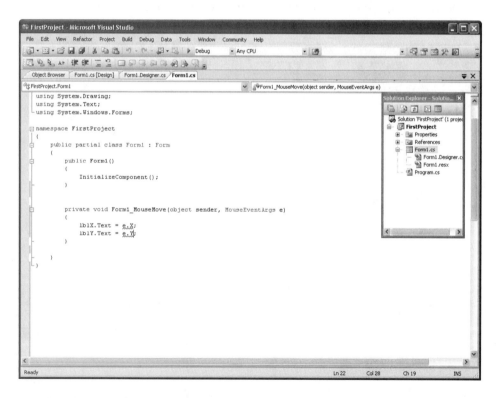

Figure 3-11   Incorrect code highlighted.

Undeterred by this warning, you nevertheless attempt to build the project. As Figure 3-12 shows, an Error List should display, reporting the following, similarly to the ToolTip: "Cannot implicitly convert type 'int' to 'string.'" Additionally, the lines containing this error are identified.

NOTE *If the Error List does not automatically display, you can display it with the menu command View | Other Windows | Error List.*

ToString Method

Of course, you still need to correct the code. To do so, you need to convert the integer value on the right side of the assignment operator to its string representation. In other words, if the integer is 123, its string representation is "123".

All classes have a ToString method. What that method does depends on the class. In the case of the Int32 class, which represents an integer, the ToString method

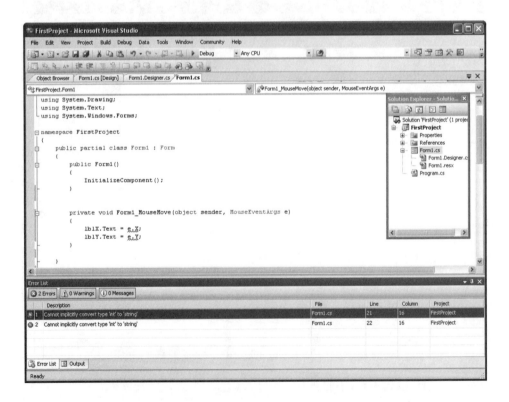

Figure 3-12   Error List reporting an error.

converts an integer to the string representation of the integer, so it can be assigned to the Text property of the Label controls.

The ToString method is preceded by the integer value to be converted and a dot or period. It is followed by empty parentheses because this method has no parameters.

NOTE *Though the parentheses are empty, do not omit them because a compiler error will result.*

Delegate

Figure 3-12 shows Solution Explorer with the expander next to Form1.cs to show two files under it, one of which is Form1.Designer.cs. (You may need to click the Show All Files button to obtain this view.) Right-click that file name and choose View Code from the shortcut menu. This will display the code in Form1.Designer. cs, as shown in Figure 3-13.

One of the lines of code reads (here on three lines because of its length):

```
this.MouseMove +=
new System.Windows.Forms.MouseEventHandler
   (this.Form1_MouseMove);
```

As explained in Chapter 2, when the .NET Framework that underlies Visual C# 2005 detects an event, such as the mouse button being held down, that happens to an object such as a form, its searches for an event procedure that handles that event for that object. If the .NET Framework finds such an event procedure, it calls that event procedure, and the code inside the event procedure executes.

MouseEventHandler, part of the System.Windows.Forms namespace, is a delegate. A delegate is used to specify which procedure handles an event that happens to a particular object. MouseEventHandler in particular specifies the procedure that will handle the MouseDown, MouseUp, or MouseMove event of a form, control, or other component.

The += operator is explained in Chapter 5 on arithmetic operators. For now, treat it as an assignment operator.

On the left side of the += operator is this.MouseMove. The "this" keyword refers to the current object of the Form1 class—that is, the form over which the mouse button is being held down. MouseDown is the event. Accordingly, this.MouseMove specifies the event to be handled, which is the mouse moving over the form.

On the right side of the += operator, the MouseEventHandler delegate is followed in parentheses by the name of the procedure that will handle the event, Form1_MouseMove.

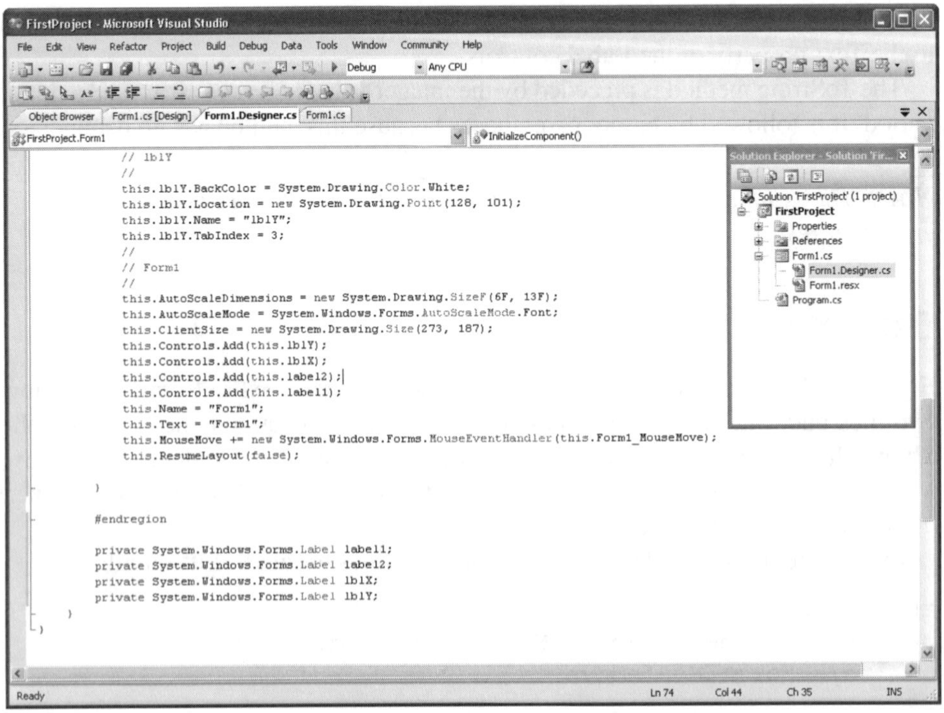

Figure 3-13 Code view of Form1.Designer.cs.

NOTE *If you delete an event procedure, you will get a compiler error if you don't delete the line concerning the corresponding delegate in Form1.Designer.cs.*

Conclusion

The form is perhaps the most important control. However, a single form without controls could only satisfy the requirements of the simplest Windows application. The form does not permit the typing of text, listing data, selecting of choices, and many other tasks that an application may need to perform. You need other, specialized controls for that additional functionality. Indeed, the form's primary role is to serve as a host, or container, for controls such as menus, toolbars, and buttons, which enrich the GUI of Windows applications.

This chapter showed you how to add controls to your form using the Toolbox. You then learned how to use the Forms Designer to change the size and location of the controls. The project also showed you how to control the size and location of multiple controls relative to each other.

The Label class, like the Form class, has properties. Perhaps the most important properties of the Label class are its Name and Text properties.

The Name property determines how you refer to a label in code. You should use a naming convention when naming a label that you will refer to in code. This chapter suggested a naming convention using a prefix, usually all lowercase and consisting of three letters, that indicates the type of control it is, followed by a word, first letter capitalized, that suggests its purpose.

The Text property determines the value of the text displayed by the label. Like the Text property of the Form class, you can change the value of the Label control's Text property either at design time or through code. You generally will use the Properties window if the purpose of the label is to identify the purpose of another control because that information usually will not change during the running of the application. By contrast, you generally will use code if the purpose of the label is to display data that may change during the running of the application. This code often will be located inside of an event procedure.

This chapter included a project that uses the Label control for both purposes—to display data that does not change during the running of the application and to display data that does change during the running of the application. Finally, you learned how to use information called parameters that's available to an event procedure.

Although it is impressive that you can create a working Visual C# 2005 program that displays information using controls by writing only two lines of code, most programs need to save information, or data. The next chapter will teach you about the different data types as well as how to create and use information storage locations called variables.

Quiz

1. What are examples of controls?
2. What is the purpose of the Toolbox?
3. How do you add a control from the Toolbox onto your form?
4. What is the purpose of the Name property of a control?
5. What is a naming convention?
6. What characteristic of the Label control does its Text property determine?
7. What are purposes of the text displayed by a Label control?
8. Can a single statement in C# take up two or more lines in the code editor?
9. What is a parameter of an event procedure?
10. What is a delegate?

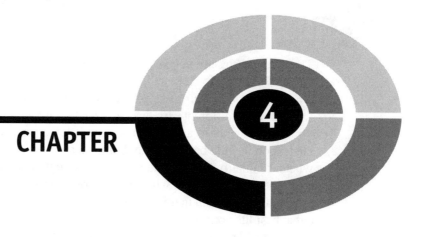

CHAPTER 4

Storing Information— Data Types and Variables

I often am asked for my autograph. Unfortunately, my autograph usually is requested by those who want my money, such as on credit card receipts when I purchase groceries or gas, or on checks to pay my mortgage or auto insurance.

These companies that love sending me bills could not possibly keep track of their thousands of customers using pencil and paper. Instead, they use computer programs, which harness the computer's unparalleled ability to store information and make computations using that data.

These companies are not the only ones that need to store and retrieve data. Visual C# 2005 also needs to store and retrieve data, such as the height, width, and background color of your startup form, necessary in order for your projects to run.

Data comes in different varieties. Some data is numeric, such as the amount of my gas bill or the height of a form. Some data is text, such as my name on my gas bill or the text on the title bar of a form. Some data is Boolean (either true or false), such as whether I qualify for the senior citizen discount or whether a form is visible.

The type of information, whether numeric, text, or Boolean, is referred to as the *data type*. I will explain in this chapter the different data types and how to select the one that best fits your purpose.

You also will need to store data. Visual C# forms and controls have many built-in properties to store data, such as the Text property of a Label or TextBox control. However, these properties are limited to storing the information they were designed for. The Height property of a form only can store a form's height, not some other information you need to store.

Visual C# 2005 enables you to create your own information storage locations, called *variables*. I will show you in this chapter how to create and use variables.

Finally, certain values never change while a program is running. For example, if you are writing a program to calculate the cost of a transaction, the percentage of sales tax will not change while your program is running. Values that do not change while your program is running are called *constants*. I will also show you in this chapter how to create and use constants.

Data Types

Think of all the different types of information that you need to keep in your mind. For example, if you as a student were driving to school for the first day of class, you would not want to be late. Therefore, you would consider the number of miles to school in deciding what time to leave. You may wonder if you will be able to get into the class and try to remember the name of the teacher you need to ask. Also, the class will be tough, so you think about the effect the class might have on your grade point average.

Some of these items of information are numeric, such as the number of miles to school and your grade point average. However, the name of the teacher is not numeric, but text, and the answer to whether you will be able to get into the class will be yes or no. The type of information, whether text, numeric, or yes/no, is referred to as the *data type*.

Numeric Data Types

Visual C# has a number of data types—int (for integer) being the most common—that may be used for whole numbers. A whole number may be positive (say, 55) or negative (−55) or zero. However, the int data type should not be used for floating-point numbers—that is, those that have numbers to the right of the decimal point, such as −.5, .5, and 5.5.

The int keyword, for an integer data type, is an alias for the System.Int32 data type in the .NET Framework. Indeed, each of the Visual C# data type keywords we will be discussing is an alias for a corresponding .NET Framework data type.

An int would be a good choice for the number of miles to school. Normally, you would think it is 8 miles to school, for example, not 8.3 miles, because there is no need to be so precise as to figure out tenths of miles.

Visual C# has three floating-point data types—float, double, and decimal—that may be used for floating-point numbers, such as −.5, .5, and 5.5. One of these data types would be a good choice for your grade point average (for example, 3.91), because for a grade point average you want to take into account the digits to the right of the decimal point. After all, if you worked hard to earn a 3.91 grade point average, you would not want the .91 ignored, thus making your grade point average 3.0.

NOTE *The int and double data types can handle almost all numbers you may use in a program. However, some numbers are too large for either data type to handle, such as distances between galaxies in the universe. Also, some numbers may be too small for the double data type to handle, such as the size of an atom. However, these circumstances are relatively rare.*

The bool (for Boolean) data type has only two possible values: True and False. The bool data type would be a good choice to report whether or not you got into the class, because there are only two alternatives, yes (True) and no (False).

Text Data Types

The string and char data types are used for text. A string is simply one or more characters, usually enclosed in double quotes to indicate that a string is intended. The characters may be alpha (A–Z or a–z), numeric (0–9), or virtually any other character you can type from your keyboard. For example, the name "R2D2" is a string even though it includes the numeric character 2. The string data type would be a good choice for the teacher's name, such as "Genghis Khent," my students' fond (?) nickname for me.

The char data type represents a single character, enclosed in single rather than double quotes ('A', not "A") to indicate that it is a character rather than a string. As with a string, a char may be alpha (A–Z or a–z), numeric (0–9), or virtually any other character you can type from your keyboard. The char data type would be a good choice for the grade you hope to earn in the class, such as an 'A'.

There are other data types, some of which will be mentioned in later chapters. However, these five data types—int, double, string, char, and bool—are the ones principally used.

Data Types of Visual C# Properties

Visual C# 2005 needs to keep track of a lot of information. Take a look at the Properties window of the form in your project. The form has many different properties. These properties determine the form's height and width, background color, caption, visibility, and so on. Visual C# 2005 uses these properties when you start a project to determine the form's size, background color, and so forth.

Each of these properties stores a particular value. The Height property stores a number that represents the height of the form. The Text property stores a string that represents the title displayed by the form. The Visible property stores a Boolean value that represents whether the form is visible (True) or hidden (False).

You can access the value of many properties when designing your application (design time) simply by viewing their values in the Properties window. You also can access the values of many properties while your application is running through code (run time). In Chapter 2, we changed the Text property of the form at run time, and in Chapter 3, we changed the Text property of labels at run time.

However, whether you are at design time or run time, the new value of the property must be of the correct data type. To confirm this, in the Properties window of the form, type **Jeff** next to the Height property, which you can access by expanding the Size property, as shown in Figure 4-1. Then press ENTER. A dialog box will display, as in Figure 4-2, warning you of an "Invalid property value."

Click the Details button of the dialog box in Figure 4-3. The dialog box then will display the message, "Jeff is not a valid value for Int32." As discussed earlier, System.Int32 is the name used in the .NET Framework for the int data type.

That Visual C# 2005 prevents you from changing the value of the Height property to "Jeff" makes sense. The height must be a number. Visual C# does not know how to make the form of the height "Jeff."

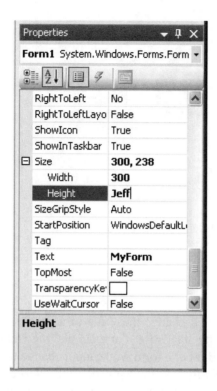

Figure 4-1   Setting the Form's Height property to an invalid value.

Try exploring the properties of the form in the Properties window. You will see there are many different data types for the different properties.

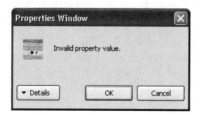

Figure 4-2   Invalid property value warning.

Figure 4-3   Details of "Invalid property value" warning.

Variables

You can store, access, and change the value of a property. However, you cannot change what the property stands for. For example, the Height property of a Form object represents the height of a form; you cannot change that property so it instead represents the width of a form or the name of your favorite ice cream.

Instead, you can create a variable to store data of your choosing, such as the name of your favorite ice cream, your social security number, and so on.

Declaring a Variable

Visual C# knows that the form's Height property stands for the height of the form and that its data type is numeric, because the Height property is built into the .NET Framework class library. However, because you, not Visual C#, create a variable, you need to tell Visual C# information about the variable. You do so by declaring the variable.

You declare a variable with the following syntax:

```
[Access Specifier] [Data Type] [Variable Name];
```

To make this syntax more understandable, here are two examples of declaring a variable:

```
public int intScore;
private string strName;
```

In the first example, public is the access specifier, int is the data type, and intScore is the variable name. In the second example, private is the access specifier, string is the data type, and strName is the variable name. In either case, the statement declaring the variable is terminated with a semicolon, as are other statements in C#.

The access specifier is used when the variable is declared as a class member, not when it is declared locally. The section "Where Do I Declare a Variable?" later in this chapter discusses declaring a variable locally or as a class member, and the effect of the various access specifiers.

You can choose any of the data types discussed in the preceding section on data types, though logically, you should choose a data type that is appropriate for the purpose of the variable. For example, if the variable represents someone's name, you likely will choose string as the data type, whereas if the variable represents someone's age, you instead may choose the int data type.

Naming a Variable

Variables, like people, have names. These names are used to identify the variable to which you want to refer. There are only a few limitations on how you can name a variable:

- The variable name cannot begin with any character other than a letter of the alphabet (A–Z or a–z) or an underscore (_). Secret agents may be code-named 007, but not variables.

- The variable name cannot contain embedded spaces, such as My Variable, or punctuation marks other than the underscore character (_), such as a question mark (?), a comma (,), a period (.), a backslash (\), a forward slash (/), or a parenthesis.

- The variable name cannot be longer than 255 characters (not that you would want to create a variable name that long).

- The variable name cannot be the same as a keyword, such as int or string, because that would confuse the compiler.

- The variable name cannot have the same name as another variable of the same scope, because that also would confuse the compiler. Scope is discussed later in this chapter.

Besides these limitations, you can name a variable pretty much whatever you want. However, it is a good idea to give your variables names that are meaningful. If you name your variables var1, var2, var3, and so on, through var17, you may find it difficult to remember later the difference between var8 and var9. And if *you* find it difficult, imagine how difficult it would be for another programmer who has to make sense of your code.

In Chapter 3, I recommended you use a naming convention when naming controls. I similarly recommend that you use a naming convention when naming your variables. Analogous to Chapter 3, the convention I suggest is to name a variable with a prefix, usually all lowercase and consisting of three letters, that indicates its data type, followed by a word, first letter capitalized, that suggests its purpose.

Here are some suggested prefixes for data types:

Data Type	Prefix
int	int
string	str
bool	bln
double	dbl

Here are some examples that use these prefixes:

- **intScore**   Integer variable representing a score, such as on a test
- **strName**   String variable representing a name, such as a person's name
- **blnResident**   Boolean variable representing whether or not someone is a resident
- **dblGPA**   Double variable representing a student's GPA

If you need more than one word to describe the variable's purpose, you should combine them into one word (because you cannot have embedded spaces) but capitalize the first letter of each word, such as blnDidUserQuit.

What Happens If I Don't Declare a Variable?

Visual C# 2005 requires you to declare a variable before you refer to it in code. For example, in either a new or existing Windows application, insert the code

```
intVar = 10;
```

at the beginning of the class. This code, which attempts to assign 10 to intVar without previously declaring intVar as a variable, will not compile:

```
public partial class Form1 : Form
{
```

```
intVar = 10;
// remainder of code
```

Instead, on the line

```
intVar = 10;
```

the compiler will complain with the following error message: "Invalid token '=' in class, struct, or interface member declaration." Although this error message is not very illuminating, it tells you that your code is wrong.

Where Do I Declare a Variable?

You can declare a variable in one of two places: inside a procedure or at the top of the code module. Where you declare a variable affects its scope.

Local Variable

If you declare a variable inside a procedure, you can refer to that variable only in that procedure. Stated in programming parlance, the variable is a *local* variable, having scope only inside the procedure in which it was declared. No access specifier is used for local variables.

Assume the code in the Load and Click event procedures of the form read as follows:

```
private void Form1_Load(object sender, MouseEventArgs e)
{
    int intVar;
}

private void Form1_Click(object sender, MouseEventArgs e)
{
    intVar = 10;
}
```

When you attempt to compile your project, the result will be a compile error ("the name 'intVar' does not exist in the current context") concerning the line intVar = 10 inside the Click event procedure. The reason is that intVar only has scope inside the Load event procedure in which it was declared, and therefore is not visible in the Click event procedure. This is why no access specifier is used for local variables; access to them already is restricted to the procedure in which they are declared.

By contrast, assigning 10 to intVar inside the Load event is okay because intVar was declared inside that event procedure. Try this by deleting the line of code in the Click event procedure of your form and changing the code in the Load event procedure of your form so it reads as follows:

```
private void Form1_Load(object sender, MouseEventArgs e)
{
    int intVar;
    intVar = 10;
}
```

In this example, the variable intVar was declared in the first statement and assigned a value in the second statement. You also can combine the two statements as follows:

```
int intVar = 10;
```

Combining the declaration and assignment of a variable in one statement is called *initialization*.

NOTE *When you compile a program that either declares or initializes a variable (here, intVar) but thereafter does not use that variable, you may get the following warning: "The variable 'intVar' is declared but never used." A warning is not a compile error. The program still will run. Instead, a warning means that Visual C# is bringing to your attention, as the programmer, that the issue may or may not be a problem, and it is up to you to decide whether it is.*

Class Member Variable

You also can declare a variable as a member of the class. In the following code snippet, intMember is a class member variable because it is declared within the class but not within an event procedure. By contrast, intLocal is a local variable because it is declared within the Load event procedure for the form.

```
public partial class Form1 : Form
{
    int intMember;
    // more code
    private void Form1_Load
        (object sender, MouseEventArgs e)
    {
        int intLocal;
        intMember = 10;
    }
    // more code
}
```

Additionally, the statement intMember = 10 within the Load event procedure for the form compiles because intMember, as a class member variable, has scope throughout the class. By contrast, the scope of intLocal is limited to the event procedure in which it was declared.

Also unlike local variables, class member variables may be declared with access specifiers. Table 4-1 lists the access specifiers.

At this point in the book, we are writing code in only one class, so the access specifier currently is unimportant as a practical matter. However, when you later create more complex applications, the issue of the appropriate access specifier will be revisited. As a general rule, you should use the most restrictive access specifier consistent with the needs of your program, as discussed in the next section, "Why Not Always Declare Variables as Class Members?"

If an access specifier is omitted, as in the following code, the access specifier then is the default, private:

```
public partial class Form1 : Form
{
    int intMember;    // public access implied
    // more code
```

The following code illustrates the syntax of the various access specifiers:

```
public partial class Form1 : Form

{
    int intHeight;    // private access implied
    public int intWeight;
    protected int intAge;
    internal int intShoeSize;
    protected internal int intShirtSize;
```

Declared Accessibility	Meaning
public	Access is unrestricted (that is, this type of access is without any of the limitations of the other access specifiers).
protected	Access is limited to the class in which the variable was declared or classes inherited from that class.
internal	Access is limited to the classes in the current assembly (or solution).
protected internal	Combines access for protected and internal.
private	Access is limited to the class in which the variable was declared.

Table 4-1   Access Specifiers

```
    private int intPinCode;
    // more code
}
```

You may declare a class-level variable using initialization:

```
    private int intPinCode = 111;
```

However, you can assign a value to an already-declared variable only inside a procedure; you cannot do so at the class level:

```
    private int intPinCode;
    intPinCode = 111;    // compiler error
```

Instead, you will get the following compile error: "Invalid token '=' in class, struct, or interface member declaration."

Why Not Always Declare Variables as Class Members?

Given the potential for compiler errors resulting from variables being referenced outside their scope, the temptation is to give your variables the widest possible scope, to make them class members instead of local, and to make their access public. Resist temptation! Indeed, as a general rule, you should make the scope of your variables the least possible.

One reason is, when you're debugging your code, if a variable can be accessed only from one location in your program, you only need to check the code in that one place. However, if the variable can be accessed from ten different locations in your program, you need to check the code in all ten places, as well as determine the effect of any interrelationships between the ten locations. In other words, the less scope the variable has, the easier your task as a programmer. Why make your job harder than it has to be?

Of course, there often will be circumstances in which a variable should be a class member. There also will be circumstances in which a class member variable should be public rather than private. The point is that in determining whether to declare a variable locally in an event procedure or instead as a class member, or in determining the access specifier for a class member variable, you need to justify to yourself any added scope you give the variable before you do so.

Constants

A constant is similar to a variable, except that a constant's value cannot change during the life of the program.

Declaring a Constant

The syntax of declaring a constant is similar to declaring a variable (the syntax is split into two lines because of the width of the printed page):

```
[Access Specifier] const [Data Type]
[Variable Name] = [value];
```

For example, the following statement declares a constant, MAX_SCORE, of the int data type, whose value, 100, is the maximum score that can be obtained on a test:

```
public const int MAX_SCORE = 100;
```

Let's analyze the component parts of the constant declaration:

- **public**   This is the access specifier. Access specifiers work the same way with constants as they do with variables.

- **const**   This is a keyword that indicates you are declaring a constant instead of a variable.

- **int**   This is the data type, again the same as with variables.

- **MAX_SCORE**   This is the name of the constant. Constants, like variables, have names. However, the naming convention for constants may be different from the one for variables. By one convention which I use, constant names, unlike variable names, do not have a prefix such as int or str to specify the data type, but instead are entirely descriptive. Additionally, by convention, the name consists of uppercase characters, so words are separated by an underscore character (_), such as in BRIBE_PAID.

- **= 100**   This assigns a value to the constant. The main difference in syntax between declaring a variable and declaring a constant, other than the const keyword, is that a constant must be assigned a value when declared. The reason why a constant must be assigned a value when it is declared is that the value of a constant cannot be changed after it is declared. Therefore, a constant must be given a value when it is declared; otherwise, it can never be given a value at all. Declaring a constant without assigning a value (public const int MAX_SCORE;) will result in the following compiler error: "A const field requires a value to be provided."

Where Do I Declare a Constant?

You can declare a constant locally or as a class member. The reasons why I recommend you declare a variable locally, unless you have a specific reason to declare the variable as a class member, don't apply to constants because, as the next section shows, you can't change the value of a constant after you declare it.

Where Do I Assign a Value to a Constant?

The answer is that you only can assign a value to a constant when you declare it (that is, via initialization).

Because a constant's value cannot be changed during the life of the program, even attempting to assign a value to a constant will cause an error. Try this code in the Windows application you have been using in this chapter. The result will be the following compile error: "Invalid token '=' in class, struct or interface member declaration."

```
public partial class Form1 : Form
{
   public const int MAX_SCORE = 100;
   // more code
   private void Form1_Load
      (object sender, MouseEventArgs e)
   {
      MAX_SCORE = 200;        //error
   }
   // more code
}
```

Why Use Constants?

Although it is important to know how a constant differs from a variable and how to declare constants, you may be wondering, Why use constants at all? The reason is that constants make your code easier to read and maintain.

Although constants are useful for values that never will change, constants perhaps are even more useful for values that someday may change. For example, we've all paid sales tax on purchases. Assuming the tax rate is 8%, the amount of the tax is price * .08. Thus, throughout your code for a store you may have calculations such as the following:

```
[price variable] * .08;
```

One day the government decides to increase the sales tax to 8.25%. Now you have to find all the places in your code where you referred to the sales tax rate and change all those references from .08 to .0825. This not only is a pain, but the potential for error is obvious.

Alternatively, you could have declared the sales tax rate as a constant:

```
const double SALES_TAX_RATE = .08;
```

Thus, the tax calculation in your code would be this:

```
[price variable] * SALES_TAX_RATE;
```

Then, when the government increases the sales tax to 8.25%, you only have to make the change in one place in your code, and you're done:

```
const double SALES_TAX_RATE = .0825;
```

Conclusion

Most programs need to keep track of information. That information may be about the subject of the program, such as the names and addresses of customers, or it may be about the program itself, such as the height, caption, or visibility of a form.

Data comes in different forms. Data may be numeric (such as the height of a form), text (such as the caption on a form), or Boolean (such as whether a form is visible). The type of information, whether number, string, or Boolean, is referred to as the *data type*.

Although the .NET Framework class library has many built-in properties to store data, Visual C# 2005 also enables you to create your own information storage locations, called *variables*. Variables must be declared before they are used.

Variables may be declared at the top of the code module, in which case they are called *module level* and will be available to all procedures in that module. Variables also may be declared inside a procedure, in which case they are called *local* and their scope is limited to the procedure in which they were declared.

Finally, certain values never change during the life of the program. These unchanging values are represented by constants, which are declared similarly to variables. However, unlike variables, constants must be initialized when they are declared, and their value cannot thereafter change during the lifetime of the program.

In this chapter, you used the assignment operator to provide values to variables. In the next chapter, you will learn about arithmetic operators, which enable you to use the computer's unparalleled ability to quickly and accurately perform mathematical calculations.

Quiz

1. What does a data type signify?

2. What is a floating-point number?

3. Can you change the data type of a built-in property of a form, such as Height or Text?

4. What is the purpose of a variable?

5. Does C# require you to declare a variable before you refer to it in code?

6. What is a local variable?

7. What is a class member variable?

8. Do you have to assign a value to a variable when you declare it?

9. What is a difference between a constant and a variable?

10. Do you have to assign a value to a constant when you declare it?

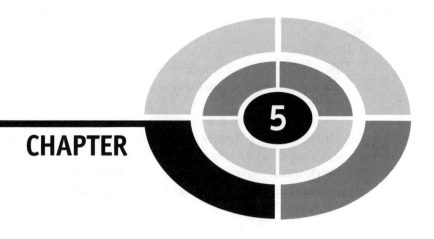

Letting the Program Do the Math— Arithmetic Operators

It is only fair that since my students have to listen to my recycled jokes, you have to read my recycled introductions. Back in Chapter 2, I complained that nowadays students don't need to be able to calculate arithmetic in their heads because they can rely on calculators. However, despite my complaining about calculators,

they certainly are far faster and more accurate than I could ever hope to be. The reason is that a calculator is a computer, and computers are superstars when it comes to calculating.

You harness the computer's calculating ability using arithmetic operators. You will learn in this chapter how to enable your applications to make fast and accurate calculations using arithmetic operators. At the end of this chapter, you will put what you learned into practice with the Change Machine project, a type of calculator that converts a number of pennies into dollars, quarters, dimes, nickels, and pennies.

Arithmetic Operators

Visual C# 2005 can do your arithmetic, and because a computer is involved, it can do so much faster and more accurately than any human could! Even better, the code is relatively easy to write, because the syntax for arithmetic is quite similar to how you would write the arithmetic calculation on paper or how you would use a calculator.

Table 5-1 lists the arithmetic operators.

The Addition Operator

The addition operator works exactly as you would expect it to with numeric values. In the following code snippet, the third line of code adds the values of the variables a and b and assigns the sum, 5, to variable a, changing its value from 2 to 5:

```
int a = 2;
int b = 3;
a = a + b;
```

The addition operator also works with string variables by concatenating, or appending, one string to another. In the following code snippet, the third line of code

Operator	Name	What It Does
+	Addition	Performs addition.
−	Subtraction	Performs subtraction.
*	Multiplication	Performs multiplication.
/	Division	Performs division; the remainder is preserved and expressed as a decimal unless both operands are whole-number data types.
%	Modulus	Used to obtain the remainder from division.

Table 5-1   Arithmetic Operators

adds the values of the variables a and b and assigns the concatenated string, "JeffKent", to variable a, changing its value from "Jeff" to "JeffKent":

```
string a = "Jeff";
string b = "Kent";
a = a + b;
```

The Subtraction Operator

The subtraction operator also works exactly as you would expect it to with numeric values. In the following code snippet, the third line of code subtracts the value of variable b from variable a and assigns the difference, −1, to variable a, changing its value from 2 to −1:

```
int a = 2;
int b = 3;
a = a - b;
```

The Multiplication Operator

The multiplication operator also works exactly as you would expect it to with numeric values. In the following code snippet, the third line of code multiplies the value of variable a by the value of variable b and assigns the product to variable a, changing its value from 2 to 6:

```
int a = 2;
int b = 3;
a = a * b;
```

The Division Operators

Whereas there is only one addition, subtraction, and multiplication operator, there are two division operators. The operators / and % both involve division. However, the two division operators differ on how they report the results of the division. The % operator, also referred to as the *modulus* operator, reports only the remainder. The / operator reports the decimal equivalent of the quotient and remainder unless integer division (explained next) is involved, in which case it reports only the quotient.

NOTE *For those of us whose arithmetic classes are far in the past, assuming the operation 11 divided by 4, the result of the division is 2, remainder 3, with 2 being the quotient and 3 the remainder.*

Let's start first with the / operator by looking at the following code snippet:

```
double a = 11;
double b = 4;
a = a / b;
```

The value of a after division is 2.75, the result you would expect.

Let's now change this example so both a and b are int instead of double variables:

```
int a = 11;
int b = 4;
a = a / b;
```

The value of a after division is 2, not 2.75. The reason is that if both operands of the division (here, 11 and 4) are int (or another whole-number data type), the division operator reports only the quotient, 2, and drops the remainder, 3.

This effect of division dropping the remainder when both operands are a whole number data type is called *integer division*. Note that integer division does not round off. If it did, 11 / 4 would be 3, not 2. Because integer division reports only the quotient, the result necessarily is a whole number.

Let's move on now to the % operator by looking at the following code snippet:

```
int a = 11;
int b = 4;
a = a % b;
```

The value of a after division is 3, which is the remainder.

Operator Precedence

So far the arithmetic expressions have been simple, involving just one arithmetic operator. However, sometimes arithmetic expressions are more complex, involving two or more arithmetic operators. For example, does the arithmetic expression 2 + 3 * 4 equal 20 (by performing addition before multiplication) or 14 (by performing multiplication before addition)?

One and only one of these two answers can be correct. Rules of operator precedence are necessary to determine which of the two answers is correct.

Table 5-2 lists the order of precedence, or priority, among arithmetic operators.

Priority	Operator(s)	Description
1	–	Unary negation operator (not subtraction)
2	*, /, %	Multiplication, division, and modulus
3	+, –	Addition and subtraction

Table 5-2   Operator Precedence

Thus, 2 + 3 * 4 equals 14, because multiplication has a higher priority than addition and therefore is performed first.

Because multiplication and division have equal priority, when both operators occur together in an expression, priority goes from left to right, so whichever of the two operators is on the left is performed before the one on the right. The same left-to-right priority rule applies between addition and subtraction. Priority, either left to right or right to left, between operators of equal precedence is called *associativity*.

Parentheses can be used to override the order of precedence and force some parts of an expression to be evaluated before others. Operations within parentheses are always performed before those outside the parentheses. Thus, (2 + 3) * 4 equals 20, not 14, because the parentheses force addition to be performed first.

Combining Arithmetic and Assignment Operators

As discussed earlier in this chapter, in the following code snippet, the third line of code adds the values of the variables a and b and assigns the sum, 5, to variable a, changing its value from 2 to 5:

```
int a = 2;
int b = 3;
a = a + b;
```

A precedence issue arises in the third line of code. Even though there is only one arithmetic operator, there are two operators—one arithmetic and the other assignment. However, the precedence issue is easily resolved. Addition is performed before assignment because all arithmetic operators have precedence over the assignment operator.

The third statement can be shortened and still accomplish the same result:

```
a += b;
```

The combined arithmetic/assignment operators are shown in Table 5-3.

Operator	Use	Alternative
+=	a += b;	a = a + b;
−=	a −= b;	a = a − b;
*=	a *= b;	a = a * b;
/=	a /= b;	a = a / b;
%=	a %= b;	a = a % b;

Table 5-3   Combined Arithmetic/Assignment Operators

These shorthand arithmetic/assignment operators make your code more readable. The purpose of the following statement is to increment (increase by 1) the value of variable a:

```
a += 1;
```

The purpose of the preceding statement is more readable (as well as shorter to type) than the following statement:

```
a = a + 1;
```

Increment and Decrement Operators

The last code snippet in the preceding section uses the combined arithmetic and assignment operator to increase the value of a by 1:

```
a += 1;
```

The same result could be achieved by the increment operator ++ :

```
a++;
```

The increment operator can follow the value it is increasing, as in the last example, or precede it, as follows:

```
++a;
```

Prefix increment refers to the increment operator preceding the value it is incrementing. Postfix increment refers to the increment operator following the value it is incrementing. Here are two examples:

```
++a;    //prefix increment
a++;    //postfix increment
```

The only difference between prefix and postfix increment is precedence. If the increment operator is used in the same statement as other operators, incrementing occurs first if prefix, last if postfix.

The counterpart to the increment operator is the decrement operator, --. The second and third statements, using prefix and postfix decrement, are equivalent to the first, which uses the combined subtraction and assignment operator:

```
a -= 1;
--a;
a++;
```

Prefix and postfix work the same way with the decrement operator as they do the increment operator, affecting precedence with other operators.

The increment and decrement operators often are used with loops, which are covered in Chapter 8.

The Parse Method

As discussed earlier in this chapter, the addition operator works with string values as well as with numeric values. With string values, the addition operator concatenates, or appends, one string to another.

The ability of the addition operator to perform double-duty with string as well as numeric values can backfire on you. To illustrate, assume your application has two TextBox controls, txtOp1 and txtOp2, in which the user types two numbers to be added, with the sum displayed in a Label control named lblResult. The application may use the following code:

```
lblResult.Text = txtOp1.Text + txtOp2.Text;
```

The user wants to add 2 + 2 and therefore types 2 in each text box. However, the answer is not the expected 4, but instead 22! This is not new math. Instead, Visual C# assumed you intended to concatenate two strings ("2" + "2" = "22") instead of adding two numbers (2 + 2 = 4) because the data type of the Text property of the two text boxes is a string, not a number.

The solution is to explicitly direct, through code, that Visual C# convert the string representation of these integers (the Text properties of txtOp1 and txtOp2) into actual integer values before performing addition and then assign that sum to be displayed in lblResult. This is the converse of the ToString method discussed in Chapter 3, which converted an integer into the string representation of an integer.

You can accomplish this conversion through the Parse method of the Int32 structure. As discussed in Chapter 4, the int keyword, for an integer data type, is an alias for the System.Int32 data type in the .NET Framework. A structure is quite similar to a class. Although there are differences between a structure and a class, for present purposes they are essentially the same, so the two terms will be used interchangeably.

The Parse method of the Int32 structure converts its argument, the string representation of an integer, into an actual integer value before that value is assigned to an integer variable. The first statement in the following code snippet converts the string representations of both of the two integers (the Text properties of txtOp1 and txtOp2) to actual integer values before adding those values and assigning the resulting sum to another integer variable, intSum. The second statement uses the ToString method to convert the integer value into its string representation before assigning it to the Text property of a Label control:

```
int intSum = Int32.Parse(txtOp1.Text) +
    Int32.Parse(txtOp2.Text);
lblResult.Text = intSum.ToString();
```

Now 2 + 2 = 4, not 22!

NOTE *The Double class also has a Parse method. It converts the string representation of a floating-point number into an actual number (for example, "123.45" into 123.45).*

Class Methods

In previous chapters we have discussed how classes have properties and events. A property is a characteristic of an object of a class, such as the Text property of the Button class being the text displayed on the button, such as "Calculate" or "Clear." An event is something that happens to an object of a class, such as the Click event of the Button class being the event that occurs when a button is clicked.

Parse and ToString are not properties or events, but methods of a class or structure, such as Int32. A method is something an object of a class does. For example, as objects of the Person class, our methods could include breathe, walk, talk, and so on. The Form class (among others) also has methods, as you will learn in later chapters.

Change Machine Project

My mother was not above using a change machine to distract cranky or mischievous young grandchildren. The youngsters poured hundreds of pennies into the top of the machine, and they watched with fascination (fortunately youngsters are easily fascinated) as the machine sorted the pennies into amounts of change that could be taken to the bank and exchanged for dollars, quarters, and so on. The youngsters were motivated as well as fascinated, because guess who got to keep the quarters?

Your project will ask the user to input the number of pennies. You can assume the user will input a positive whole number and then click the Calculate button. The code then will output in controls the number of dollars, quarters, dimes, nickels, and pennies. Figure 5-1 shows the result of running the program and inputting 392 for the number of pennies:

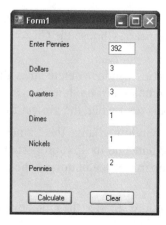

Figure 5-1   Change Machine project in action.

Creating the Project

Implement the following steps to create the application:

1. Start a new Windows application. I called my project name Change Machine.

2. Using the Toolbox, add controls to the form so it appears as shown in Figure 5-1. All the controls are labels except for the two buttons on the bottom of the form and the text box across from the label caption "Enter pennies."

3. Using the Properties window, change the Name property of the TextBox control to txtPennies and then delete any value in its Text property.

4. Using the Properties window, change the AutoSize property of all labels from the default (True) to False. This can be done by selecting all the labels first, which changes the AutoSize property of each. This step will make easier the customization of the labels in the following steps.

5. Using the Properties window, change the Text properties of the labels on the left so they are captioned as they appear in Figure 5-1.

6. Using the Properties window, change the Name properties of the labels on the right to lblDollars, lblQuarters, lblDimes, lblNickels, and lblPennies, respectively.

7. Again using the Properties window, change the BackColor property of the labels on the right to White (so they will be more visible after we delete their

text in the next step). When you click the value of the BackColor property, a tabbed dialog box appears. Choose the Custom tab and then click on a box that is white.

8. Also using the Properties window, delete any value in the Text properties of the labels on the right so they are blank, to avoid these labels' names displaying as the labels' text when the project first starts up.

9. Using the Properties window, change the Name property of the button on the left to btnCalculate and its Text property to Calculate. Similarly, change the Name property of the button on the right to btnClear and its Text property to Clear.

10. Create an event procedure stub for the Click event of btnCalculate and write the following code (to be explained in the following section, "The Algorithm") inside the event procedure:

```csharp
private void btnCalculate_Click
    (object sender, EventArgs e)
{
    int intLeftover;
    intLeftover = Int32.Parse(txtPennies.Text);
    lblDollars.Text = (intLeftover / 100).ToString();
    intLeftover = intLeftover % 100;
    lblQuarters.Text = (intLeftover / 25).ToString();
    intLeftover = intLeftover % 25;
    lblDimes.Text = (intLeftover / 10).ToString();
    intLeftover = intLeftover % 10;
    lblNickels.Text = (intLeftover / 5).ToString();
    intLeftover = intLeftover % 5;
    lblPennies.Text = intLeftover.ToString();
}
```

11. Create an event procedure stub for the Click event of btnClear and write the following code inside the event procedure:

```csharp
private void btnClear_Click(object sender, EventArgs e)
{
    txtPennies.Text = "";
    lblDollars.Text = "";
    lblQuarters.Text = "";
    lblDimes.Text = "";
    lblNickels.Text = "";
    lblPennies.Text = "";
}
```

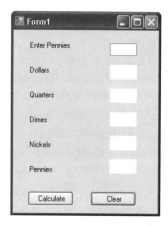

Figure 5-2   Form at run time after the Clear button is clicked.

This code simply resets the Text properties of the TextBox and the Label controls on the right to blank, as they were when the application first started. The result is shown by Figure 5-2.

The Algorithm

As you learned in Chapter 1, the purpose of Visual C# 2005, and indeed programming languages generally, is to enable you, as the programmer, to give instructions to the computer to carry out. Before you can formulate those instructions in code, you first need to be able to articulate those instructions in English or whatever other language you think in.

To write the Change Machine project, you need to come up with a step-by-step logical procedure to convert the pile of pennies into neater stacks of dollars, quarters, dimes, nickels, and pennies. A step-by-step logical procedure for solving a problem is called an *algorithm*, pronounced "Al Gore rhythm."

One algorithm for converting the pile of pennies into dollars, quarters, dimes, nickels, and pennies is to first determine how many stacks of 100 pennies you can make from the pile. Each stack of 100 pennies would then represent one dollar. You then would work with the number of pennies left over to determine the number of quarters, dimes, nickels, and pennies.

For example, assume there are 392 pennies in the pile. You might use the following steps to determine the number of quarters, dimes, nickels, and pennies in 392 pennies:

- There are 100 pennies in a dollar. You can make three stacks of 100 pennies from 392 pennies. That means there are three dollars, with 92 pennies left over, from which you will determine the number of quarters, dimes, nickels, and pennies.

- There are 25 pennies in a quarter. You can make three stacks of 25 pennies from 92 pennies. That means there are three quarters, with 17 pennies left over, from which you will determine the number of dimes, nickels, and pennies.

- There are ten pennies in a dime. You can make one stack of ten pennies from 17 pennies. That means there is one dime, with seven pennies left over, from which you will determine the number of nickels and pennies.

- There are five pennies in a nickel. You can make one stack of five pennies from seven pennies. That means there is one nickel, with two pennies left over, which is the number of pennies.

Let's now convert this algorithm from English to code.

The first step is to store the number of pennies entered by the user in the text box txtPennies into the int variable intLeftover. The following code does this, first using the Parse method of the Int32 structure (discussed in the earlier section "The Parse Method") to convert the string representation of an integer (the Text property of txtPennies) to the actual integer value before that value is assigned to the int variable (intLeftover):

```
intLeftover = Int32.Parse(txtPennies.Text);
```

When you divide the number of pennies (stored in intLeftover) by 100 (the number of pennies in a dollar), the quotient is the number of dollars in the pennies, and the remainder is the number of pennies left over. This division is integer division, because both intLeftover and 100 are integers, so it provides you with the quotient but no remainder. The % operator provides you with the remainder:

```
lblDollars.Text = (intLeftover / 100).ToString();
intLeftover = intLeftover % 100;
```

NOTE *As explained in Chapter 3, the ToString method converts a number (intLeftover / 100) into the string representation of that number so it can be displayed as text in the Label control.*

The quotient, representing the number of dollars in the pile of pennies, is displayed in lblDollars. The remainder is stored in intLeftover, which will be used in the code to determine the number of quarters, dimes, nickels, and pennies.

Next, you follow the same procedure, with two differences. First, you are not dividing the total number of pennies, but instead the number of pennies left over, represented by the current value of the variable intLeftover. Second, you are not dividing by 100, but instead 25, the number of pennies in a quarter. We already have determined the number of dollars in the pile of pennies. Now we want to determine the number of quarters in the remaining pennies. Accordingly, the code reads as follows:

```
lblQuarters.Text = (intLeftover / 25).ToString();
intLeftover = intLeftover % 25
```

The remainder of the code follows the same process, except that next the divisor is 10, the number of pennies in a dime, then 5, the number of pennies in a nickel:

```
lblDimes.Text = (intLeftover / 10).ToString();
intLeftover = intLeftover % 10;
lblNickels.Text = (intLeftover / 5).ToString();
intLeftover = intLeftover % 5;
```

The number of pennies left over after division by 5 cannot be converted into any higher change, so there is no need for further division:

```
lblPennies.Text = intLeftover.ToString();
```

You frequently will need to create and implement algorithms in writing a computer program. Creating algorithms is a skill that can be developed from any field that requires analytical thinking, including but not limited to mathematics as well as computer programming.

Conclusion

Computers, in addition to being able to store vast amounts of data, can calculate far faster and more accurately than we can. You harness the computer's calculating ability using arithmetic operators. Most of the arithmetic operators, such as those for addition and multiplication, work the same as the arithmetic operators you use with pencil and paper. However, there are two division operators: one the familiar / operator, the other the modulus operator, %. The / operator reports the decimal equivalent of the quotient and remainder (as does the / operator you use with pencil and paper or a calculator) unless both operands (dividend and divisor) are a whole number data type such as an int, in which case it's called *integer division* and reports only the quotient. The % operator reports only the remainder.

In the next chapter, you will learn about relational and logical operators, which enable your program to take different actions depending on choices the user makes while the program is running.

Quiz

1. Which arithmetic operator works with string as well as numeric variables?
2. What is the significance of operator precedence?
3. How can you override default operator precedence?
4. Which operator increases the value of a numeric variable by one?
5. What is integer division?
6. Which operator provides only the remainder resulting from division?
7. Which operator has precedence, an arithmetic operator or the assignment operator?
8. What is the purpose of the Parse method of the Int32 class?
9. What is the purpose of the ToString method of the Int32 class?
10. What is a method of a class?

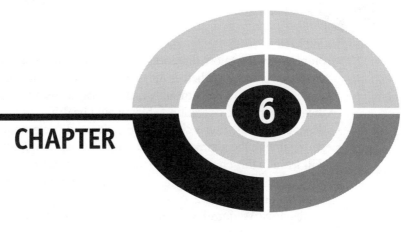

CHAPTER 6

Making Comparisons— Comparison and Logical Operators

Can you imagine going to a restaurant that had only one item on its menu? Although this would make it easy for you to decide what you want to order, this one-item restaurant likely would not be in business long, because people like choices. Indeed, life is full of choices—some pleasant (a good menu) and some not so pleasant (do you want to pay by cash, check, or credit card).

Up to now the programs we have discussed have been like the one-item restaurant, offering no choices. However, as programs become more sophisticated, they often branch in two or more directions. For example, a calculator program would first give the user a choice of whether they want to add, subtract, multiply, or divide. The code then would need to determine which choice the user made before performing the indicated arithmetic operation, which would be different, and lead to a different result, depending on the user's choice. The code would determine the user's choice by comparing it with the alternatives—addition, subtraction, multiplication, or division. You will learn in this chapter how to make that comparison using comparison operators.

A comparison operator can make only one comparison at a time. Sometimes you need to combine several comparisons. For example, some years ago car washes had Ladies Free Wednesdays, which meant that on Wednesdays (evidently a slow day for car washes) women could have their cars washed for free. The car wash would need to make two comparisons to determine eligibility for a free car wash. The customer's gender must be equal to female, and the day of the week must be equal to Wednesday. Either comparison just by itself would not be enough to determine eligibility for a free car wash; the two comparisons must be done together. You will learn in this lesson how to combine several comparisons using logical operators.

The comparison and logical operators lay the groundwork for the following chapters on control structures and loops, which use these operators to determine whether a condition, or a combination of conditions, evaluates as true or false.

Debugging

Before discussing the comparison and logical operators, let's take a brief detour into debugging. The immediate benefit of debugging is that it will enable you to test code in this chapter without going to the trouble of adding controls to your form. The longer-term benefit of debugging, which you will use in later chapters, is that it enables you to identify and solve "bugs," a term that usually means a logic error in your code (such as $2 + 2 = 22$ instead of 4).

Note *The origin of the term "bug" is in dispute. One story is that during the pre-PC era, when mainframe computers ruled the earth, a mainframe was producing illogical results. The programmers checked and rechecked their punch cards but could find no errors. In desperation, they opened up the mainframe. Inside they saw a moth fried on one of the circuits.*

One useful class for debugging is named, not surprisingly, the Debug class. The Debug class is part of the System.Diagnostics namespace. Accordingly, you should import this namespace at the beginning of your code as follows:

```
using System.Diagnostics;
```

Now you can refer in your code just to Debug rather than the much longer System. Diagnostics.Debug.

The Debug class has a WriteLine method. The syntax of the WriteLine method is

```
Debug.WriteLine(parameter)
```

The WriteLine method outputs the value of its parameter to the Output window, which you may display with the menu command View | Other Windows | Output. For example, the following code outputs 10 to the Output window:

```
private void Form1_Load(object sender, EventArgs e)
{
   int A = 10;
   Debug.WriteLine(A);    // Outputs 10
}
```

The WriteLine method only outputs to the Output window if you start your application with the Debug | Start Debugging menu command. There will be no output to the Output window if you instead start your application with the Debug | Start Without Debugging menu command. This is logical because you need to be debugging to use the Debug class.

Finally, the output to the Output window from the WriteLine output usually is not the only output in the Output window. The Output window normally also contains information generated by Visual C# 2005. As Figure 6-1 shows, the output to the Output window from WriteLine usually is the last output in the Output window.

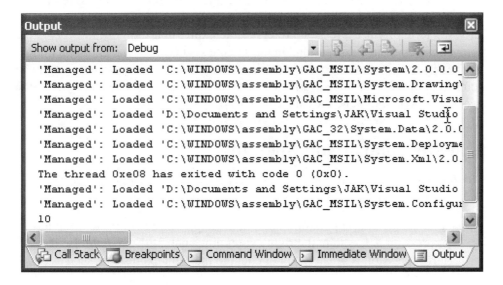

Figure 6-1   Output window.

When you're finished debugging, choose Stop Debugging from the Debug menu to stop the running of the application.

Comparison Operators

Often your programs will need to compare two values. The comparison may be whether the two values are equal, or whether one value is greater than (or less than) another. Regardless of which comparison is being made, the comparison may have only one of two possible results, either true or false.

The earlier example of a calculator program was used to show one use of comparisons—to determine which of several choices the user has made. Comparisons also are used for error prevention. For example, in the calculator program, before performing division, the program should compare the divisor to zero, because division by zero is illegal and, if performed, will result in a run-time error. If the divisor is equal to zero, the user should be warned and the division not performed. Otherwise, the division may be performed.

Comparison operators usually are used to compare numerical values, but some of them also may be used to compare strings, as discussed later in this chapter.

The syntax of a comparison is shown here:

```
[Expression1] [comparison operator] [Expression2];
```

In the following discussion, the term "left expression" refers to the expression on the left side of the comparison operator (Expression1 in the sample syntax). Similarly, the term "right expression" refers to the expression on the right side of the comparison operator (Expression2 in the sample syntax).

The left and right expressions both may be anything that has a value that can be compared: literals, constants, variables, or properties. However, the data type of the two expressions should be the same.

Numeric Comparison Operators

The following list describes the comparison operators used to compare numbers and the circumstances under which they evaluate to true or false:

- The < (less than) operator results in the expression being true if the left expression is less than the right expression, such as 4 < 5, but false if the left expression is greater than or equal to the right expression, such as 5 < 4 or 5 < 5.

- The <= (less than or equal to) operator results in the expression being true if the left expression is less than or equal to the right expression, such as 4 <= 5 or 5 <= 5, but false if the left expression is greater than the right expression, such as 5 <= 4.

- The > (greater than) operator results in the expression being true if the left expression is greater than the right expression, such as 5 > 4, but false if the left expression is less than or equal to the right expression, such as 4 > 5 or 5 > 5.

- The >= (greater than or equal to) operator results in the expression being true if the left expression is greater than or equal to the right expression, such as 5 >= 4 or 5 >= 5, but false if the left expression is less than the right expression, such as 4 >= 5.

- The == (equality) operator results in the expression being true if the left expression is equal to the right expression, such as 5 == 5, but false if the left expression is less than or greater than the right expression, such as 4 == 5 or 5 == 4.

NOTE *A common rookie mistake is to use = for equality comparison. The = operator is the assignment operator; it does not compare for equality.*

The != (inequality) operator works the opposite of the equality operator. The inequality operator results in the expression being true if the left expression is less than or greater than the right expression, such as 4 != 5 or 5 != 4, but false if the left expression is equal to the right expression, such as 5 != 5.

Try running the following code in a new or existing project. The output for each Debug.WriteLine statement, true or false, is in the comment accompanying that line:

```
private void Form1_Load(object sender, EventArgs e)
{
    int A = 10;
    int B = 8;
    int C = 10;
    Debug.WriteLine(A > B);   // Outputs True
    Debug.WriteLine(A >= B);  // Outputs True
    Debug.WriteLine(A == B);  // Outputs False
    Debug.WriteLine(A != B);  // Outputs True
    Debug.WriteLine(A < B);   // Outputs False
    Debug.WriteLine(A <= B);  // Outputs False
    Debug.WriteLine(A > C);   // Outputs False
    Debug.WriteLine(A >= C);  // Outputs True
```

```
Debug.WriteLine(A == C);   // Outputs True
Debug.WriteLine(A != C);   // Outputs False
Debug.WriteLine(A < C);    // Outputs False
Debug.WriteLine(A <= C);   //   ' Outputs True
}
```

String Comparisons

Programs often need to make string comparisons. For example, code that authenticates users who are logging in needs to compare the user name entered with a list of user names, and the password entered with the password for that user name. Another example is the Find feature in Microsoft Word, Internet Explorer, and other applications, which enables you to search text for specific words.

You can use two of the comparison operators, equality and inequality, with strings. For example, "Jeff" == "Jeff" evaluates to true, "Jeff" != "Jeff" evaluates to false, and "Jeff" == "Kent" evaluates to false.

NOTE *Conversely, the other comparison operators (>, >=, <, and <=) cannot be used with strings.*

The following code shows the use of the equality and inequality comparison operators with strings:

```
private void Form1_Load(object sender, EventArgs e)
{
    string name1 = "Jeffrey";
    string name2 = "Jeffery";
    string name3 = "Jeff";
    string name4 = "Jeffrey";
    Debug.WriteLine(name1 == name2);   //outputs False
    Debug.WriteLine(name1 != name3);   //outputs True
    Debug.WriteLine(name1 == name4);   //outputs True
}
```

Let's discuss how the equality and inequality operators work behind the scenes.

String comparisons are based on positive integer values of the characters in the string. For the English language, the character set adopted by ANSI (American National Standards Institute) and ASCII (American Standards Committee for Information Interchange) use the numbers 0–255 to cover all alphabetical characters (upper- and lowercase), digits and punctuation marks, and even characters used in graphics and line drawings. Table 6-1 lists the ASCII values of commonly used characters:

Characters	Values	Comments
0 through 9	48–57	0 is 48; 9 is 57.
A through Z	65–90	A is 65; Z is 90.
a through z	97–122	A is 97; Z is 122.

Table 6-1 ASCII Values of Commonly Used Characters

NOTE *The result of the comparison of string representations of numbers may not always be what you expect. As you might expect, "5" is greater than "4" because the ASCII value of 5 (53) is greater than the ASCII value of 4 (52). However, "5" also is greater than "4444" for the same reason.*

Precedence

The comparison operators (<, >, <=, and >=) are of equal precedence and are evaluated from left to right.

The equality and inequality operators (== and !=) are below the comparison operators in precedence, but are of equal precedence between themselves. They also are evaluated from left to right.

The comparison, equality, and inequality operators all rank lower than the arithmetic operators discussed in the previous chapter and higher than the logical operators discussed in the next section.

Logical Operators

Sometimes a first comparison and a second comparison both must evaluate as true for an action to take place. For example, a person may vote only if their age is at least 18 *and* they are a citizen:

- First comparison: age >= 18
- Second comparison: USA citizenship == true
- Only if both comparisons are true: Allowed to vote
- If either comparison is false: Not allowed to vote

By contrast, at other times it is sufficient if either a first comparison or a second comparison evaluates as true for an action to take place. For example, to be admitted to a community college, the prospective student must be either at least 18 years old or have a high school diploma:

- First comparison: age >= 18
- Second comparison: High school diploma == true
- If either comparison is true: Eligible for admission
- Only if both comparisons are false: Not eligible for admission

The combining of comparisons in either the conjunctive (and) or disjunctive (or) involves logical operators.

The && Operator

As Table 6-2 shows, the && operator performs an "And" comparison and returns false unless both comparisons are true.

The following code shows the && operator in action:

```
private void Form1_Load(object sender, EventArgs e)
{
    int A = 10;
    int B = 8;
    int C = 6;
    Debug.WriteLine(A > B && B > C);  // Outputs True
    Debug.WriteLine(A > B && C > B);  // Outputs False
    Debug.WriteLine(B > A && B > C);  // Outputs False
}
```

In the first use of the && operator (A > B && B > C), 10 > 8 is true, and 8 > 6 is true. Because both expressions are true, the output is true.

By contrast, in the second use of the && operator (A > B && C > B), whereas 10 > 8 is true, 6 > 8 is false. Because only one expression is true, and the other is false, the output is false.

Similarly, in the third use of the && operator (B > A && B > C), 8 > 10 is false, so even though 8 > 6 is true, because one of the two expressions is false, the output

If First Expression Is	And Second Expression Is	Result Is
true	true	true
true	false	false
false	true	false
false	false	false

Table 6-2   The && Operator

is false. Actually, because the first expression is false, the second expression is not evaluated. The overall expression will be false whether the second expression is true or false.

Of course, if both expressions are false, the output is false.

The voting eligibility example discussed earlier is a good case of when you would use the && operator, because both conditions (adult age and citizenship) must be true or the result (eligibility to vote) is false.

The & Operator

The & operator is almost identical to the && operator in comparing two Boolean expressions. The only difference is that if the first expression is false, the second expression still is evaluated. By contrast, with the && operator, if the first expression is false, the second expression is not evaluated, because the overall expression will be false whether the second expression is true or false.

Because with the && operator the evaluation of the second expression is conditional on the evaluation of the first expression being true, the && operator is referred to as the *conditional* And operator, whereas the & operator is referred to as the *logical* And operator.

The || Operator

As Table 6-3 shows, the || operator performs an "Or" comparison and returns true unless both comparisons are false.

The following code, which is the same as used for the && operator (except || is substituted for &&), shows the || operator in action:

```
private void Form1_Load(object sender, EventArgs e)
{
    int A = 10;
    int B = 8;
    int C = 6;
    Debug.WriteLine(A > B || B > C);   // Outputs True
```

If First Expression Is	And Second Expression Is	Result Is
true	true	true
true	false	true
false	true	true
false	false	false

Table 6-3   The || Operator

```
Debug.WriteLine(A > B || C > B);   // Outputs True
Debug.WriteLine(B > A || B > C);   // Outputs True
}
```

In the first use of the || operator (A > B || B > C), 10 > 8 is true, and 8 > 6 is true. Because both expressions are true, the output is true.

In the second use of the || operator (A > B || C > B), 10 > 8 is true, so even though 6 > 8 is false, because at least one expression is true, the output is true. Actually, because the first expression is true, the second expression is not evaluated. The overall expression will be true whether the second expression is true or false.

Similarly, in the third use of the || operator (B > A || B > C), whereas 8 > 10 is false, 8 > 6 is true, so again because at least one expression is true, the output is true.

Of course, if both expressions are false, the output is false.

The community college admission example discussed earlier is a good case of when you would use the || operator, because only one of the two conditions (adult age or a high school diploma) need be true for the result (eligibility for admission) to be true.

The || operator is implied in the comparison operators (>= and <=). For example, the expression

```
A >= B;
```

is the same as

```
A > B || A == B;
```

The | Operator

The | operator is almost identical to the || operator in comparing two Boolean expressions. The only difference is that if the first expression is true, the second expression still is evaluated. By contrast, with the || operator, if the first expression is true, the second expression is not evaluated, because the overall expression will be true whether the second expression is true or false.

Because with the || operator the evaluation of the second expression is conditional on the evaluation of the first expression being false, the || operator is referred to as the *conditional* Or operator, whereas the | operator is referred to as the *logical* Or operator.

The ^ Operator

The ^ operator performs a logical exclusion operation on two Boolean expressions and returns a Boolean value, which as Table 6-4 shows, is true if one and only one of the expressions evaluates to true; otherwise, it is false.

If First Expression Is	And Second Expression Is	Result Is
true	true	false
true	false	true
false	true	true
false	false	false

Table 6-4   The ^ Operator

The following code shows how the ^ operator works with Boolean expressions:

```
private void Form1_Load(object sender, EventArgs e)
{
    int A = 10;
    int B = 8;
    int C = 6;
    Debug.WriteLine(A > B ^ B > C);   // Outputs false
    Debug.WriteLine(A > B ^ C > B);   // Outputs true
    Debug.WriteLine(B > A ^ B > C);   // Outputs true
}
```

In the first use of the ^ operator (A > B ^ B > C), 10 > 8 is true, and 8 > 6 is true. Because both expressions are true, the output is false.

In the second use of the ^ operator (A > B ^ C > B), 10 > 8 is true, and 6 > 8 is false. Because only one of the expressions is true, the output is true.

Similarly, in the third use of the ^ operator (B > A ^ B > C), whereas 8 > 10 is false, 8 > 6 is true. Because only one of the expressions is true, the output is true.

Of course, if both expressions are false, the output is false.

The ^ operator also is known as the Xor operator, which is an acronym for the exclusive Or operator.

The ! Operator

The ! (logical Not) operator changes true to false and false to true. An example is when my youngest daughter tells me, "Dad, you look like Tom Cruise...NOT!"

The ! operator is useful in situations whether Not true appears more intuitive than false. For example, in the calculator program discussed earlier in this chapter, in verifying whether the divisor is equal to zero (division by zero being illegal), it may be more intuitive to say that division may be performed if the divisor is not equal to zero than to say that division may be performed if the divisor is greater than zero.

The ! operator is a unary operator, which means it operates on one operand. This is different from the preceding operators, which are binary, operating on two operands.

Precedence

Logical operators rank lower than the comparison operators discussed earlier in this chapter. Table 6-5 lists the order of precedence among comparison operators, from highest to lowest.

If logical operators of equal priority appear in the same statement, precedence between them is from left to right.

Why && and || in Addition to & and |?

As previously discussed, the only difference between the & and && operators is that the && operator does not evaluate the second expression if the first expression is false. Similarly, the only difference between the | and || operators is that the || operator does not evaluate the second expression if the first expression is true.

Not yet discussed is what difference it really makes whether you use & or &&, or | or ||.

The answer is, there is no real difference if the second expression is simply a comparison, other than a slight savings in processor time for sometimes skipping the evaluation of the second expression. However, the second expression may be more complex, such as a function call that changes values. In that event, variables may have different values depending on whether the second expression was evaluated.

Priority	Operator(s)	Description
1	!	Not
2	&	Logical And
3	^	Logical Xor
4	|	Logical Or
5	&&	Conditional And
6	||	Conditional Or

Table 6-5　Precedence among Logical Operators

Conclusion

As programs become more sophisticated, they often branch in two or more directions based on whether a condition is true or false. For example, as discussed at the beginning of this chapter, a calculator program, before performing division, should check to see if the divisor is equal to zero (division by zero being illegal) and, if performed, result in a run-time error. The program branches by performing the division if the divisor is not equal to zero, but warning the user if the divisor is equal to zero.

You use comparison operators to determine if the divisor is equal to (or is not equal to) zero. There are comparison operators to test for equality and inequality, as well as whether one value is greater than or less than another.

A comparison operator can make only one comparison at a time, and sometimes you need to combine several comparisons. For example, to determine if someone is eligible to vote, you have to compare both their age to the minimum voting age and their country of citizenship to the United States. In this case, both comparisons must evaluate as true or the person is not allowed to vote. However, in other comparisons, only one of two conditions need be true. For example, you may be permitted to attend a movie without having to pay for a ticket if you are either a child or a senior citizen.

You use logical operators to combine several comparisons. The logical operators include And, when both comparisons must evaluate as true for an action to be taken, and Or, when only one of two comparisons must evaluate as true for an action to be taken. There are other logical operators as well.

The comparison and logical operators lay the groundwork for the following chapters, which use these operators to determine if a condition, or a combination of conditions, evaluates as true or false.

Quiz

1. What does the WriteLine method of the Debug class do?
2. What is the data type of the result of a comparison performed by a comparison operator?
3. May the = operator be used for equality comparison?
4. Which comparison operators can you use with strings as well as with numeric data types?

5. What is the ANSI or ASCII value of a character?

6. What is the difference between the && and & operators?

7. Which operators have precedence, comparison or arithmetic?

8. What is the purpose of a logical operator?

9. Which logical operator operates on only one operand rather than two?

10. Which operators have precedence, comparison or logical?

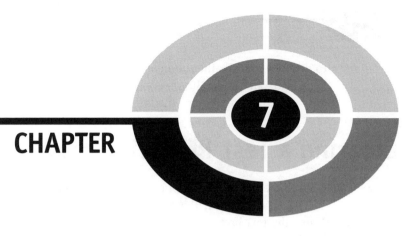

CHAPTER

7

Making Choices—if and switch Control Structures

I showed you in Chapter 6 how to use comparison and logical operators to evaluate an expression as true or false. I will show you in this chapter how to use that information by employing a control structure—specifically an if control structure or a switch control structure—so that different blocks of code execute depending on whether an expression evaluates as true or false.

The application user interacts with your code, including if and switch control structures, through the GUI of your application. You will learn in this chapter how

to use two controls that often are utilized with if and switch control structures: the CheckBox and RadioButton controls.

Creating a Test Project

Create a new Windows application so you can run the code in this chapter.

The default form will have two controls: a TextBox control and a Button control. Name the text box txtInput and delete its Text property (if any). Name the button btnTest and change its Text property to Test.

When you run the project, in Debug mode, you will enter a value in the text box, click the button, and then view the output in the Output window. Figure 7-1 shows the form at run time with the value "George" entered.

The if Control Structure

The if control structure comes in three varieties, depending on the number of alternative blocks of code:

- You use the if statement if you want a block of code to execute if a condition is true but no block of code to execute if the condition is false. For example, if a purchaser is eligible for a senior citizen discount, you adjust the price, but if not, there is no price change to make.

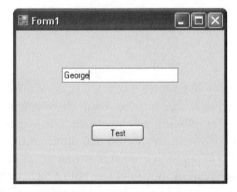

Figure 7-1   Test form.

- You use the if...else statement if you want one block of code to execute if a condition is true, and a second, different block of code to execute if the condition is false. This code structure often is used when there are two alternatives, such as yes or no, or male or female.

- The if...else if statement is similar to the if...else statement except that the if...else if statement is used when there are more than two choices. For example, if your test score is 90 or better, your grade is an A. If your test score is between 80 and 89, your grade is a B. If your test score is between 70 and 79, your grade is a C, and so on.

The if Statement

You use an if statement to execute code if, and only if, a condition is true. If the condition is false, the code dependent on the if statement does not execute. After the if statement finishes executing, execution continues with the code, if any, following the statement.

The syntax of an if statement is shown here:

```
if (condition)
    [Code];
```

Both lines together are called an if statement. The first line consists of the if keyword followed by an expression, such as a relational expression, that evaluates to a Boolean value (true or false). The relational (or other Boolean) expression must be in parentheses, and it should not be terminated with a semicolon.

The next line is called a conditional statement. The statement is conditional because the statement executes only if the value of the relational expression following the if keyword is true. If the value of the relational expression is false, the conditional statement is not executed (in effect, it's skipped).

NOTE *There may be more than one conditional statement. If so, the multiple conditional statements must be encased in curly braces. This is illustrated in the following section "Multiple Conditional Statements."*

Try the following code. It displays "You entered a positive number" to the Output window only if the input is a positive number (greater than zero). However, it displays "This line will always print" whether or not the input is a positive number, because after the if statement finishes executing, execution continues with the code following the if statement.

NOTE *Because the Debug class is part of the System.Diagnostics namespace, you should import that namespace with a using statement as you did in Chapter 6.*

```
private void btnTest_Click(object sender, EventArgs e)
{
    string strScore;
    int intScore;
    strScore = txtInput.Text;
    intScore =  Int32.Parse(strScore);
    if (intScore > 0)
        Debug.WriteLine("You entered a positive number");
    Debug.WriteLine("This line will always print");
}
```

NOTE *This code assumes that the user entered a number in the text box before clicking the Test button. Otherwise, an error would result. The "Input Validation" section later in this chapter will discuss how to guard against this error.*

The comparison may also use logical operators, as in the following code, which validates a test score as being between 0 and 100:

```
private void btnTest_Click(object sender, EventArgs e)

{
    string strScore;
    int intScore;
    strScore = txtInput.Text;
    intScore = Int32.Parse(strScore);
    if (intScore >= 0 && intScore <= 100)
        Debug.WriteLine
        ("You entered a valid test score (0 - 100)");
    Debug.WriteLine("This line will always print");
}
```

This code displays "You entered a valid test score (0–100)" in the Output window only if the input is between 0 and 100. However, it displays "This line will always print" whether or not the input is between 0 and 100.

Multiple Conditional Statements

The first Debug.WriteLine statement in each of the preceding two examples ("You entered a positive number" and "You entered a valid test score (0–100)," respectively) is indented to show that it is conditional (that is, it will execute only if the if condition is true). This indenting is not required by the compiler. Rather, it is helpful to the programmer to see the flow of the code, and will be used in this and later chapters. Often the Visual C# 2005 IDE will add the indentation for you.

The second Debug.WriteLine statement ("This line will always print") is not indented because it is not conditional (that is, it will execute whether the condition is true or false).

As mentioned in the opening discussion on the if statement, unless you use curly braces, only the first statement following the if keyword and relational expression is conditional. That is fine in the preceding two examples, because logically the second Debug.WriteLine statement should not be conditional. However, sometimes you want more than one statement to be conditional.

For example, in the following code, only the first Debug.WriteLine statement is conditional. The second Debug.WriteLine statement is not, so it will execute whether the relational expression is true or false:

```
private void btnTest_Click(object sender, EventArgs e)
{
    string strScore;
    int intScore;
    strScore = txtInput.Text;
    intScore = Int32.Parse(strScore);
    if (intScore % 2 == 0)
        Debug.WriteLine("The number is even");
    Debug.WriteLine("And the number is not odd");
}
```

Thus, if the user enters an odd number such as 17 in the text box, the statement "The number is even" will not display because the statement is conditional and the relational expression is false. So far, so good. However, the following statement "And the number is not odd" will display even on input of an odd number because that statement is not conditional. This is not the logical result; we want this second statement also to be conditional.

If you want more than one statement to be conditional, you must encase these statements in curly braces:

```
private void btnTest_Click(object sender, EventArgs e)

{
    string strScore;
    int intScore;
    strScore = txtInput.Text;
    intScore = Int32.Parse(strScore);
    if (intScore % 2 == 0)
    {
        Debug.WriteLine("The number is even");
        Debug.WriteLine("And the number is not odd");
    }
}
```

Now the second statement, "And the number is not odd," will execute only if the if expression is true.

Common Mistakes

During years of teaching introductory programming classes, I have noticed several common mistakes in the writing of if statements. Some of these mistakes may result in compiler errors and therefore are easy to spot. However, other mistakes are harder to spot because they do not cause an error, either at compile time or run time, but rather give rise to illogical results.

Don't Put a Semicolon after the Relational Expression!

The first common mistake is to place a semicolon after the relational expression:

```
private void btnTest_Click(object sender, EventArgs e)
{
    int num = Int32.Parse(txtInput.Text);
    if ( num % 2 == 0 );  // don't put a semicolon here!
        Debug.WriteLine("The number is even");
}
```

Because the compiler generally ignores blank spaces, the following if statement would be the same, and better illustrates visually the problem:

```
if ( num % 2 == 0 )
    ;  // don't put a semicolon here!
Debug.WriteLine("The number is even");
```

No compiler error will result, though there will be a warning about a possible mistaken empty statement. The compiler will assume from the semicolon that it is an empty statement. An empty statement does nothing. An empty statement is perfectly legal in C#, and indeed sometimes has a purpose. Here, however, it is not intended.

One consequence is that the empty statement will execute if the relational expression is true. Of course, nothing will happen. So far, there is no harm done.

However, there is an additional consequence: an illogical result. The Debug.WriteLine statement "The number is even" will execute whether or not the relational expression is true. In other words, even if an odd number is entered in the text box, the program will output "The number is even."

The reason the Debug.WriteLine statement "The number is even" will execute whether or not the relational expression is true is that this statement is not conditional. As explained in the preceding section, "Multiple Conditional Statements," unless you use curly braces, only the first statement following the if keyword and relational expression is conditional. That first, conditional statement is the empty statement by virtue of the semicolon following the if expression. And this leads us to the next common mistake.

Don't Forget Curly Braces for Multiple Conditional Statements

This issue already has been discussed in the preceding section "Multiple Conditional Statements," but it bears repeating here because it is a very common mistake. If you intend multiple statements to be conditional, you must encase them in curly braces.

Don't Mistakenly Use the Assignment Operator!

The third common syntax error is to use the assignment operator instead of the relational equality operator because the assignment operator looks like an equals sign:

```
private void btnTest_Click(object sender, EventArgs e)
{
    int num = Int32.Parse(txtInput.Text);
    if ( num % 2 = 0 )  // wrong operator!
        Debug.WriteLine("The number is even");
}
```

The result is a compiler error, because you are attempting to use an integer value (01) in a Boolean expression.

The if...else Statement

You use the if...else statement if you want one block of code to execute if the condition is true, and a second, different block of code to execute if the condition is false. This differs from the if statement in that some code in the if...else statement will execute; the only question is which. By contrast, with the if statement, if the condition is false, no code dependent on the if statement executes.

After the if...else statement completes executing, execution continues with the code following the statement.

The syntax of an if...else statement is shown here:

```
if (condition)
    [Code];
else
    [Code];
```

No express condition follows the else statement because the condition is implied as being the negation of the condition following the if statement. In other words, the code following the else statement executes if the condition following the if statement is not true.

Try the following code. It displays in the Output window "You entered a valid test score (0 - 100)" if the input is between 0 and 100, and it displays "You did not enter a valid test score" if the input is less than 0 or greater than 100.

```
private void btnTest_Click(object sender, EventArgs e)
{
   string strScore;
   int intScore;
   strScore = txtInput.Text;
   intScore = Int32.Parse(strScore);
   if (intScore >= 0 && intScore <= 100)
      Debug.WriteLine
      ("You entered a valid test score (0 - 100)");
   else
      Debug.WriteLine
      ("You did not enter a valid test score");
   Debug.WriteLine("This line will always print");
}
```

Although you can have an if without an else, as with the if statement, you cannot have an else without an if. This is logical because else means "none of the above," and without an if there is no "above."

Common Mistakes

Just as with the if statement, I have noticed while teaching introductory programming classes several common syntax mistakes with the if...else statement.

No else Without an if Expression

You can have an if expression without an else part. However, you cannot have an else part without an if part. The else must be part of an overall if statement. This requirement is logical. The else part works as "none of the above." Without an if part, there is no "above."

As a consequence, in the following code example, placing a semicolon after the Boolean expression following the if keyword will result in a compiler error. Because curly braces are not used, the if statement ends after the empty statement created by the incorrectly placed semicolon. The Debug.WriteLine statement "The number is even" is not part of the if statement. Consequently, the else part is not part of an if...else statement and therefore will be regarded as an else part without an if part.

```
private void btnTest_Click(object sender, EventArgs e)
{
   int num = Int32.Parse(txtInput.Text);
   if ( num % 2 == 0 );  // don't put a semicolon here!
      Debug.WriteLine("The number is even");
   else
      Debug.WriteLine("The number is odd");
}
```

Don't Put a Relational Expression after the else Keyword!

Another common mistake is to place a relational expression in parentheses after the else keyword:

```
private void btnTest_Click(object sender, EventArgs e)
{
   int num = Int32.Parse(txtInput.Text);
   if ( num % 2 == 0 )
      Debug.WriteLine("The number is even");
   else ( num % 2 == 1 ) // don't do this!
      Debug.WriteLine("The number is odd");
}
```

The program will not compile, and the end of the else expression will be highlighted with an error description such as "; expected."

Actually, the error description is misleading. The problem is not that a semicolon is missing. Instead, no relational expression should follow the else keyword. The reason is that the else acts like "none of the above" in a multiple-choice test. If the if expression is not true, the conditional statements connected to the else part execute.

Don't Put a Semicolon after the else Expression!

Another common mistake is to place a semicolon after the else expression. This will not cause a compiler or run-time error, but it often will cause an illogical result.

For example, in the following code, the Debug.WriteLine statement "The number is odd" will output even if the number input is even:

```
private void btnTest_Click(object sender, EventArgs e)
{
   int num = Int32.Parse(txtInput.Text);
   if ( num % 2 == 0 )
      Debug.WriteLine("The number is even");
   else;  // don't put a semicolon here!
      Debug.WriteLine("The number is odd");
}
```

The Debug.WriteLine statement "The number is odd" will execute whether or not the relational expression is true because that Debug.WriteLine statement no longer is part of the if…else statement. Unless you use curly braces, as explained already in connection with the if statement, only the first statement following the else keyword is conditional. That first, conditional statement is the empty statement by virtue of the semicolon following the if expression. Therefore, the Debug.Write-Line statement "The number is odd" is not part of the if…else statement at all.

Curly Braces Needed for Multiple Conditional Statements

As with the if expression, if you want more than one conditional statement to belong to the else part, you must encase the statements in curly braces.

The if…else if Statement

You use the if…else if statement if you have more than two alternative blocks of code, the maximum possible with an if…else statement.

With an if…else if statement, the first block of code whose condition is true executes, and all following blocks of code are skipped. The first block of code follows the if clause, and each succeeding block of code coupled with a condition is an else if clause. You can have as many else if clauses as you want. Finally, you may optionally have an else clause that, as with an if…else statement, acts as "none of the above." After the if…else if statement finishes executing, execution continues with any code following the statement.

The syntax of an if…else if statement is shown here:

```
if (condition)
    [Code];
else if (condition)
    [Code];
else  // optional
    [Code];
```

Try the following code. It displays in the Output window "The test score is valid" if the input is between 0 and 100, "Test score cannot be less than zero" if the input is less than 0, or "Test score cannot be greater than 100" if the input is greater than 100.

```
private void btnTest_Click(object sender, EventArgs e)
{
    string strScore;
    int intScore;
    strScore = txtInput.Text;
```

```
    intScore = Int32.Parse(strScore);
    if (intScore >= 0 && intScore <= 100)
        Debug.WriteLine("The test score is valid");
    else if (intScore < 0)
        Debug.WriteLine
        ("Test score cannot be less than zero");
    else
        Debug.WriteLine
        ("Test score cannot be greater than 100");
    Debug.WriteLine("This line will always print");
}
```

Although you can have as many else if clauses as you want, none can appear after an else clause. The else clause is optional; it serves the function of "none of the above."

Common Syntax Errors

The common syntax errors for the if part discussed earlier in this chapter apply to the else if part also. Don't put a semicolon after the relational expression, and you must enclose multiple conditional statements in curly braces.

Additionally, just as you cannot have an else part without a preceding if part, you cannot have an else if part without a preceding if part.

You are not required to have an else part. The downside in omitting the else part is you will not have code to cover the "none of the above" scenario in which none of the relational expressions belonging to the if part and else if parts is true.

Input Validation

The code used in the preceding section "The if...else if Statement" involves the entry of a student's test score. No matter how badly a student performs on a test, that student will do no worse than 0. Similarly, no matter how well a student performs on a test, that student will do no better than 100.

However, it is not prudent to assume that the application user will enter a number between 0 and 100 in the input box and click the OK button. Human error is inevitable. An application user may not even read directions, much less follow them. Further, even a conscientious application user will make data-entry errors.

For example, if the application user enters in the input box a number less than 0 or larger than 100, that input necessarily is incorrect. If that incorrect input is stored as the student's test score, the student's records will be wrong. Even worse, under the saying "garbage in, garbage out," any calculation based on that test score also will be wrong.

Accordingly, your code should guard against the possibility that the application user's input is incorrect. This is called validating the user's input, or input validation.

The code used in the preceding section "The if…else if Statement" does perform input validation. The following portion of that code checks that the user's input is between 0 and 100, and it warns the user that the input is incorrect if the input isn't between 0 and 100:

```
if (intScore >= 0 && intScore <= 100)
   Debug.WriteLine("The test score is valid")
else if (intScore < 0)
   Debug.WriteLine("Test score cannot be less than zero");
else
   Debug.WriteLine
   ("Test score cannot be greater than 100");
```

Exceptions

The code used in the preceding section "The if…else if Statement" performs some input validation, but not enough. For example, that code does not guard against the possibility that the application user could enter a nonnumeric string and click the OK button. To demonstrate this, run the project with the Debug | Start Without Debugging menu command, or simply press CTRL-F5. Enter **Jeff** in the text box and click the Test button. Your application will halt, and the message box shown in Figure 7-2 will display with the message "Input string was not in a correct format."

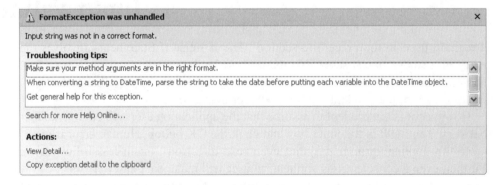

Figure 7-2 The exception "Input string was not in a correct format".

Stop the project by clicking the Quit button. Run the project again with Debug | Start Without Debugging menu command. Click the Test button without entering anything in the text box. Your application will halt, and the message box shown in Figure 7-2 again will display.

What Is an Unhandled Exception?

Figure 7-2 refers to an "unhandled exception." An exception is a problem that occurs while the program is executing that must be dealt with before the program can proceed. Examples of exceptions include the inability to open a file because it cannot be found, the application not putting in the floppy drive the floppy disk that contains the file, the file being corrupt, the operating system not having enough available memory remaining to open the file, and so on. The exception may be due to faulty code, application user error, or circumstances beyond the control of either the programmer or the application user, such as a crash of the operating system. Regardless of the cause, the program cannot proceed until the exception is resolved.

It is possible through code to "handle" an exception. For example, if the application user forgot to put in the floppy drive the floppy disk that contains the file, code warns the user and gives the user an opportunity to either put the floppy disk in the floppy drive or quit the application.

Exception handling is an advanced subject and therefore is not covered here. For present purposes, exceptions generally do not crash programs; instead, unhandled exceptions crash programs. That is why Figure 7-2 refers to an "unhandled exception."

Determining Where the Exception Occurred

Although this explains what an unhandled exception is generally, what remains to be explained is what caused the unhandled exception in this code. You can determine the details of the exception by clicking the Details button. Figure 7-3 shows the result of clicking the Details button of the message box depicted in Figure 7-2.

The line of our code highlighted (in yellow) when the exception occurred is

```
intScore = Int32.Parse(strScore)
```

The reason for the error is that the Parse method of the Int32 class requires for its parameter a string representation of an integer. Neither "Jeff" nor an empty string is a string representation of an integer. Therefore, the Parse method is unable to properly execute, and an exception occurs.

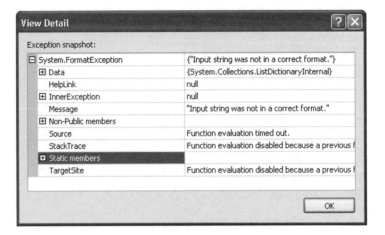

Figure 7-3 Exception details.

TryParse Method

The Int32 class has a TryParse method in addition to a Parse method. Both methods convert the string representation of an integer into an integer. However, the TryParse method also returns a Boolean value (true or false) indicating whether the conversion was successful. If the conversion is not successful—for example, because the argument is "Jeff" or an empty string—no exception occurs. Rather, the return value is false.

NOTE *Other numeric classes, such as Double, also have a TryParse method. In the case of the Double class, the method attempts to convert the string representation of a double into a double.*

The syntax of the TryParse method of the Int32 class is shown here:

```
[Boolean] = Int32.TryParse([string], out [integer]);
```

The first parameter, the string, is the string representation of an integer. When the TryParse method is called, the first argument usually is a variable, though it also could be a property of the String data type, such as the Text property of a Label control.

The second parameter, an integer, is where the integer equivalent of the string representation will be stored. When the TryParse method is called, the second argument usually is a variable, though it also could be a property of the Int32 data type.

The second parameter is preceded by the out keyword. The out keyword indicates that the method may change the value of the argument. This is the case here, because when the TryParse method is called, the value of the second argument will be changed to the integer value of the first argument's string representation of that integer. By contrast, the first argument need not be preceded by the out keyword because the string representation only is being evaluated, not being changed.

The return value is Boolean and usually stored in a variable of that data type.

The following code snippet illustrates the TryParse method in action:

```
string strScore;
int intScore;
strScore = txtInput.Text;
bool blnInput;
blnInput = Int32.TryParse(strScore, out intScore);
if (blnInput == false)
    // Conversion unsuccessful.
    // Don't use intScore in further code
else
    // Conversion successful. Use intScore in further code
```

The following code implements this logic and modifies the code used in the preceding section on the if...else if statement:

```
private void btnTest_Click(object sender, EventArgs e)
{
    string strScore;
    int intScore;
    strScore = txtInput.Text;
    bool blnInput;
    blnInput = Int32.TryParse(strScore, out intScore);
    if (blnInput == false)
        Debug.WriteLine
        ("Input does not evaluate to an integer");
    else if (intScore >= 0 && intScore <= 100)
        Debug.WriteLine("The test score is valid");
    else if (intScore < 0)
        Debug.WriteLine
        ("Test score cannot be less than zero");
    else
        Debug.WriteLine
        ("Test score cannot be greater than 100");
    Debug.WriteLine("This line will always print");
}
```

Controls Used for the if Control Structure

The application user interacts with your code, including the if control structure, through the graphical user interface (GUI) of your application. Two controls in particular are used in conjunction with the if control structure. The CheckBox control is used when a particular decision has only two choices, as in true or false, yes or no, and so on. The RadioButton control is used when there are multiple, mutually exclusive choices, such as whether a student's grade is an A, B, C, D, or F.

CheckBox Control

CheckBox controls are commonly used in Windows applications. For example, in the Print dialog box shown in Figure 7-4, there are check boxes for Print to File and Collate.

The reason that CheckBox controls are often used is that they are ideal for situations in which there are only two choices, such as yes or no, male or female, and so on. The CheckBox control being checked is considered true, yes, or on, with unchecked being false, no, or off.

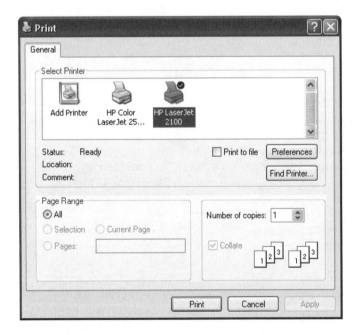

Figure 7-4 Print dialog box.

Each CheckBox control is independent of the others. They may all be checked, or all unchecked, or any combination of checked and unchecked.

The CheckBox control has two properties you will use often: Text and Checked.

The Text property essentially is a label, built into the CheckBox control, that identifies to the application user the purpose of the check box. When you add the CheckBox control to the form, you have to draw it large enough (after first setting AutoSize to False in the Properties window) to show the text portion as well as the check box portion. The Text properties of the two CheckBox controls in Figure 7-4 are Print to File and Collate, respectively. The Text property usually is set at design time.

The Checked property is of a Boolean data type. If the check box is checked, the value of the Checked property is True. If the check box is not checked, the value of the Checked property is False.

Because the Checked property has only two possible values, True and False, often you use an if...else statement based on the Checked property, as the following code snippet illustrates:

```
if (chkPizza.Checked == true)
   Debug.WriteLine("I want pizza!");
else
   Debug.WriteLine("I don't want pizza.");
```

RadioButton Control

RadioButton controls also are commonly used in Windows applications. Taking again the example of the Print dialog box in Figure 7-4, there are radio buttons for printing all pages, printing the current page, printing a range of pages, and printing just the selected text.

The primary difference between CheckBox and RadioButton controls is that whereas each check box is independent of another, all radio buttons in a group are related in that only one of them can be chosen at any one time. Therefore, the RadioButton control is ideal for situations in which there are choices, and one choice, but only once choice, must be chosen.

NOTE *If radio buttons are contained within a GroupBox or Panel control, those radio buttons are in a group independent of any other radio buttons on the form. This is useful when one set of radio buttons that, say, concerns age is logically independent of another set of radio buttons that, say, concerns income level.*

As with the CheckBox control, the two properties you will use often with the RadioButton control are Text and Checked. As with the CheckBox control, the Checked property for a RadioButton control has only two possible values: True and False.

In the event you have more than two RadioButton controls, often you use an if…else if statement based on the Checked property, as shown here:

```
if (radLarge.Checked == true)
    Debug.WriteLine("I want a large pizza.");
else if (radMedium.Checked == true)
    Debug.WriteLine("I want a medium pizza.")
else
    Debug.WriteLine("I want a small pizza.");
```

Pizza Calculator

This project calculates the cost of the programmer's food of choice, pizza, using radio buttons and check boxes. The cost of the pizza is based initially on whether the pizza is a small ($5.00), medium ($7.50), or large ($10.00). There is an additional cost of 50 cents for each topping.

Figure 7-5 shows the project in action. Because the application user has selected a large pizza ($10.00) with pepperoni and anchovies ($1.00 for two toppings), the total cost is $11.00.

Figure 7-5   Pizza Calculator project.

Creating the Project

Radio buttons are used to represent the three alternative pizza sizes: small, medium, and large. The radio buttons are named radSmall, radMedium, and radLarge, respectively. Similarly, their Text properties are, respectively, Small, Medium, and Large.

Check boxes are used to represent each topping choice—mushrooms, pepperoni, and my favorite, anchovies (because no one else wants anchovies, I get the whole pizza for myself). The check boxes are named chkMushroom, chkPepperoni, and chkAnchovy, respectively. Similarly, their Text properties are, respectively, Mushroom, Pepperoni, and Anchovy.

There are two Button controls. One is named btnCalculate, and its Text property is Calculate. The other is named btnClear, and its Text property is Clear.

There also are two Label controls. The one that displays the total in Figure 7-5 is named lblTotal. Its Text property initially is blank. I also have set its AutoSize property to False and its BackColor property to white using the Properties window to give it its white background. The other label has a Text property of Total. It is not involved in the code, so you can retain its default name (mostly likely, Label1 or Label2).

How the Project Works

The cost of the pizza is based initially on whether the pizza is a small ($5.00), medium ($7.50), or large ($10.00). There is an additional cost of 50 cents for each topping.

Clicking the Calculate button calculates and displays the cost in the Label control named lblTotal. Clicking the Clear button returns the application to its default settings (large size, all toppings unchecked, cost blank).

The Code

The code will consist of three sections:

- Declaring constants to represent the cost of the pizza sizes and toppings. This will be done in the Click event procedure of the Calculate button.

- Calculating the cost of the pizza. This also will be done in the Click event procedure of the Calculate button.

- Restoring the application to its default settings. This will be done in the Click event procedure of the Clear button.

Declaring the Constants

Declare the following constants in the Click event procedure of the Calculate button:

```
private void btnCalculate_Click
    (object sender, EventArgs e)
{
    const double LARGE = 10;
    const double MEDIUM = 7.5;
    const double SMALL = 5;
    const double TOPPING = 0.5;
}
```

These constants represent the costs of the different sizes of pizza and the extra cost of each topping. The actual values instead could have been used in the code. However, using constants makes the code easier to change if the costs of the different sizes or the toppings ever change, because only one change would need to be made (the value of the constant) rather than changing the value in all places it is used in the code. Similarly, the constants LARGE and SMALL are declared as a double instead of an integer because someday the price may involve cents, such as the price of a large pizza changing from $10.00 to $10.50.

NOTE *These constants do not need to have broader scope than the Click event procedure of the Calculate button because they only are referred to in that event procedure.*

Calculating the Price

Add the following code in the Click event procedure of the Calculate button after the declaration of the constants:

```
private void btnCalculate_Click
    (object sender, EventArgs e)
{
    const double LARGE = 10;
    const double MEDIUM = 7.5;
    const double SMALL = 5;
    const double TOPPING = 0.5;
    double dblTotal;
    if (radLarge.Checked == true)
        dblTotal = LARGE;
    else if (radMedium.Checked == true)
```

```
      dblTotal = MEDIUM;
   else
      dblTotal = SMALL;
   if (chkMushroom.Checked == true)
      dblTotal += TOPPING;
   if (chkPepperoni. Checked == true)
      dblTotal += TOPPING;
   if (chkAnchovy. Checked == true)
      dblTotal += TOPPING;
   lblTotal.Text = dblTotal.ToString("c");
}
```

The variable dblTotal is used to store the total price. The data type of this variable is a double instead of an integer because the number may be a floating-point number (that is, it may have cents as well as dollars).

An if ... else if statement is used to assign to dblTotal the cost of the size of pizza selected, based on which radio button's value is true. An if ... else if statement is appropriate because one, and only one, of the radio buttons can be selected.

By contrast, independent if statements are used to determine whether to add 50 cents for each topping, based on whether each check box's value is true. Independent if statements are appropriate because the value of each check box is independent from that of the others. The user may choose all toppings, no toppings, or any combination.

Finally, the value of dblTotal is displayed in the Total label. This involves two steps. First, the value is converted from a double to a string data type using the ToString method because that value is being assigned to a property (Text) that is a string data type. Second, the argument "c" is passed to the ToString method so the total is formatted as currency, starting with the dollar sign ($) and having two numbers, no more and no less, to the right of the decimal point.

NOTE *The argument "c" to the ToString method is a format specifier. There are other format specifiers, such as "e" for exponential or scientific notation, and "p" for a percentage.*

Restoring the Application to its Initial Settings

Finally, the following code in the Click event procedure of the Clear button returns the application to its default settings (large size, all toppings unchecked, cost blank):

```
private void btnClear_Click(object sender, EventArgs e)
{
   radLarge.Checked = true;
   radMedium.Checked = false;
```

```
radSmall.Checked = false;
chkMushroom.Checked = false;
chkPepperoni.Checked = false;
chkAnchovy.Checked = false;
lblTotal.Text = "";
}
```

The switch Control Structure

The switch control structure is quite similar to the if ... else if statement, but they are not the same. The primary difference is that, in the if ... else if statement, the if and else if clauses each may evaluate completely different expressions, whereas a switch control structure may evaluate only one expression, which then must be used for every comparison.

For example, the condition of an if clause could be whether Night > Day, the condition of the following else if clause whether Citizenship == U.S., the condition of the next else if clause whether NumberOfClasses >= 4, and so on. Usually the conditions evaluated by the if and else if clauses are related, but they can be completely independent of each other.

By contrast, the switch control structure evaluates one test expression, and that test expression is used for all the following comparisons.

Syntax

The syntax of a switch control structure is shown here:

```
switch [test expression]
{
    case [integer literal constant]:
        [code];
        break;
    // More case statements optional
    default: //also optional
        [code];
        break;
}
```

The test expression must be capable of being evaluated as an integer. A character also may be evaluated as an integer because of its ANSI or ASCII value, discussed in the last chapter. The grade program in the next section demonstrates the use of a character as a test expression.

Each case keyword must be followed by an integer expression that is either a literal (such as 5) or a constant. Consequently, a variable cannot follow a case keyword. In the grade program in the next section, the constant is a character literal, such as 'A', 'B', and so on. A character literal works following the case keyword because, as mentioned in the previous paragraph, the character's ANSI or ASCII value is an integer value.

The default keyword serves the same purpose as an else part in an if ... else or if ... else if statement, and therefore is not followed by an integer constant or literal.

Each case block, and the default block, usually must be terminated by a break statement. The exception to this rule is discussed in the later section on the break keyword.

The switch Control Structure in Action

Although the switch control structure differs from the if ... else if statement in that it may evaluate only one expression that then must be used for every comparison, it otherwise behaves quite similarly to the if ... else if statement:

If the condition following an if (or else if) clause in an if ... else if statement evaluates as true, the code following that clause executes, and none of the following else if (or else) clauses are evaluated. Similarly, if the literal or constant following a case clause matches the test expression, the code following the case clause executes, and any remaining case clauses are not evaluated because of the break keyword at the end of the case clause. (An exception to this is discussed in the later section on the break keyword).

If the condition following an if (or else if) clause in an if ... else if statement instead evaluates as false, the code following that clause does not execute, and each of the following else if (or else) clauses is evaluated in order. Similarly, if the expression or expression list following a case clause does not match the test expression, the code following that clause does not execute, and each of the following case clauses is evaluated in order.

If none of the conditions following the if and else if clauses in an if ... else if statement evaluates as true, the code following the else clause executes if there is an else clause. Similarly, if none of the literals or constants following the case clauses in a switch control structure match the test expression, the code following the default clause executes if there is a default clause. The default clause is analogous to the else clause, covering the "none of the above" circumstance.

Once execution of the if ... else if statement is completed, the program continues to the code following the if control structure. Similarly, once execution of the switch control structure is completed, the program continues to the code following the switch control structure.

Open the Windows application you created at the beginning of this chapter. Comment out the existing code in the Click event of the button btnTest and then insert the following code in that event procedure:

```
private void btnTest_Click(object sender, EventArgs e)
{
   char grade;
   grade = Convert.ToChar(txtInput.Text);
   switch (grade)
{
      case 'A':
         Debug.WriteLine("Test score between 90-100");
         break;
      case 'B':
         Debug.WriteLine("Test score between 80-89");
         break;
      case 'C':
         Debug.WriteLine("Test score between 70-79");
         break;
      case 'D':
         Debug.WriteLine("Test score between 60-69");
         break;
      case 'F':
         Debug.WriteLine("Test score between 0-59");
         break;
      default:
         Debug.WriteLine("Invalid grade");
         break;
   }
}
```

The one line of code that requires further explanation is

```
grade = Convert.ToChar(txtInput.Text);
```

The Text property returns a string, but the grade variable's data type is a character. The ToChar method of the Convert class returns the first character in the string as a character, which then is assigned to the grade variable.

Run the project and input a letter for a grade. The switch control structure evaluates the value of that variable and then either outputs the test score based on that value or outputs "Invalid grade" if the grade is not an A, B, C, D, or F.

The break Keyword

In an if … else if statement, each if, else if, or else part is separate from all the others. By contrast, in a switch control structure, once a matching case statement is reached, unless a break statement is reached, execution tries to "fall through" to the following case statements.

If a case or default statement contains at least one executable statement, such as Debug.WriteLine, the lack of a following break statement would result in the following compiler error: "Control cannot fall through from one case label to another."

This "falling through" behavior is not necessarily bad. In the following modification of the grade program, the falling through behavior permits the user to enter a lowercase grade in addition to an uppercase grade. There is no compiler error because each case that lacks a break statement (such as case 'a') has no executable statement.

```
private void btnTest_Click(object sender, EventArgs e)
{
    char grade;
    grade = Convert.ToChar(txtInput.Text);
    switch (grade)
    {
        case 'a':
        case 'A':
            Debug.WriteLine("Test score between 90-100");
            break;
        case 'b':
        case 'B':
            Debug.WriteLine("Test score between 80-89");
            break;
        case 'c':
        case 'C':
            Debug.WriteLine("Test score between 70-79");
            break;
        case 'd':
        case 'D':
            Debug.WriteLine("Test score between 60-69");
            break;
        case 'f':
        case 'F':
            Debug.WriteLine("Test score between 0-59");
            break;
```

```
        default:
            Debug.WriteLine("Invalid grade");
            break;
    }
}
```

You could not achieve the same result with a case statement such as the following:

```
case: 'a' || 'A'
```

The reason is that the case keyword must be followed by an integral or character literal (such as 4 or 'a') or constant.

Choosing Between if...else if and switch

The if ... else if statement and the switch control structure are similar. However, in deciding whether to use if ... else if or switch, you may not have a choice.

Although any code you write using a switch control structure also can be written using an if control structure, the reverse is not also true. If you need to evaluate several different expressions in a block of code, you cannot use a switch control structure, which may evaluate only one expression that then must be used for every comparison.

Additionally, the switch control structure does not work well with ranges of values. A statement such as

```
if (var >= 90 && var <= 100)
```

tests if the value of the variable var is between 90 and 100. You can't write the same statement so easily in a switch statement because the case keyword must be followed by an integer or constant. There would need to be a separate case for 90, 91, 92, 93, and so forth to 100.

If you do have a choice, the decision is one of personal preference, concerning which way is easier to write and easier to understand. Your choice may be the switch statement in processing a menu choice such as 1, 2, or 3, or A, B, or C.

Conclusion

In Chapter 6, you learned how to use comparison and logical operators to evaluate an expression as true or false. You learned in this chapter how to use that information by employing control structures—specifically an if or switch control structure—so that different blocks of code execute depending on whether an expression evaluates as true or false.

The application user interacts with your code, including if and switch control structures, through the GUI of your application. You learned in this chapter how to use two controls that often are utilized with if and switch control structures—the CheckBox and RadioButton controls.

In the next chapter, I will show you how to apply this information with loops, which enable you to repeat the execution of code statements.

Quiz

1. What does modal mean?

2. What is the converse of modal?

3. What is a conditional statement?

4. Which namespace should you import to use the Debug class?

5. What are the three varieties of an if control structure?

6. What is an exception?

7. What does the TryParse method of the Int32 class do?

8. Which two controls are commonly used with the if control structure?

9. What is the primary difference between the if . . . else if statement and the switch control structure?

10. What part of a switch control structure performs the same purpose as an else clause in an if control structure?

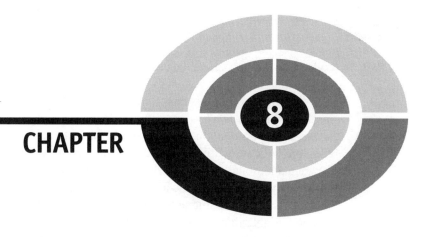

CHAPTER

Repeating Yourself—Loops and Arrays

Parents customarily remind their children not to repeat themselves. Indeed, parents often illustrate another saying ("Do as I say, not as I do") by continually repeating that reminder.

Sometimes you want your code to repeat itself. For example, if the user enters invalid data, you may want to ask the user whether they want to retry or quit. If they retry and still enter invalid data, you again would ask the user whether they want to retry or quit. This process keeps repeating until the user either enters valid data or quits.

You use a loop to repeat the execution of code statements. A loop is a structure that repeats the execution of code until a condition becomes false. In the preceding example, the condition is that the data is invalid and the user should retry. The repeating code is the prompt asking the user whether they want to retry or quit and then permitting them to retry if they want to.

I will show you in this chapter the different types of loops available and how to implement them.

An array permits you to use a single variable to store many values. The values are stored at consecutive indexes, starting with zero and then incrementing by one for each additional element of the array. For example, to store sales for each day of the week, you can create one array with seven elements, rather than declaring seven separate variables. Using an array has several advantages. It is easier to keep track of one variable than seven. Additionally, you can use a loop to access each consecutive element in an array, whether to assign a value of that element or to display that value.

I will show you in this chapter how to create and use arrays.

Loops

This section will introduce four loop statements: for, foreach, while, and do while. These loop statements differ in syntax and other details, but they all have in common that they repeat the execution of code until a condition becomes false, each repetition being called an *iteration*.

The for Statement

If you wanted to output the numbers between 1 and 10, you could write a program such as the following, which will output 1 through 10, followed by "This line will always print."

```
private void Form1_Load(object sender, EventArgs e)
{
    int num = 1;
    Debug.WriteLine(num++);
    Debug.WriteLine(num++);
    Debug.WriteLine(num++);
    Debug.WriteLine(num++);
    Debug.WriteLine(num++);
    Debug.WriteLine(num++);
    Debug.WriteLine(num++);
    Debug.WriteLine(num++);
    Debug.WriteLine(num++);
```

```
    Debug.WriteLine(num++);
    Debug.WriteLine("This line will always print");
}
```

NOTE *Because the Debug class is part of the System.Diagnostics namespace, you should import that namespace with a using statement as you did in Chapter 6.*

However, you could write the same program with far less code by using a for statement:

```
private void Form1_Load(object sender, EventArgs e)
{
    for (int num = 1; num <= 10; num++)
        Debug.WriteLine(num);
Debug.WriteLine("This line will always print");
}
```

NOTE *As with the if control structure, only the first statement following the for statement is conditional on the for statement unless curly braces are used to enclose multiple conditional statements.*

The difference between using and not using a loop structure becomes more pronounced if you change the specification from outputting the numbers between 1 and 10 to outputting the numbers between 1 and 100. I won't rewrite the first program because it would take up too many pages; suffice it to say you would have to add 90 more Debug.WriteLine(num++) statements. However, here's the same program using a for statement:

```
private void Form1_Load(object sender, EventArgs e)
{
    for (int num = 1; num <= 100; num++)
        Debug.WriteLine(num);
    Debug.WriteLine("This line will always print");
}
```

Indeed, by using the for statement, the same code could output the numbers between 1 and 1000 or even 1 and 10000; you just would need to change the 100 in the code to 1000 or 10000.

Syntax

Let's discuss the syntax of the for statement. The for keyword is followed by parentheses that contain three expressions that will be discussed in a moment. This line of code is followed by one or more statements.

```
for ([DataType counter] = [start value];
[comparison]; [update counter])
    statement;
```

If the execution of more than one statement is conditional on the for statement, the statements must be enclosed with curly braces, as is the case with the if control structure:

```
for ([DataType counter] = [start value];
[comparison]; [update counter])
    {
        statement;
        statement;
    }
```

The three expressions contained in the parentheses following the for keyword are separated by semicolons; there is no semicolon after the third expression because no expression follows it.

Let's use as an example the following portion of the code in the preceding section, which displays the numbers 1 through 10:

```
for (int num = 1; num <= 10; num++)
    Debug.WriteLine(num);
Debug.WriteLine("This line will always print");
```

The first expression is

```
int num = 1;
```

This expression may be referred to as the *initialization* part because its purpose usually is to initialize the value of a variable (as explained shortly, there are alternatives), typically referred to as a *counter*, to provide that variable with a starting value. In this example, the integer variable num is the counter, and it is initialized to the starting value of 0. This initialization is the first action performed by the loop, and it's only performed once.

The second expression is

```
num <= 10;
```

This expression may be referred to as the *comparison* part because its purpose usually is to make a comparison involving the counter. The result of this comparison will evaluate to a Boolean value (true or false). The result must be true for the conditional statements to execute. In this example, the condition is whether the current value of num is less than or equal to 10.

The third expression is

```
num++
```

This expression is referred to as the *update* part because its purpose usually is to update the value of the counter. In this example, the integer variable num is incremented. This expression executes at the end of each iteration, and only executes if the condition was true at the beginning of the iteration.

NOTE *Postfix incrementing was used in this example and generally is employed by convention. However, the result would be the same if prefix incrementing were used, because only one operator is involved in this expression.*

The conditional statement is

```
Debug.WriteLine(num);
```

This statement will execute only if the result of the comparison is true.

The following statement is not conditional, so it will execute once—no more, no less:

```
Debug.WriteLine("This line will always print");
```

As mentioned earlier, similar to the if control structure, only the first statement following the for statement is conditional on the for statement unless curly braces are used to enclose multiple conditional statements. Here, no curly braces were used, so this statement is not conditional.

Initialization and updating need not occur in the parentheses following the for statement. In the following variation of the program that outputs from 1 through 10, num is initialized before the for statement and is incremented inside the body of the loop:

```
private void Form1_Load(object sender, EventArgs e)
{
    int num = 1;
    for (; num <= 10;)
    {
        Debug.WriteLine(num);
        num++;
    }

    Debug.WriteLine("This line will always print");
}
```

Even though initialization and incrementing are not done within the parentheses, two semicolons nevertheless must be within the parentheses to indicate where the three expressions would be. Although an expression may be empty, the following semicolon nevertheless is necessary.

Although there are syntax variations, following the parentheses with a semicolon is not one of them. Instead, this is simply is a mistake. The semicolon is interpreted as an empty statement. Accordingly, in the following code fragment, the only number that would output is 11:

```
private void Form1_Load(object sender, EventArgs e)
{
    int num;
    for (num = 1; num <= 10; num++); // no semi-colon
        Debug.WriteLine(num);
    Debug.WriteLine("This line will always print");
}
```

The reason the only number that would output is 11 is that the loop continues, and the empty statement executes, until the condition fails when num is 11. The Debug.WriteLine(num) statement is not part of the for loop, so it executes when the for loop completes, outputting 11, the value of num after the loop finishes.

How the for Statement Works

Let's now analyze how the following for statement works, step by step:

```
for (int num = 1; num <= 10; num++)
    Debug.WriteLine(num);
Debug.WriteLine("This line will always print");
```

Here is the order of execution in the first iteration of the loop:

1. The integer variable num is initialized to 1.

2. The current value of num, 1, is compared to 10.

3. Because the comparison is true, num is less than or equal to 10. The current value of num, 1, is output.

4. The value of num is incremented, becoming 2.

And here is the order of execution in the second iteration of the loop:

1. The current value of num, 2, is compared to 10.

2. Because the comparison is true, the current value of num, 2, is outputted.

3. The value of num is incremented, becoming 3.

Note that the initialization that occurred during the first iteration of the loop did not occur during the second iteration of the loop. As discussed previously, initialization occurs only once, in the first iteration of the loop. Were it otherwise, an endless loop would result.

This order of execution in the second iteration of the loop repeats during the third and following executions of the loop, each time incrementing the value of num through the tenth iteration of the loop, which executes in the following order:

1. The current value of num, 10, is compared to 10.

2. Because the comparison is true (10 is less than or equal to 10), the current value of num, 10, is outputted.

3. The value of num is incremented, becoming 11.

In the next iteration of the loop, the current value of num, 11, is compared to 10. Because the comparison is false (11 is not less than or equal to 10), the for loop ends. The code inside the for loop does not execute, the value of num is not incremented, and the code following the for loop executes:

```
Debug.WriteLine("This line will always print");
```

If you wanted the execution of this statement to be conditional on the for statement, then it and the preceding conditional statement would be enclosed in curly braces:

```
for (int num = 1; num <= 10; num++)
{
    Debug.WriteLine(num);
    Debug.WriteLine("This line will always print");
}
```

Table 8-1 summarizes the execution of the loop.

Value of x	x <= 10	Value of x Prints?	New Value of x
1	True	Yes	2
2	True	Yes	3
3	True	Yes	4
4	True	Yes	5
5	True	Yes	6
6	True	Yes	7
7	True	Yes	8
8	True	Yes	9
9	True	Yes	10
10	True	Yes	11
11	False	No	11

Table 8-1   Summary of Execution of for Statement

The numbers need not be outputted in ascending order. Changing the for statement to read as follows would result in the numbers between 1 and 10 being outputted in reverse:

```
for (int num = 10; num >= 1; num—)
   Debug.WriteLine(num);
Debug.WriteLine("This line will always print");
```

Beware the Infinite Loop

Let's return to the program that outputs the numbers 1 through 10:

```
private void Form1_Load(object sender, EventArgs e)
{
   for (int num = 1; num <= 10; num++)
      Debug.WriteLine(num);
   Debug.WriteLine("This line will always print");
}
```

If the statement num++ is omitted, the loop would never stop:

```
private void Form1_Load(object sender, EventArgs e)
{
   for (int num = 1; num <= 10;)
      Debug.WriteLine(num);
   Debug.WriteLine("This line will always print");
}
```

The reason is that the condition num <= 10 would never become false because num would start at 1 and its value would never change because the statement num++ is omitted.

This loop that never stops executing is called an *infinite loop*. Usually, it manifests itself by nothing happening for a protracted period, with the application never ending.

You would not intend to have an infinite loop in your code, but mistakes do happen; I have made this mistake a lot more than once. If it happens to you, don't panic. You can use the Stop Debugging button to end the program. Knowing you have encountered an infinite loop, you then can correct the code error that caused it.

A Factorial Example

So far, use of the for loop has been relatively trivial, counting numbers in ascending or descending order. However, the for loop can be used for more sophisticated programs.

The following program calculates the factorial of 5. A factorial is the product of all the positive integers from 1 to that number. For example, the factorial of 3 is 3 * 2 * 1, which is 6. Similarly, the factorial of 5 is 5 * 4 * 3 * 2 * 1, which is 120:

```csharp
private void Form1_Load(object sender, EventArgs e)
{
    int total = 1;
    for (int num = 2; num <= 5; num++)
        total *= num;
    Debug.WriteLine("The factorial of 5 is " + total);
}
```

Breaking Out of the Loop

We previously used the break keyword in a switch statement. You also can use the break keyword in a for statement. The break keyword is used within the code of a for statement, commonly within an if statement nested inside the for statement.

The break statement transfers control immediately to the statement following the for statement. Stated another way, the break statement prematurely ends the execution of the for statement before its condition becomes false.

For example, the following code will output only 5 through 7, not 5 through 10, because the loop ends prematurely when x equals a number evenly divisible by 4 (here, 8):

```csharp
private void Form1_Load(object sender, EventArgs e)
{
    for (int num = 5; num <= 10; num++)
    {
        if (num % 4 == 0)
            break;
        Debug.WriteLine(num);
    }
    Debug.WriteLine("This line will always print");
}
```

Although the break keyword is part of the C# language, I recommend you use it sparingly. Normally, the for statement has one exit point—the condition when it becomes false. However, when you use one or more break statements, the for statement has multiple exit points. This makes your code more difficult to understand and can result in logic errors.

In the following program, the logical && (And) operator is an alternative to using the break keyword:

```
private void Form1_Load(object sender, EventArgs e)
{
    for (int num = 5; num <= 10 && num % 4 > 0; num++)
        Debug.WriteLine(num);
    Debug.WriteLine("This line will always print");
}
```

Before leaving the discussion of the break keyword, one additional use of it (in conjunction with the parentheses following the for keyword being empty of all three expressions) deserves mention simply because you may encounter it. The following program is a variant of the one that outputs numbers between 1 and 10, with the first and third expressions inside the parentheses being empty because num is initialized before the for loop and incremented inside the body of the loop. In this program, the second expression—the condition—is missing as well. Instead, the break keyword inside the if/else structure substitutes for that condition.

```
private void Form1_Load(object sender, EventArgs e)
{
    int num = 1;
    for (;;)
    {
        if (num > 10)
            break;
        else
        {
            Debug.WriteLine(num + " ");
            num++;
        }
    }
}
```

Without the break keyword, the for loop would be infinite due to the lack of a second expression. Again, however, I do recommend against this use of the break keyword, and point it out simply because other programmers believe differently, and therefore you're likely to encounter it at some point in time.

The continue Keyword

You also can use the continue keyword in a for statement. The continue keyword, like the break keyword, is used within the code of a for statement, commonly within an if/else structure. If the continue statement is reached, the current iteration of the loop ends, and the next iteration of the loop begins.

For example, in the following program, the user is charged $3 an item, but not charged for a "baker's dozen." In other words, every 13th item is free (the user is charged for only a dozen items, instead of 13). The program assumes a project like the one we used in Chapter 7, in which the form contains two controls, a TextBox control named txtInput (where the user will enter the number of items) and a Button control named btnCalculate:

```
private void btnTest_Click(object sender, EventArgs e)
{
    string strItems;
    int intItems, total = 0;
    strItems = txtInput.Text;
    intItems = Int32.Parse(strItems);
    for (int counter = 1; counter <= intItems; counter++)
    {
        if (counter % 13 == 0)
            continue;
        total += 3;
    }
    Debug.WriteLine
    ("Total for " + intItems + " items is $" + total);
}
```

The price for 12 or 13 items is the same, $36. However, on the 14th item the user again is charged an additional $3, for a total of $39. The reason why the code charges the user no additional price for the 13th item is that the continue statement is reached, preventing $3 from being added to the total.

Although the continue keyword is part of the C# language, I recommend, as I do with the break keyword, that you use it sparingly. Normally, each iteration of a for statement has one end point. However, when you use a continue statement, each iteration has multiple end points. This makes your code more difficult to understand, and can result in logic errors.

In the following program, the logical ! (Not) operator is an alternative to using the continue keyword:

```
private void btnTest_Click(object sender, EventArgs e)
{
    string strItems;
    int intItems, total = 0;
    strItems = txtInput.Text;
    intItems = Int32.Parse(strItems);
```

```
for (int counter = 1; counter <= intItems; counter++)
{
   if (! (counter % 13 == 0 ))
      total += 3;
}
Debug.WriteLine
("Total for " + intItems + " items is $" + total);
}
```

NOTE *You also could use the relational != (not equal) operator, changing the if statement to if (counter % 13 != 0).*

Nesting

You can nest a for statement just as you can nest if statements. For example, the following program prints five rows of ten X characters:

```
private void Form1_Load(object sender, EventArgs e)
{
   for (int x = 1; x <= 5; x++)
   {
      for (int y = 1; y <= 10; y++)
         Debug.Write("X");
      Debug.WriteLine("");
   }
}
```

The for loop

```
for (int x = 1; x <= 5; x++)
```

is the outer for loop, and the for loop

```
for (int y = 1; y <= 10; y++)
```

is the inner for loop.

With nested for loops, for each iteration of the outer for loop, the inner for loop goes through all its iterations. By analogy, in a clock, minutes are the outer loop, seconds the inner loop. For each iteration of a minute, there are 60 iterations of seconds.

In the rows and columns example, for the first iteration of the outer for loop, the inner for loop goes through all ten of its iterations, printing ten X characters. Then, for the next iteration of the outer for loop, the inner for loop again goes through all ten of its iterations, again printing ten X characters. The same thing happens on the third, fourth, and fifth iterations of the outer for loop, resulting in five rows of ten X characters. The outer for statement represents the rows, and the inner for statement represents the columns.

The foreach Statement

The foreach statement is similar to the for statement, but it executes the statement block for each element in a collection, instead of a specified number of times. A collection is a group of usually like objects. The syntax is shown here:

```
foreach ([Data Type] [variable] in [Collection])
   //code
```

For example, a form has a Controls collection, which is a collection of all the controls on a form. The following code displays in the Output window the name of each control in the form, which is represented by the this keyword:

```
private void Form1_Load(object sender, EventArgs e)
{
    foreach (Control ctl in this.Controls)
        Debug.WriteLine(ctl.Name);
}
```

The while Statement

The while loop is similar to a for loop in that both have the typical characteristic of a loop: The code inside each continues to iterate until a condition becomes false. The primary syntax difference between them is in the parentheses following the for and while keywords.

The parentheses following the for keyword consists of three expressions: initialization, condition, and update. By contrast, the parentheses following the while keyword consists only of the condition; you have to take care of initialization and update elsewhere in the code.

The following program first introduced earlier in this chapter outputs the numbers between 1 and 10 using the for loop:

```
private void Form1_Load(object sender, EventArgs e)
{
    for (int num = 1; num <= 10; num++)
        Debug.WriteLine(num);
    Debug.WriteLine("This line will always print");
}
```

The same program using the while loop could be written like this:

```
private void Form1_Load(object sender, EventArgs e)
{
    int num = 1;
    while (num <= 10)
    {
        Debug.WriteLine(num);
        num++;
    }
}
```

With the while loop, the integer variable num had to be declared and initialized before the loop because this cannot be done inside the parentheses following the while keyword. Further, num was updated inside the code of the loop using the increment operator. This update also can be done inside the parentheses following the while keyword, as shown by an example later in this section.

The update of the variable is particularly important with the while loop. Without that update, the loop would be infinite. For example, in the following excerpt from this program, if num is not incremented, the loop would be infinite. The value of num would not change from 1, so the condition num <= 10 always would remain true.

```
int num = 1;
while (num <= 10)
    Debug.WriteLine(num);
```

Forgetting to update the value of the variable you are using in the condition is a common mistake with a while statement. Forgetting the update is less common with a for statement because that update is the usual purpose of the third expression in the parentheses following the for keyword.

Otherwise, the syntax rules discussed earlier in this chapter concerning the for statement apply equally to the while statement. For example, if more than one conditional statement belongs to the while statement, the statements must be contained within curly braces. That is why in the program that outputs the numbers between 1 and 10 using the while loop, the two statements in the body of the while loop are contained within curly braces:

```
while (num <= 10)
{
    Debug.WriteLine(num);
    num++;
}
```

In the program we just analyzed, the update of the value of num was done within the body of the loop. The update could also be done within the condition itself:

```
private void Form1_Load(object sender, EventArgs e)
{
   int num = 0;
   while (num++ < 10)
      Debug.WriteLine(num);
}
```

Updating the counter within the condition requires two changes from the previous code. First, the value of num has to be initialized to 0 instead of to 1 because the increment inside the parentheses during the first iteration of the loop would change that variable's value to 1. Second, the relational operator in the condition is < rather than <= because the value of num is being incremented before it is outputted.

Updating the counter within the condition raises the question, Given the condition num++ < 10, which comes first, the comparison or the increment? Because the increment is postfix, the answer is the comparison.

The counter also could be updated within the condition using a prefix increment. However, then the condition should be ++num <= 10 to obtain the desired output.

As with the for statement, the statement or statements following the while keyword and parentheses will not execute if the parentheses are followed by a semicolon, because that would be interpreted as an empty statement. Test yourself on this; what would be the output if we placed a semicolon after the while condition, as in the following code fragment?

```
int num = 0;
while (num++ < 10);
   Debug.WriteLine(num);
```

The only number that would output is 11. The reason is that the loop continues, and the empty statement executes, until the condition fails when num is 10. The value of num still is incremented to 11 (the increment is postfix so it occurs after the comparison), at which time the statement following the loop executes and the value of num (11) is outputted.

Given the similarities between the for and while statements, a program that uses one usually could have used the other as well. As a general rule, the for statement often is preferred when the number of iterations is known in advance, such as counting from 1 through 10. The while statement instead is preferred if the number of iterations cannot be known in advance, such as if the loop structure must continue until the user enters a valid input.

The Do While Construct

The do while loop is similar to the while loop. The primary difference is that with a do while loop, the condition is tested at the bottom of the loop, unlike a while loop where the condition is tested at the top. This means that a do while loop will always execute at least once, whereas a while loop may never execute at all if its condition is false at the outset.

The syntax of a do while loop is

```
do {
    statement(s);
} while (condition);
```

The do keyword starts the loop. The statement or statements belonging to the loop are enclosed in curly braces. After the closing curly brace, the while keyword appears, followed by the condition in parentheses, terminated by a semicolon.

A do while loop often is preferred over a while loop in situations where the loop structure must iterate at least once before the comparison may be made.

Arrays

In previous chapters, I showed you how to declare variables of different data types, such as int and double. Those variables are *scalar* variables. They can store only one value at a time.

An array permits you to use a single variable to store many values. The values are stored at consecutive indexes. The index is a positive integer, starting with zero and then incrementing by one for each additional element of the array.

Declaring Arrays

Array variables are declared the same as other variables, with one difference. The data type is followed by empty square brackets, indicating that the variable name that follows is an array rather than a scalar variable.

The following example will declare an array that represents sales for each day of a week. I have chosen the name arrSalesPerDay for the array, and an integer data type, though a floating-point data type also would be appropriate. The following statement declares the array, starting with the data type (here, int), followed by empty square brackets to indicate that an array rather than a scalar variable is being declared, followed by the name of the variable that represents the array, arrSalesPerDay:

```
int[] arrSalesPerDay;
```

The next step is to specify the size of the array—that is, the number of elements it will contain. Because this array is supposed to represent sales for each day of the week, it should have seven elements (we'll assume our store is open every day).

The following statement creates seven elements for the array. The array name (here, arrSalesPerDay) is followed by the assignment operator, which in turn is followed by the new keyword, followed by the data type (here, int), followed by the number of elements in the array within square brackets (here, seven):

```
arrSalesPerDay = new int[7];
```

You also can declare the array and its size in one statement rather than in two:

```
int[]arrSalesPerDay = new int[7];
```

NOTE *You also can assign values to the array at the same time as you declare the array. This is discussed in the later section on initialization.*

Assigning Values to the Array

Our array has seven elements, but we have not yet assigned values to any of them. That does not mean that the array elements do not have a value. When you first declare an array, each element of the array has a default value. The specific default value depends on the data type of the array. If, as here, the data type is integer, each element of the array has a default value of 0.

However, you rarely want to use the default value. Instead, you want to assign your own values to the array elements. You can do so at two times—via initialization when the array is declared and via assignment after the array is declared.

Initialization

Initialization is when you assign values to a variable when you declare it. The following example initializes the arrSalesPerDay array:

```
int[]arrSalesPerDay = new int[7] {8, 5, 7, 3, 2, 9, 11};
```

The values being assigned are enclosed in curly braces and separated by commas.

You also may omit the size of the array during initialization:

```
int[]arrSalesPerDay = new int[] {8, 5, 7, 3, 2, 9, 11};
```

This works because the number of values assigned (here, seven) tells the compiler to allocate memory to hold seven integer elements.

Another syntax variation is that you can also omit the new operator if you are using initialization:

```
int [] arrSalesPerDay = {8, 5, 7, 3, 2, 9, 11};
```

Assignment

You assign a value to an element of an array by using the index of the element. The index of the first array element is always 0. Accordingly, the index of the last array element is always one less than the total number of elements. Thus, if the array has seven elements, the index of the last array element is six.

The following code fragment assigns 73 to the second element of the array:

```
arrSalesPerDay [1]  = 73;
```

Again, the index 1 indicates the second element of the array, not the first, because the starting index of the array is 0.

You can use a loop to efficiently assign values to each element of the entire array. Try the following code, which uses two loops. The first loop assigns an arbitrary value (double the amount of the index) to that array element. The second loop outputs these elements:

```
private void Form1_Load(object sender, EventArgs e)
{
    int [] arrSalesPerDay = new int [7];
    for (int x = 0; x < 7; x++)
    arrSalesPerDay [x]  = x * 2;
    for (int x = 0; x < 7; x++)
        Debug.WriteLine(arrSalesPerDay [x]);
}
```

The counter variable x starts at 0 because 0 is always the starting element of the array. The comparison is true so long as x is less than 7. Although 7 is the number of elements in the array, the highest index of the array is 6, not 7, because the starting index is 0, not 1.

Setting the comparison to the counter being <= the number of elements in the array rather than the counter being < the number of elements is a common rookie mistake. The consequences of attempting to access arrSalesPerDay[7], which is a nonexistent element of the array, are unpredictable, though never good, because you are attempting to access an area of memory not reserved for the array. One possibility is a run-time error if the area of memory you are attempting to access is reserved, such as for the operating system.

You also can use arrays with loops to obtain a running total. Try the following code, which outputs the total of the seven daily sales amounts entered by the user:

```
private void Form1_Load(object sender, EventArgs e)
{
   int total = 0;
   int[] arrSalesPerDay = new int[7];
   for (int x = 0; x < 7; x++)
   {
      arrSalesPerDay[x] = x * 2;
      total += arrSalesPerDay[x];
   }
   Debug.WriteLine("Total Sales: " + total);
}
```

NOTE *In the examples in this section, the lower and upper bounds of the array (0 and 6, respectively) were known. You also can obtain these values through code with the GetLowerBound and GetUpperBound methods of the Array class (which represents arrays), and you can get the number of elements in the array with the Length property of that class:*

As you can see, loops are very useful with arrays.

The arrays in this chapter have one dimension. You can have arrays with two or more dimensions, two often representing rows and columns in a table or spreadsheet, three representing a cubic space, and so forth. You also can use loops with a multidimensional array. For example, a two-dimensional array would be accessed by a loop nested within another loop!

Conclusion

Loops are used to repeat the execution of code statements. The for statement is used to repeat code execution a fixed number of times. The foreach statement is similar to the for statement, but it executes the statement block for each element in a collection (a group of usually like objects), instead of a specified number of times.

The while statement is more flexible than the for statement because the number of times a while statement executes does not have to be determined when you write the code, but may depend on user input. The do while statement has the additional flexibility that it tests the condition at the bottom rather than at the top of the loop, important when the loop must execute at least once to obtain a value to compare.

An array permits you to use a single variable to store many values. The values are stored at consecutive indexes, which start with zero and end at an index that is one less than the number of elements in the array.

In the next chapter, you will learn how to use subroutines and functions to organize your code more efficiently.

Quiz

1. What is a loop?
2. What is a difference between a while statement and a for statement?
3. What is a difference between the do . . . while statement and the for and while statements?
4. What is a difference between the for and foreach statements?
5. What are examples of nesting?
6. What is an array?
7. What is the difference between declaring an array variable and declaring a scalar variable?
8. What is the lowest index of an array?
9. What is the relationship between the number of elements in an array and the highest index in that array?
10. If you declare an array without assigning a value to its elements, do its elements have a default value?

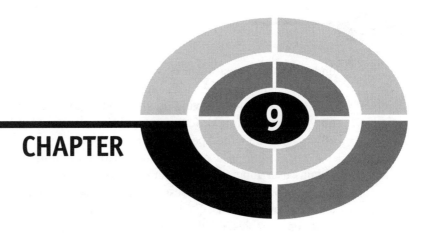

Organizing Your Code with Methods

A method is a group of statements that together perform a task. So far, the methods we have written have been event procedures, often the Load event procedure of the form.

As you write more complex and sophisticated programs, you may find that the code in your event procedures becomes extremely long.

Neither the compiler nor the Runtime cares if the code in an event procedure is short or long. However, you should care. An event procedure that continues for pages is difficult to understand or fix if errors arise.

By analogy, this book is a few hundred pages long. It would be harder to understand if each chapter was not divided into sections. This book would be still harder to understand if it consisted of only one, very long chapter. By dividing this book's content into chapters, and each chapter into sections, this book is easier to understand.

Similarly, you can divide up your code into separate methods. How you divide up your code among different methods is up to you, but logically the division usually is so each method performs a specific task.

For example, in a program that performs arithmetic calculations, one method obtains user input, another method performs the calculation, and a third method performs the output of the result. This is analogous to how a book is divided up into chapters and sections. Each chapter explores a different subject. One chapter focuses on variables, another (this one) on methods.

There are advantages to dividing your code into separate methods in addition to making your code easier to understand. For example, if a method performs a specific task, such as sending output to a printer, which is performed several times in a program, you only need to write once in a method the code necessary to send output to the printer, and then you can call that method each time you need to perform that task. Otherwise, the code necessary to send output to the printer would have to be repeated each time that task was to be performed. Further, if you later have to fix a bug in how you perform that task, or simply find a better way to perform the task, you only have to change the code in one place rather than many.

Hopefully I have persuaded you that organizing your code into separate methods can be useful. I will now show you how to do it.

Defining and Calling a Method

Implementing any method involves two steps:

1. Defining the method.
2. Calling the method.

The explanation of these steps uses terminology we have not discussed before, so that terminology is reviewed first.

Terminology of a Method

Let's look at a simple program with one method, the event procedure or handler for the Load event of the form:

```
private void Form1_Load(object sender, EventArgs e)
{
    Debug.WriteLine("Hello world");
}
```

NOTE *Up until now I have used the term "event procedure." A method that handles an event, such as this one, which handles the Load event of the form, also may be referred to as an "event handler." Now that we are discussing methods, I prefer and will be using in this chapter the term "event handler" because I believe it better distinguishes this type of method from others. However, the term "event procedure" also is acceptable; the issue really is one of personal preference.*

The first line is the header. The header is the "signature" of the method, describing its attributes or characteristics , and it consists of the following four parts:

- **Access specifier**   Here, the access specifier is private. Access specifiers were discussed in Chapter 4 with respect to variables. They serve the same purpose with methods.

- **Return type**   Here, the return type is void, which indicates the lack of a return value. Return values are discussed later in this chapter.

- **Name**   Here, the name is Form1_Load. The name of an event handler follows the Object_Event syntax. In this case, the object is Form1 and the event is Load.

- **Parameter list**   Here, the parameter list is (object sender, EventArgs e). Parameters are information provided to a method so that it may perform its task. Chapter 3 involved a project that used parameters of an event handler to report mouse coordinates. Parameters also are discussed in a later section of this chapter.

When you're declaring and implementing a method, a header always is followed by an open curly brace, which begins the body of the method, which correspondingly ends with a closing curly brace.

The method body consists of one or more statements. In this example, the method body consists of one statement, which writes "Hello World" to the Output window. The method body may contain additional curly braces, such as to enclose multiple statements that belong to an if statement or a loop.

The method body must contain a return statement unless the return type is void, as it is here, in which case the return statement is optional. Further examples in this chapter will show you how to implement a return statement.

The method header and body together are referred to as the method definition. A method cannot execute until it is first defined. Once defined, a method executes when it is called.

A method may be called by the occurrence of an event, code, or the .NET Runtime. The Form1_Load event handler is called by the occurrence of an event, namely the loading of the startup form.

The header of an event handler is predefined by the .NET Framework. You cannot change it. In order to invoke the event procedure, the .NET Runtime needs to find the event handler signature it expects for that event.

By contrast, you have relative freedom in writing the header of methods you create. This includes naming the methods, which we'll discuss next.

Naming a Method

The rules for naming a method are similar to those for naming a variable. There are only a few limitations, such as no embedded spaces within the method name. For example, Print Message is not a valid method name.

Although Visual C# imposes few limitations on how you name a method, as with naming variables, you should name your methods so that what they do is reasonably clear to you and other programmers who may have to review your code. Method names such as Method1, Method2, Method3, and so on, are not very helpful. You, and even more so your fellow programmers, will have trouble remembering which of them does what. By contrast, descriptive method names such as PrintName, PrintAddress, PrintCity, and so on, are quite helpful in describing what each method does.

I agree with Microsoft's recommendation that you use the NounVerb or Verb-Noun style to create a name that clearly identifies what the method does. For example, the method name PrintName is a concatenation of the verb "Print," which indicates the action the method takes, and the noun "Name," which indicates the information printed. You might have more than one noun, such as PrintCustomer-Name. In any event, the first letter of each noun and verb is capitalized when naming public methods. For private methods, the first word by convention often is lowercase, such as the printMessage method in the following examples.

The next sections will explain how to define your own method and then call it.

Defining a Method

Let's take our "Hello world" example and divide the code into two methods: the Load event handler and a printMessage method that outputs "Hello world."

The comments (beginning with //) indicate the beginning and end of the definition of the printMessage method and where that method is called.

```
private void Form1_Load(object sender, EventArgs e)
{
    printMessage(); // calls printMessage method
}
// begins definition of printMessage method
private void printMessage ()
{
    Debug.WriteLine("Hello world");
}
// ends definition of printMessage method
```

NOTE *As mentioned in previous chapters, because the Debug class methods are being used, you should import, with a using statement, the System.Diagnostics namespace.*

Let's first examine the definition of the printMessage method. The void keyword preceding the method printMessage means that this method does not return a value. The empty parentheses following the method name means this method has no arguments.

The body of the printMessage method has one statement, which outputs "Hello world." The method body does not need to contain an explicit return statement because, since the return type is void, the return statement is implied. However, you may include an explicit return statement. If you did, then the printMessage method would read as follows:

```
void printMessage ()
{
    Debug.WriteLine("Hello world");
    return;
}
```

Calling a Method

Firefighters put out fires. However, they generally do not drive around looking for fires. Instead, they go out to a fire when called upon to do so.

In the same way, a method does not just execute by itself. The statements within a method do not execute until and unless the method is called, usually by code, though also it could be by the occurrence of an event or by the .NET Runtime. Indeed, unless the printMessage method is called, it is the programming analogy of the tree that falls in the forest without anyone seeing or hearing it; it is there in the program, but it doesn't do anything.

The printMessage method may be called in the Load event handler of the form with the following line:

```
printMessage();
```

In this example, printMessage is the called method, because it is the method being called from the Load event handler of the form. The empty parentheses indicate that no arguments are being passed to this method. I will show you later in this chapter how to pass arguments, as well as how to use return values.

The order of execution is as follows:

1. Execution starts with the Load event handler of the form.

2. The first statement in the Load event handler, printMessage(), is executed. This calls the printMessage method.

3. Execution next shifts to the printMessage method and then begins with the first statement in that method, which outputs "Hello world."

4. After the printMessage method completes executing, execution returns to the Load event handler, which then ends execution because there are no further statements in that event handler.

Continuing the firefighter analogy, when firefighters arrive at the scene of the fire, they take control and maintain that control until they put out the fire. Similarly, once the method is called, whether by user action or code, it takes control of the application, and no other code executes without being called by the method, until the method is finished. Thus, control does not return to the Load event handler while the printMessage method is executing.

NOTE *An exception is that two methods may execute independently in a multithreaded application. Such an application is an advanced topic far beyond the introductory scope of this book.*

Completing the analogy, when the firefighters successfully put out the fire, they pack up their equipment and go back to the fire station, relinquishing control of the fire scene. Similarly, when the method finishes executing, it relinquishes control of the application, and whatever code (or user action) follows the call of the method determines the further flow of the application. Thus, control returns to the Load event handler when the printMessage method finishes executing.

Parameters—Sending Information to a Method

As discussed earlier in this chapter, the parentheses following the method name in the header contain the method's parameters. Parameters are information that is provided to a method so that it may perform its task.

Returning to our firefighter analogy, when firefighters are called to a fire, they need to know the location of the fire, the type of fire (house fire, chemical fire, and so on) so they know what equipment to bring, and other pertinent information. The particular location and type of fire may well vary from call to call, but in each case this information is necessary in order for the firefighters to do their job.

Similarly, a method often needs information in order to perform its task. For example, a method that outputs the square of a number to the Output window needs to know the number to be squared. The value of that number may vary from call to call, but in each case the method will need to know the particular number to be squared. This information is called an argument.

Some methods don't need further information to do their job. One example has been the printMessage method, which simply outputs "Hello world." It does not need any further information to do its job.

However, when we want to modify the printMessage method so that it does not always output "Hello world" but instead outputs whatever message we ask it to, we need to tell it the message we want it to output. We can do so by passing the method an argument that specifies the message.

This chapter will discuss two ways of passing arguments—by value and by reference.

Passing Arguments by Value

The following is a modification of the program that uses the printMessage method to output a message. This time, the content of the message to be output (here, the Text property of the form) is passed to the printMessage method as an argument:

```
private void Form1_Load(object sender, EventArgs e)
{
    printMessage(this.Text);
}
private void printMessage (string msg)
{
    Debug.WriteLine("The form's Text property is " + msg);
}
```

Using the Argument

The following code calls the printMessage method:

```
printMessage(this.Text);
```

The Text property of the form (represented by the "this" keyword) is passed as an argument to the printMessage method. The value of this Text property then is passed to the string variable msg, which is the parameter name in the header of the printMessage method:

```
void printMessage (string msg)
```

The string variable msg then is used in the body of the printMessage method to output the message:

```
Debug.WriteLine("The form's Text property is " + msg);
```

The header must include a parameter name as well as a data type so the value being passed by the method call (this.Text in the Load event handler) may be stored in a variable that can be used in the printMessage method. Otherwise, the value passed would have no place to be stored for use in the printMessage method.

Note *As with variables and methods, you should name the parameter descriptively.*

Using Multiple Arguments

The program we just discussed uses one argument. However, a method may have two or even more method arguments.

The following modification of the printMessage method uses two arguments—the first for the form's Text property, the second for the number of controls on the form:

```
private void Form1_Load(object sender, EventArgs e)
{
    printMessage(this.Text, this.Controls.Count);
}
private void printMessage (string txt, int count)
{
    Debug.WriteLine _
    ("The form's Text property is " + txt);
    Debug.WriteLine
    ("The form contains " + count + " controls");
}
```

Here is some sample output (the form I used has two controls):

```
The form's Text property is Form1
The form contains 2 controls
```

As this example illustrates, the only difference between declaring a procedure with a single parameter and declaring a procedure with more than one parameter is that a comma separates the parameters:

```
(string txt, int count)
```

Similarly, when you call the procedure, a comma separates the arguments:

```
(this.Text, this.Controls.Count);
```

The Parameters and Arguments Must Match

The order of arguments in the call to the method must correspond to the order of the arguments in the header. Here are the call and the header for this example:

```
printMessage(this.Text, this.Controls.Count);
private void printMessage (string txt, int count)
```

The first variable in the method call is this.Text. Therefore, the value of the form's Text property is copied into the first parameter in the printMessage header, txt. Similarly, because the second argument in the call is this.Controls.Count, the value of that Count property is copied into the second parameter in the printMessage header, count.

If the arguments in the method call were reversed, as in

```
printMessage(this.Controls.Count, this.Text);
```

the result would be the following compiler errors:

```
cannot convert argument 1 from 'string' to 'int'
```

and

```
cannot convert argument 2 from 'int' to 'string'
```

This is because the compiler was expecting from the method header that the first argument would be a string, not an int, and that the second argument would be an int, not a string.

Similarly, when you call a method, you must pass the same number of arguments as the number of parameters specified in the method's parameter list. For example, if you tried to call the printMessage method with only one argument, as in

```
printMessage(this.Text);
```

the compiler would complain as follows:

```
No overload for method 'printMessage' takes 1 argument
```

This means that the compiler could not find a header for printMessage that takes only one argument.

Too many arguments are no better than too few arguments. If you tried to call the printMessage method with three arguments, as in

```
printMessage(this.Text, this.Controls.Count, "oops");
```

the compiler would similarly complain:

```
No overload for method 'printMessage' takes 3 arguments
```

Passing Arguments by Reference

Passing arguments by value is fine when you don't want to change their value in the called method. The printMessage method did not change the value of its arguments; it simply outputs them.

However, sometimes the intent of a method is to change the value of the argument passed to it. Consider the following example, in which the doubleIt method is supposed to double the value of the argument passed to it:

```
private void Form1_Load(object sender, EventArgs e)
{
    int num =5;
    Debug.WriteLine
    ("Num in Form1_Load before call = " + num);
    doubleIt(num);
    Debug.WriteLine
    ("Num in Form1_Load after call = " + num);
}
void doubleIt (int x)
{
    Debug.WriteLine
    ("x in doubleIt before doubling = " + x);
    x *= 2;
    Debug.WriteLine("x in doubleIt after doubling = " + x);
}
```

Here is some sample output:

```
num in Form1_Load before call = 5
x in doubleIt before doubling = 5
x in doubleIt after doubling = 10
num in Form1_Load after call = 5
```

As the sample input and output reflects, the value of num in the Load event handler was not changed by the doubling of its counterpart argument in the doubleIt method.

The reason the value of num was not changed in the Load event handler is that a copy of it was passed to doubleIt. The change was made to the copy, but the original, the variable num in the Load event handler, was not affected by the doubling of the copy. The logic is the same as if I gave you a copy of this page, which you then proceeded to rip up. The original I kept would be unaffected.

In order for the called method to change the value in the Load event handler of a variable passed to it, the variable must be passed by reference. The variable in the called method is called a reference variable. The reference variable is not a copy of the variable in the Load event handler. Instead, the reference variable is an alias for the variable in the Load event handler. You may recall from television that an alias is another name a person may use, such as James Bond's alias of 007. However, whether you refer to him as James Bond or 007, you are still referring to the same person.

In order to pass a variable by reference, the data type in the argument, both in the method header and in the call, is preceded either by ref or out.

The ref Keyword

The following program passes the variable to be doubled by reference:

```
private void Form1_Load(object sender, EventArgs e)
{
    int num =5;
    Debug.WriteLine
    ("Num in Form1_Load before call = " + num);
    doubleIt(ref num);
    Debug.WriteLine
    ("Num in Form1_Load after call = " + num);
}
void doubleIt (ref int x)
{
    Debug.WriteLine
    ("x in doubleIt before doubling = " + x);
    x *= 2;
    Debug.WriteLine("x in doubleIt after doubling = " + x);
}
```

Here is some sample output:

```
num in Form1_Load before call = 5
x in doubleIt before doubling = 5
x in doubleIt after doubling = 10
num in Form1_Load before call = 10
```

There are two changes from the program that passed a parameter by value. First, the header was changed to insert the ref keyword:

```
void doubleIt (ref int x)
```

Second, the call also was changed to insert the ref keyword:

```
doubleIt(ref num);
```

You can pass multiple values by reference as well as by value. Indeed, you can pass some values by reference and others by value. You pass by reference those values you need to change, and you pass by value those values you are not changing.

NOTE *There is another difference between passing by value and passing by reference. You can pass by value expressions and constants as well as variables. However, you can only pass variables by reference.*

The out Keyword

The preceding program would not work with the out keyword instead of the ref keyword. If the method header and call were changed respectively to

```
void doubleIt (out int x)
doubleIt(out num);
```

the result would be a compiler error. In the method

```
void doubleIt (out int x)
{
    Debug.WriteLine
    ("x in doubleIt before doubling = " + x);
    x *= 2;
    Debug.WriteLine _
    ("x in doubleIt after doubling = " + x);
}
```

the compiler would complain about the use of the unassigned out parameter x. This means that x was not assigned an explicit value before its value was to be outputted in the first Debug.WriteLine statement. This is a requirement for using the out keyword.

Although out would not be a good choice in the doubleIt program, it does have an advantage over the ref keyword in that a variable passed with the ref keyword must already have an assigned value, whereas one passed with the out keyword need not.

For example, in Chapter 7, the following code, which assumes a Button control named btnTest, uses the TryParse method of the Int32 class to check if a value entered by the user in a TextBox named txtInput may evaluate as an integer:

```
private void btnTest_Click(object sender, EventArgs e)
{
    string strScore;
    int intScore;
    strScore = txtInput.Text;
    bool blnInput;
    blnInput = Int32.TryParse(strScore, out intScore);
    if (blnInput == false)
        Debug.WriteLine
        ("Input does not evaluate to an integer");
    else if (intScore >= 0 && intScore <= 100)
        Debug.WriteLine("The test score is valid");
    else if (intScore < 0)
        Debug.WriteLine
        ("Test score cannot be less than zero");
    else
        Debug.WriteLine
        ("Test score cannot be greater than 100");
    Debug.WriteLine("This line will always print");
}
```

When the TryParse method is called, its second argument, intScore, has no existing value. Rather, the TryParse method assigns intScore an integer value, corresponding to the string representation of that integer in strScore, if strScore is the string representation of an integer. Thus, the actual header of the TryParse method uses the out keyword rather the ref keyword:

```
public static bool TryParse(string s, out int result)
```

Passing an Array as an Argument

You can also pass an array as an argument. To illustrate, let's start with this program from Chapter 8, which uses two loops in the Load event handler. The first loop assigns an arbitrary value (double the amount of the index) to that array element. The second loop outputs these elements.

```
private void Form1_Load(object sender, EventArgs e)
{
    int[]arrSalesPerDay = new int[7];
```

```
    for (int x = 0; x < 7; x++)
        arrSalesPerDay[x] = x * 2;
    for (int x = 0; x < 7; x++)
            Debug.WriteLine(arrSalesPerDay[x]);
}
```

Let's now revise this program by creating two additional methods, one, assign-Values, to assign values to the array elements, the other, outputValues, to output those values:

```
private void Form1_Load(object sender, EventArgs e)
{
    int[] arrSalesPerDay = new int[7];
    assignValues(arrSalesPerDay);
    outputValues(arrSalesPerDay);
}

private void assignValues(int[] arr)
{
    for (int x = 0; x < 7; x++)
        arr[x] = x * 2;
}

private void outputValues(int[] arr)
{
    for (int i = 0; i < 7; i++)
        Debug.WriteLine(arr[i]);
}
```

The output of this program is the same as the version where all the code was in the Load event handler. Several aspects of this revised program are significant.

First, the parameter of the two new methods have empty square brackets after the data type, int[], rather than just int. This signifies that the parameter is an integer array rather than a single integer.

Second, when the two new methods are called, the argument is the name of the array in the Load event handler, arr. Thus, the entire array, or in reality its address in memory, is passed to the methods.

Third, the assignValues method did change the value of the corresponding argument in the Load event handler. However, the parameter seemingly was not passed by reference; no ref or out keyword is in the parameter list. The reason is that an array is a reference type; when an array name is an argument, the value of that argument is the array's address in memory. This is in contrast to when, for example, a single integer variable is an argument, when the value of that argument, absent the ref or out keyword, is the value of that variable, not its address.

Thus, with a reference type like an array, you can pass it by value and change, via the called function, the values of its elements. However, you cannot, via the called function, replace the array with a different array if you pass the array by value. To do that, you must pass the array by reference.

Returning a Value from a Method

Arguments are used to pass values to a called method. A return value may be used to pass a value from a called method back to the method that called it.

Syntax

In the previous section, the method doubleIt changed the value of its argument both in that method and in the Load event handler that called it. There, the header of the doubleIt method was

```
void doubleIt (ref int x)
```

Let's modify the doubleIt method by passing its one parameter by value rather than by reference (because we are not going to change its value in this example) but also by adding a return value to the method. The return value is added by indicating its data type (here, an int) in front of the method name in the header:

```
int doubleIt (int x)
```

Thus, the return value is changed from void, indicating no return value, to int, indicating that a value is returned, and its data type is an integer.

We will now implement this revised doubleIt method in the following program:

```
private void Form1_Load(object sender, EventArgs e)
{
    int num =5;
    int newNum = doubleIt(num);
    Debug.WriteLine
    ("newNum in Form1_Load after call = " + newNum);
}
int doubleIt (int x)
{
    return x *= 2;
}
```

The output should be the following:

```
newNum in Form1_Load after call = 10
```

How the Value Is Returned

Although the output of the preceding code shows that the variable newNum was successfully assigned 10, double the value of num, how exactly did that happen?

Let's start with the call of the doubleIt method by the following line:

```
int newNum = doubleIt(num);
```

The declaration of the doubleIt method is

```
int doubleIt (int x)
{
    return x *= 2;
}
```

Because the value of the argument passed (num) is 5, the value of the parameter in doubleIt, x, is 5. Thus, the statement

```
return x *= 2;
```

in effect is

```
return 10;
```

With the return statement, the doubleIt method finishes executing, and the value 10 is returned to the right side of the assignment statement. After the doubleIt method finishes executing, the statement

```
int newNum = doubleIt(num);
```

in effect is

```
int newNum = 10;
```

Thus, the following code outputs that the value of newNum is 10:

```
Debug.WriteLine
("newNum in Form1_Load after call = " + newNum);)
```

Saving the Return Value

It is common that a method returning a value is called on the right side of an assignment operator with a variable on the left side of the assignment operator to capture the return value. However, this is not required. In the program, the variable newNum was not necessary. Instead of the two statememts

```
int newNum = doubleIt(num);
Debug.WriteLine
("newNum in Form1_Load after call = " + newNum);
```

the return value could have been displayed in one statement:

```
Debug.WriteLine
("newNum in Form1_Load after call = " + doubleIt(num));
```

The only difference is that once this statement completes, the return value of the method cannot be used in later statements because it was not stored in a variable. In this program, that is not a problem because the return value is not used again. However, if you are going to use a return value more than once, it's generally a good idea to store that return value in a variable, as in the example in the preceding section.

Returning a Boolean Value

Methods that return a Boolean value often are called in an if control structure. For example, the following method, isEmptyString, returns true if the string that is its parameter is an empty string, and otherwise returns false:

```
private bool isEmptyString (string str)
{
    return (str == "");
}
```

The method may then be called following an if clause, and passed a string value (here, the Text property of the form). If the Text property is empty, the method will return true, and the output will be "Text property has no value." If the Text property has some value, the method will return false, and the output will be "Text property has value."

```
private void Form1_Load(object sender, EventArgs e)
{
    if (isEmptyString(this.Text))
       Debug.WriteLine("Text property has no value");
    else
       Debug.WriteLine("Text property has value");
}
```

The statement

```
if (isEmptyString(this.Text))
```

also could have been written as follows:

```
if (isEmptyString(this.Text)== true)
```

These two statements have the same effect. Because isEmptyString returns a Boolean value, it is unnecessary to compare that Boolean value to another Boolean value to obtain a Boolean result. Thus, the == true is unnecessary, though harmless.

Conclusion

A method is a group of statements that together perform a task. You implement a method by first defining it and then calling it. A method definition consists of a header and a body. The header consists of an access specifier, a return type, a method name, and an argument list. The header always is followed by an opening curly brace, which begins the method's body. The body ends with a closing curly brace and contains one or more statements. Unless the return value is void, the body must end with a return statement.

You can pass information to a method by using arguments. You may pass arguments by value or by reference. You pass an argument by value when you don't intend any change to that variable in the called method to affect that variable's value in the calling method. Conversely, you pass a variable argument by reference when you intend a change to that variable in the called method to affect that variable's value in the calling method.

The order and data type of the arguments in the method's header must correspond to the order and data type of the arguments in the call to that method.

Although arguments are used to pass values to a called method, a return value can be used to pass a value from a called method back to the method that called it. However, although multiple values can be passed to a method as arguments, multiple values cannot be returned from methods.

There are several reasons why you might want to create your own methods. As you write more complex and sophisticated programs, your code will be easier to write, understand, and fix if you divide the code up among different methods, each method performing a specific task, than if one method contains pages of code. Additionally, if you are performing essentially the same task from several places in the program, you can avoid duplication of code by putting the code that performs that task in one place, as opposed to repeating that code in each place in the program that may call for the performance of that task. Further, if you later have to fix a bug in how you perform that task, or simply find a better way to perform the task, you only have to change the code in one place rather than many.

In the next chapter we will start focusing on the "Visual" in Visual C#, the user interface.

Quiz

1. What is a method?

2. What is the significance of the void return type?

3. What is the usual return type of an event procedure?

4. What does the private access specifier do when applied to a method?

5. May there be a return statement in a function whose return type is void?

6. What does calling a method do?

7. What is the difference between passing by value and passing by reference?

8. What parameter attribute performs a similar but not exactly the same purpose as the out keyword?

9. What is the significance of an array being a reference type?

10. What are some reasons for writing your own methods?

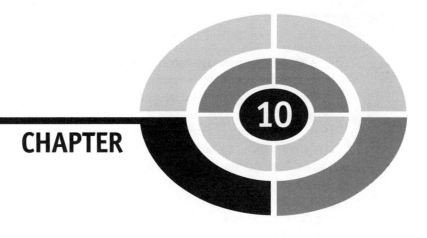

CHAPTER

Helper Forms

Forms are the most common user interface element in Visual C# applications. Indeed, it is difficult to conceptualize a Windows application without at least one form. Forms are the windows, literally, through which application users view information and interact with the application.

Visual C#'s automated creation of a new Windows application project includes a form that serves as the main application window. However, although the main application window may be the star of the show, that form needs a supporting cast of helper forms, because Windows applications generally are far too complex for the main application window to perform all the tasks required by the application.

The message box is a helper form built into the .NET Framework. The message box includes text that is either informative or a question as well as buttons, such as OK, Yes, No, Cancel, and so on, for the application user's response and to close the message box.

Message boxes are very common in Windows applications. One typical example, discussed later in this chapter, is if you make changes to a document in Microsoft Word and then try to close the document without saving the changes, you may be presented with a message box asking if you want to save the file before closing, with buttons for Yes, No, and Cancel. This chapter will show you how to create and use a message box in your application.

Although the message box is very useful, sometimes you want the helper form to have functionality that is beyond the capability of a message box to provide. For example, the text displayed by a message box is limited to a prompt. However, most Windows applications have an About dialog box, summoned by the main form's Help | About menu command, that displays more detailed information about the application than can be provided in a message box.

The About dialog box is an example of a dialog form. However, although the About dialog box simply is informational, dialog forms are not limited to the role of passive purveyors of information, and instead typically are interactive. For example, the Print dialog box displayed with the File | Print menu command enables the user to choose from among printers, decide which pages to print, the number of copies to make, and so forth, and then to start the print job by clicking the OK button. This chapter will show you how to create and display a dialog form.

The ability of the user to interact with the Print dialog box is possible because it may contain controls that a message box cannot contain, such as a drop-down list from which the user may select a printer, radio buttons and a text box from which the user may designate which pages to print, a check box through which the user can designate whether the pages should be collated, and so forth.

The ability of the user to interact with a dialog form presents programming challenges involving communication between the main and helper form. For example, the main form needs to know which button was clicked on the helper form, and it should execute different code depending on which button was clicked. Additionally, because the dialog form contains controls, the main form needs to know and take actions based on what the application user typed, checked, or selected in the controls in the helper form. This chapter will show you how to solve these programming challenges.

Message Boxes

Because the actions of the application user cause a Windows application to receive messages from the operating system, it seems only fair that a Windows application can send a message to the application user. Windows applications often use message boxes to inform and obtain a response from the application user.

Message boxes are valuable tools to use in applications. For example, one late evening, working bleary-eyed to finish a chapter under unceasing pressure from my heartless editor, I forgetfully close the document without first saving about an hour's worth of changes. Mercifully, up pops the message box shown in Figure 10-1, asking if I want to save my unsaved changes before the document is closed.

Figure 10-1　Message box in Microsoft Word.

This message box, in addition to conveying valuable information, also is able to obtain and process my response. If I choose the Yes button, the unsaved changes are saved before the document is closed. If I choose the No button (bad choice), the unsaved changes are discarded and the document is closed. If I choose the Cancel button, the state just before I attempted to close the document is restored; the document is kept open, but the unsaved changes remain unsaved.

Creating the Project

In this project, you will create the message box shown in Figure 10-2, which asks the user if they want to quit the application. If the user chooses Yes, the application closes. If the user chooses No, the application will not close.

Create the project through the following steps:

1. Create a new Windows application.

2. Using the Toolbox, add a button to the form.

3. Use the Properties window to change the Name property of the button to btnClose and the Text property of the button to Close.

4. Add this code to the Click event of btnClose:

```
private void btnClose_Click(object sender, EventArgs e)
{
    DialogResult drQuit;
    drQuit = MessageBox.Show("Do you really want to quit?",
        "Exit Confirmation",
        MessageBoxButtons.YesNo,
        MessageBoxIcon.Warning,
        MessageBoxDefaultButton.Button2);
    if (drQuit == DialogResult.Yes)
        this.Close();
}
```

Run the project and click the Close button to display the message box shown previously in Figure 10-2. This type of message box is common in Windows applications,

Figure 10-2
Project in action.

providing the application user a last chance to decide whether they really want to quit the application. If the application user chooses the Yes button, the application will end. If instead the application user chooses the No button, just the message box will close and the application user will be returned to the main form. Thus, the clicking of the No button will restore the application to its state just before the application user chose the Close button.

Message Boxes Are Modal

The code involves three logical steps:

1. Display the message box using the Show method.
2. Obtain the application user's choice (Yes or No) by the return value of the Show method.
3. If the choice is Yes, close the application.

However, before we analyze the code, let's examine a feature that message boxes share with the dialog forms discussed later in this chapter—both are modal.

The term "modal" refers to the fact that the user cannot return to the application until the message box is closed by the user clicking one of the buttons of the message box.

Message boxes are always modal. However, not all forms are modal. This issue will be discussed further in connection with dialog forms later in this chapter in the section "Modal vs. Modeless."

Show Method

You do not need to create or design the message box. The message box is a form built into the .NET Framework. All you need to do to create and display a message box, together with its buttons, icon, text, and title, is to call the aptly named Show method of the MessageBox class, which is part of the class library of the .NET Framework, and provide the appropriate arguments. The .NET Framework also takes care of closing the message box. When you click a button, the message box closes, automatically. You have to write the code that executes when the user clicks a given button.

Parameters of Show Method

The Show method is overloaded. This means that you can call it several different ways, depending on the number of parameters you include. The parameters of the Show method are listed in Table 10-1.

The only parameter that is required is Text. In that case, the message box only will have one button, OK, which closes the message box when clicked. This may be sufficient if the message box simply provides information to the application user. For example, when filling out a form in an application, you may have seen a message box popping up telling you that you forgot to fill out a required field, or that the field only takes numbers or that the password must be at least six characters, and so on.

Parameter	Description	Required?
Text	The prompt inside the message box that conveys a question or information to the application user (in this case, "Do you really want to quit?").	Yes.
Title	The title of the message box (in this case, "Exit application"), which provides a visual cue to the application user of the purpose of the message box.	No. If omitted, no title.
MessageBoxButtons	The buttons inside the message box (in this case, Yes and No). The choices are listed in Table 10-2.	No. If omitted, only one button (OK).
MessageBoxIcon	The graphic inside the message box, such as the exclamation icon in Figure 10-2. The choices are listed in Table 10-3.	No. If omitted, no graphic.
MessageBoxDefaultButton	The button outlined as a cue that pressing ENTER is the same as clicking the button (in this case, the second button, labeled No). The choices are listed in Table 10-4.	No. If omitted, first button is the default.

Table 10-1   Parameters of the Show Method

NOTE The parameters are positional. This means you can't skip or omit an argument. Therefore, if you want to specify a default button, which is the last parameter, all of the previous arguments must also be supplied.

MessageBoxButtons Enumeration

Although a message box with only an OK button is sufficient if the message box's purpose is purely information, the objective of this project is to give the application user a choice of Yes or No concerning whether they really want to quit. You use buttons—here, Yes and No buttons—to give the application user this choice. The MessageBoxButtons enumeration contains the available button combinations, which are listed in Table 10-2.

The term "enumeration" means a list of related choices, which in this case represents the various available button combinations. The syntax of an enumeration is

```
[Enumeration Name].[Choice Name]
```

For example, if the selected button combination is Yes and No, the syntax is

```
MessageBoxButtons.YesNo
```

Here, MessageBoxButtons is the name of the enumeration, and YesNo is the choice from the enumerated list.

MessageBoxIcon Enumeration

The saying that a picture is worth a thousand words, while perhaps trite, has much truth. The visual cue of an icon in a message box tells the application user the nature and importance of the message, ranging from informational to warning or error.

Similar to the button choices, the available icon choices are contained in an enumeration, this time named the MessageBoxIcon enumeration. Table 10-3 lists the available icon choices.

Name	Buttons Contained in Message Box
AbortRetryIgnore	Abort, Retry, and Ignore.
OK	OK. This is the default.
OKCancel	OK and Cancel.
RetryCancel	Retry and Cancel.
YesNo	Yes and No.
YesNoCancel	Yes, No, and Cancel.

Table 10-2 MessageBoxButtons Enumeration

Name	Icon in Message Box
Asterisk	White lowercase letter *i* in a circle with a blue background.
Error	White X in a circle with a red background.
Exclamation	Black exclamation point in a triangle with a yellow background.
Hand	White X in a circle with a red background.
Information	White lowercase letter *i* in a circle with a blue background.
None	None.
Question	Blue question mark in a circle with a white background.
Stop	White X in a circle with a red background.
Warning	Black exclamation point in a triangle with a yellow background.

Table 10-3   MessageBoxIcon Enumeration

MessageBoxDefaultButton Enumeration

The users of your application may be using the keyboard in lieu of the mouse to choose a button. This may not simply be a matter of preference. Users with certain disabilities may not be able to use a mouse and have to use the keyboard to choose a button. Accordingly, you should designate a default button, which means that the user pressing the ENTER key is the same as the user clicking that button.

The choices of the default button are contained in yet another enumeration, this time called the MessageBoxDefaultButton enumeration. Table 10-4 lists the available button choices.

There are only three buttons in the enumeration because, as Table 10-2 indicates, the maximum number of buttons is three—Abort, Retry, and Ignore, or Yes, No, and Cancel.

Usually you choose as the default button the one whose choice would have the least drastic effect, if for no other reason than if the application user absentmindedly presses the ENTER key, nothing horrible will happen. Here, the button with the least drastic effect is the No button, which will simply restore the status quo.

Member Name	Description
Button1	The first button on the message box is the default button.
Button2	The second button on the message box is the default button.
Button3	The third button on the message box is the default button.

Table 10-4   MessageBoxDefaultButton Enumeration

Using the Show Method's Return Value

The next step is to write code so the form knows if the application user clicked the Yes or No button in the message box. The programming task is that one form needs to know an action taken in another form, the other form here being the message box.

You solve this problem by using the return value of the Show method. The concept of a method returning a value is discussed in Chapter 9 in the coverage of methods.

DialogResult Enumerations

The Show method returns a value that represents the button that the application user clicked in the message box. Each button is represented by a member of the Dialog-Result enumeration listed in Table 10-5.

The DialogResult enumeration corresponds to the buttons in the MessageBox-Buttons enumeration listed previously in Table 10-2, and will be returned if the corresponding button is chosen. Thus, if the application user clicks the Yes button, the Show method returns the value DialogResult.Yes.

The return value usually is stored in a variable for later use in the application. The data type of that return value should be the same as the data type returned by the method.

Member Name	Description
Abort	The dialog box's return value is Abort, usually sent from a button labeled Abort.
Cancel	The dialog box's return value is Cancel, usually sent from a button labeled Cancel.
Ignore	The dialog box's return value is Ignore, usually sent from a button labeled Ignore.
No	The dialog box's return value is No, usually sent from a button labeled No.
None	Nothing is returned from the dialog box. This means that the modal dialog box continues running.
OK	The dialog box's return value is OK, usually sent from a button labeled OK.
Retry	The dialog box's return value is Retry, usually sent from a button labeled Retry.
Yes	The dialog box's return value is Yes, usually sent from a button labeled Yes.

Table 10-5 DialogResult Enumerations

Accordingly, you often use the DialogResult data type for the variable in which you will save the return value of the Show method. You may declare that variable as follows:

```
DialogResult drQuit;
```

Once you have declared the variable, the next step is to use it to store the return value of the Show method. The variable drQuit should be on the left side of the assignment operator, so it will receive the return value of the Show method that is called on the right side of the assignment operator:

```
drQuit = MessageBox.Show("Do you really want to quit?",
  "Exit Confirmation",
  MessageBoxButtons.YesNo,
  MessageBoxIcon.Warning,
  MessageBoxDefaultButton.Button2);
```

When this code statement executes, and the application user clicks a button in the message box, closing the message box, the value of the variable drQuit will be either DialogResult.Yes or DialogResult.No, depending on whether the application user clicked the Yes or No button.

Processing the Returned DialogResult Value

The form object has a Close method that, as its name indicates, closes the form. Because this is the only form in the project (other than the message box, which will close when the user clicks the Yes or No button), closing the form ends the application as well. However, we only want to close the form if the application user chose Yes, not if the application user chose No.

The following code closes the form if, and only if, the application user's choice was Yes:

```
if (drQuit == DialogResult.Yes)
   this.Close();
```

This code statement first compares the value of drQuit and DialogResult.Yes using the if keyword. If the user chose Yes, the value of drQuit is DialogResult.Yes, so the comparison drQuit == DialogResult.Yes will be true and the this.Close() statement is executed. However, if the user chose No, the value of drQuit is DialogResult.No, so the comparison drQuit == DialogResult.Yes will be false and the this.Close() statement will not be executed.

Dialog Forms

Although the message box is a valuable tool, it is limited in that it only can contain a text prompt, buttons, an icon, and a title. Further, the only information a message box can obtain from the application user is which button the user clicked. The message box does not permit the application user to enter text in a text box, choose an item from a drop-down list, select a check box or radio button, and so on.

If you need a user interface richer than the message box, you may create a custom and more complex version of a message box—the dialog form.

Creating the Project

A good way to illustrate how to create and use a dialog form is with a project. In this project, you will create the dialog form shown in Figure 10-3. This dialog form enables the user to change the text of the title bar of the main form, that title bar text currently being "Form1" in Figure 10-3.

Clicking either the OK or Cancel button will close the dialog form. However, if the user chooses the OK button in the dialog form, the text of the title bar of the main form will be changed to the text the user typed into the text box of the dialog form. By contrast, if the user instead chooses the Cancel button in the dialog form, the dialog form simply will close, with no change made to the text of the title bar of the main form.

Figure 10-3   Dialog form project in action.

Try the following steps to create this project:

1. Create a new Windows application.

2. Using the Properties window, change the StartPosition property of the form from the default (WindowsDefaultLocation) to CenterScreen to center the form on the screen. This change is not required for the program to function, but it will permit both forms to be centered on the screen.

3. Using the Toolbox, add a button to the form.

4. Use the Properties window to change the values of the Name property of the button to btnNewCaption and the Text property from the default (for example, Button1) to New Caption.

5. You need to add a second form to the project to serve as the dialog form. Use the Project | Add Windows Form menu command to display the Add New Item dialog box shown in Figure 10-4, highlight Windows Form, and then click the Open button. You can keep the default name Form2.cs for the new form. Figure 10-5 shows the Solution Explorer, in which the second form now appears.

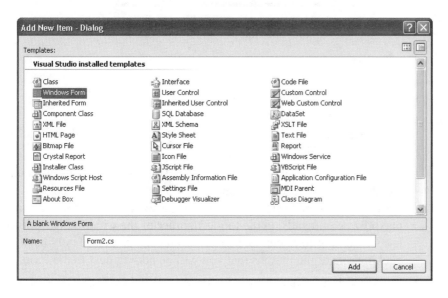

Figure 10-4   Add New Item dialog box.

Figure 10-5   Solution Explorer after the second form is added.

6. Using the Properties window, change the values of the following properties of the second form:

- **Text**   Change from Form2 to Dialog so you have a visual cue that you are looking at the dialog form.

- **ControlBox**   Change from the default (True) to False. This eliminates the close, minimize, and maximize buttons in the top-right corner of the window and the system menu, which also has close, minimize, and maximize commands, in the top-left corner of the window. The purpose is so the dialog form cannot be resized and can be closed only by clicking one of the buttons that you will be adding next to the form.

- **StartPosition**   Change from the default (WindowsDefaultLocation) to CenterParent so the dialog box is centered on the main form.

- **FormBorderStyle**   Change from the default (Sizable) to FixedDialog. This change is not required for the program to function, but does give the form a more dialog box-like appearance.

7. Using the Toolbox, add a button to the second form.

8. Use the Properties window to change the values of the following properties of the button you just added to the dialog form:

   • **Name**   Change from Button1 to btnOK.

   • **Text**   Change to OK.

   • **DialogResult**   Choose OK from the drop-down list. Because the dialog box displayed by the MessageBox.Show method is a built-in Visual C# .NET form, clicking the OK button automatically returns OK as the DialogResult value. By contrast, the dialog form is not a built-in Visual C# .NET form, but instead one that you create, so you need to correlate the clicking of the OK button with OK as the DialogResult value, both in order to return a DialogResult value and to close the dialog form when the button is clicked. You do so by setting the button's DialogResult property to OK.

9. Using the Toolbox, add a second button to the dialog form.

10. Use the Properties window to change the values of the following properties of the second button you just added to the dialog form:

    • **Name**   Change from the default name (likely Button1 or Button2) to btnCancel.

    • **Text**   Change to Cancel.

    • **DialogResult**   Choose Cancel from the drop-down list. This is done for the same reason as we set the DialogResult property of the OK button to OK.

11. Use the Properties window to change the values of the AcceptButton property of the second dialog form to btnOK and the CancelButton property of that form to btnCancel, using the drop-down list. Pressing the ENTER key is the equivalent of clicking the button designated in the AcceptButton property. Similarly, pressing the ESC key is the equivalent of clicking the button designated in the CancelButton property.

12. Using the Toolbox, add a TextBox control to the second form.

13. Use the Properties window to change the values of the following properties of the TextBox control you just added to the dialog form:

    • **Name**   Change to txtNewCaption.

    • **Text**   Delete the default so it is blank so no text shows in the text box when you run the application.

- **TabIndex**   Change to 0 so when the second form appears the cursor will start at the text box.

- **Modifiers**   Change from Private to Internal to permit the first form to access this TextBox control in the second form.

14. Add the following code to the Click event of btnNewCaption in the main form:

```
private void btnNewCaption_Click
    (object sender, EventArgs e)
{
    Form2 frmCaption = new Form2();
    frmCaption.ShowDialog(this);
    if (frmCaption.DialogResult == DialogResult.OK)
        this.Text = frmCaption.txtNewCaption.Text;
}
```

Try out this code by running the project. Click the New Caption button in the first form and then type some text in the second form. If you then click OK, the second form will close, and the first form will have a new title, the text you typed in the second form. If you instead click Cancel, the second form will still close, but the title of the first form will not change.

Showing the Dialog Form and Returning Its Result

The dialog form is similar to the MessageBox class. For example, both are displayed by another form and are modal; that is, the application user cannot return to the main form until they have dismissed the dialog form by clicking one of its buttons. Another similarity is that both the dialog form and the MessageBox class return a result based on which button was clicked. However, there are important differences between the dialog form and a message box, both in how they are shown and in how they return a result.

ShowDialog Method

You use the ShowDialog method of the Form object to display a dialog form. This method is similar to the Show method of the MessageBox class in that it will show, modally, the form that is invoking the method.

NOTE *You also could display the second form using the Show method instead of the ShowDialog method, but then the second form would not be modal. This is discussed further in the later section "Modal vs. Modeless."*

Because Form2 is a class (that is, a blueprint or template for an object), the code first declares and creates an instance of Form2 before you show it using the Show-Dialog method. You do so via the following code, which goes in the Click event procedure of the btnNewCaption button in the main form:

```
Form2 frmCaption = new Form2();
frmCaption.ShowDialog(this);
```

Let's go through this code one line at a time.

The first line creates an object named frmCaption of the Form2 class. You use a class to instantiate (create) an object of that class. The class in this example is Form2. The new keyword is used to create the object. The object is represented by a variable (here, frmCaption).

The second line of code displays the dialog form object created in the first line. The Form2 object, represented by the variable frmCaption, calls the ShowDialog method to display itself as a dialog form. The this keyword is passed as the argument. The this keyword refers to the current form, which is the main form because we are writing this code in the main form. This makes the current, main form instance the owner of the dialog form.

Returning a DialogResult

Another difference between the MessageBox class and the dialog form is that whereas the Show method of the MessageBox class indicates the button the user clicked by returning a DialogResult value, the ShowDialog method of the Form object indicates the button the user clicked by assigning that value to the dialog form's DialogResult property. Therefore, the comparison is

```
if (frmCaption.DialogResult == DialogResult.OK)
```

You can make multiple comparisons. For example, if the dialog form had three buttons, Yes, No, and Cancel, the comparison could be this:

```
if (frmCaption.DialogResult == DialogResult.Yes)
    // do action based on user clicking yes button
else if (frmCaption.DialogResult == DialogResult.No)
    // do action based on user clicking no button
else
    // do action based on user clicking cancel button
```

If the DialogResult is anything besides None, the dialog form is closed and returns a DialogResult value. However, under certain circumstances you may wish to prevent the dialog form from being closed, such as if the user has made an input error that first needs to be corrected.

To prevent the dialog form from closing, the DialogResult property of the dialog form needs to be set to None. The following code fragment sets the value of the DialogResult property of the current form (represented by the this keyword) to a DialogResult of None:

```
this.DialogResult = DialogResult.None
```

This code logically would be placed in the Click event of the OK button to handle the situation where you want the user to fix an error on that dialog form rather than closing the dialog form.

Accessing Values from the Dialog Form

If the value of the second form's DialogResult property is OK, all that is left to do is to change the title of the first form to the text you typed in the second form. The following code in the Click event procedure of btnNewCaption therefore is indicated:

```
this.Text = frmCaption.txtNewCaption.Text;
```

The this keyword refers to the main form because this code is in its code module. The Text property is the text in its title bar. It is possible to refer in the code of the main form to the TextBox control txtNewCaption in the dialog form because we changed that control's Modifiers property from Private to Internal, which permits access from anywhere in the current project.

The reference to txtNewCaption, the text box in the dialog form, is preceded by the name of the dialog form object, frmCaption. The reason why the name of the control is preceding by the name of the form that contains it is that a reference to a control, not preceded by a form object, is assumed to be to a control in the form whose code is executing. However, the current code module is for the main form, and txtNewCaption is not in that form, but instead in the dialog form. Therefore, a reference to txtNewCaption.Text instead of frmCaption.txtNewCaption.Text would result in the following compiler error message: "The name 'txtNewCaption' is not declared."

Modal vs. Modeless

Whereas all message boxes are modal, not all forms are. The second form in the application we just created is a dialog form because it was displayed with the Show-Dialog method rather than the Show method. Had we instead displayed the second form using the Show method, the second form would have been modeless. This means that the application user could return to the main form without closing the second form.

Some forms in Windows applications are modeless. Examples include the Find and Replace forms in Microsoft Word. Because the Find form is modeless, you can return to the main application window and edit a found word without having to close the Find form.

It usually is easier to write code for modal forms because you don't have to be concerned about the user returning to the main application without first closing the modal form. However, there are situations, such as the Find form in Microsoft Word, in which a modeless form may be the better choice.

Conclusion

Visual C# 2005's automated creation of a new Windows application project includes a form that serves as the main application window. The main application window often needs a supporting cast of other forms, because Windows applications generally are far too complex for the main application window to perform all the tasks required by the application.

This chapter first showed you how to display a message box and determine which button the user clicked. You also learned that a message box is modal, which means that the user cannot return to the rest of the application until the message box is closed, by clicking one of its buttons.

You next learned how to create and use a dialog form. The dialog form is similar to the MessageBox class in that it is modal and returns a value based on the button clicked to dismiss it. However, a dialog form, unlike a MessageBox, also may contain text boxes, check boxes, drop-down lists, and other controls.

There also are code differences between the dialog form and the MessageBox. You use the ShowDialog instead of the Show method to display a dialog form. Further, you first create an instance of the dialog form to use the ShowDialog method. Additionally, the return value of the MessageBox class is a DialogResult value, whereas the return value of the dialog form is in its DialogResult property. You also learned how through code in the main form to determine values in controls in the dialog form.

In the next chapter we will enhance the user interface of the form with a menu.

Quiz

1. Is a message box modal or modeless?

2. What value is returned by the Show method of the MessageBox class?

3. Do you always have to call the Show method of the MessageBox class with the same number of arguments?

4. Do buttons in a message box automatically have a DialogResult value?

5. What is the data type of a variable you use to store the return value of the Show method of the MessageBox class?

6. What is an enumeration?

7. What method do you use to display a modal form?

8. What is the return value from showing a dialog form?

9. Do buttons in a dialog form you create automatically have a DialogResult value?

10. What method do you use to display a form as modeless rather than modal?

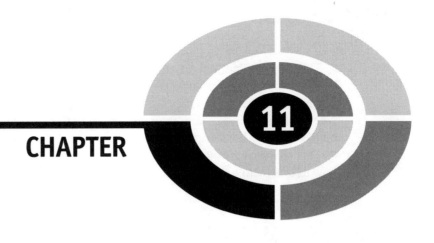

Menus

You often may encounter menus, perhaps at an elegant restaurant, or in my case, in the drive through lane of a local fast food restaurant. Regardless of the quality of the food, the menus at the two places serve the same purpose: to inform you of your choices and the corresponding prices.

A Windows application also has a menu, but that menu serves a different purpose than a restaurant menu. The application user generally knows what they want to do. The menu provides a graphical user interface (GUI) to make it easier for the application user to issue commands to the application, such as to open a file, print a document, and so on.

The menu is not the only way through which the GUI may make it easier for the application user to issue commands to the application. For example, toolbars, which are covered in the next chapter, are another alternative. However, the menu has the advantage of enabling the programmer to organize commands in a logical hierarchy. For example, commands related to file operations, such as New, Open, and Save, are under the File menu, whereas commands related to editing, such as Cut, Copy, and Paste, are under the Edit menu. Additionally, menus save valuable screen space, in that submenu items collapse unless the menu item above them is chosen. This enables your application to remain uncluttered, by hiding commands that are not immediately needed.

There are two common types of menus. One is the main menu that usually appears at the top of applications, with headings such as File, Edit, View, and Help. The main menu is represented by the MenuStrip class. The other menu that appears when you right-click, sometimes called a *shortcut* or *context menu*, is represented by the ContextMenuStrip class.

This chapter will show you how to create a main menu and a context menu and how to link them to each other.

Creating a Main Menu

The MenuStrip class represents the main menu that usually appears at the top of a Windows form. The MenuStrip object contains a collection of ToolStripMenu-Item objects, each of which is an item on the menu.

Each ToolStripMenuItem can be a command for your application. Figure 11-1 shows menu items under the File menu in Microsoft Word. Many of the menu items are commands for the application, such as to open or save a file.

However, as Figure 11-2 shows, a menu item may also be a parent menu for other menu items, each another ToolStripMenuItem. For example, Send To is the

Figure 11-1
Menu items under the File menu.

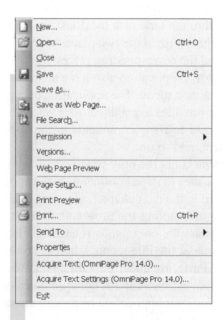

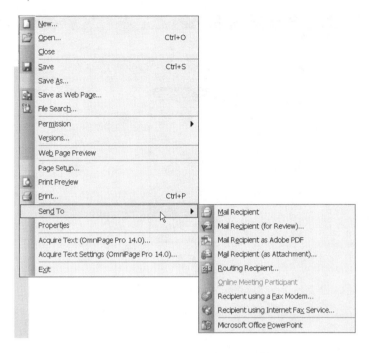

Figure 11-2   Send To menu item as a parent to other menu items.

parent menu item for other menu items, including Mail Recipient and Microsoft Office PowerPoint.

Creating a main menu is a two-step process. You first add a MenuStrip control to your form, and then you append ToolStripMenuItem objects to it.

Adding a MenuStrip Control to a Form

You add a MenuStrip control to a form using the following steps, which are similar to how you would add a control such as a Button to the form. Try the following, which you could do with an existing project, though I would recommend a new project to avoid any confusion with existing code:

1. View the form in designer view.

2. Double-click the MenuStrip component in the Toolbox. As shown in Figure 11-3, the MenuStrip component is added to the component tray below the form. When this component is selected in the component tray, a rectangular area appears underneath the top-left corner of the form displaying the text "Type Here."

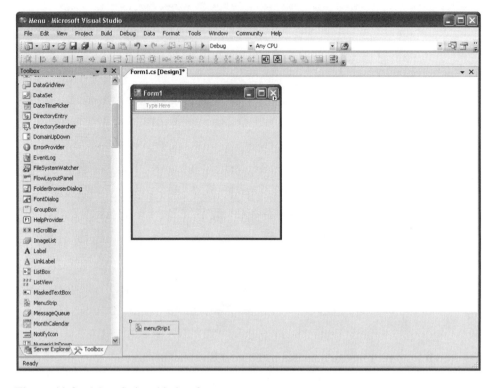

Figure 11-3   MenuStrip added to form.

3. Using the Properties window, if not already set by default, set the MainMenuStrip property of the form to the name of your MenuStrip component (by default, menuStrip1). This links the MenuStrip to your form.

Adding Menu Items to the MenuStrip

Once you have added a MenuStrip component to your Windows form, the next step is to add menu items to it. Each menu item is an object of the ToolStripMenuItem class. You can add ToolStripMenuItems to the MenuStrip by typing in the menu items or by using the Items Collection Editor.

Typing in the Menu Items

You may add a menu item to the MenuStrip component by clicking the text "Type Here" (after selecting the MenuStrip component in the component tray, as mentioned in step 2 in the preceding section) and typing the display name of the desired menu item to add it. For example, you may add a File menu item by typing **File** because the File menu usually is the first top-level item in Windows applications.

Typing the name of the menu item sets its Text property. You also should change the menu item's Name property from the default. You set the Name property of the menu item by right-clicking it, choosing Properties from the shortcut menu to display the Properties window, and then changing the Name property in the Properties window. One logical name for the File menu would be mnuFile, with the "mnu" prefix indicating a menu item and "File" indicating the purpose of the menu item.

Figure 11-4 shows the menu after the File menu item is added.

As Figure 11-4 shows, you now have "Type Here" options both below and to the right of the File menu item. You may add items below the File menu item, such as New and Open. You then should change the Name property of these menu items.

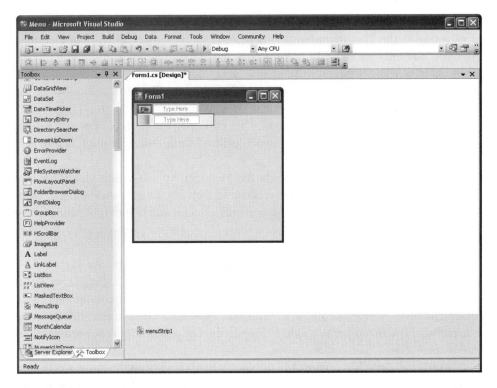

Figure 11-4   File menu item added.

For example, I would name a menu item Open under the File menu mnuFileOpen, with "mnuFile" being the name of the parent File menu and "Open" being descriptive of the subsidiary menu item's purpose.

You may add menu items to the right of the File menu as well as below it. For example, you might add an Edit menu item to the right of the File menu item to be consistent with other Windows applications. Following the same naming convention, I would name the Edit menu item mnuEdit.

TIP *If you forget a menu item, right-click the menu item before which the new one will be inserted and then choose Insert | New from the context menu. If you decide you no longer want a menu item you previously added, right-click that item and choose Delete from the context menu.*

Items Collection Editor

One of the properties of the MenuStrip component is an Items collection, which is a collection of the ToolStripMenuItems belonging to the MenuStrip. For example, after you add the File and Edit menu items, those menu items would belong to the Items collection of the MenuStrip.

Figure 11-5 shows the Items collection listed in the Properties window of the MenuStrip component.

Click the ellipsis (. . .) next to Items. This will open the Items Collection Editor, which is shown in Figure 11-6 after two ToolStripMenuItems (for the File and Edit menus) have been added.

You may add ToolStripMenuItems to the MenuStrip by choosing MenuItem (the default selection) from the drop-down box and then clicking the Add button. Once the ToolStripMenuItem is added, you then may select it and in the right pane change its Name, Text, and other properties. Figure 11-6 shows properties for the Edit menu item.

You also can add menu items to the File or Edit menu item. As Figure 11-7 shows, the File menu item (as well as the Edit menu item) has a DropDownItems collection property. This is a collection of the ToolStripMenuItems belonging to that menu item. For example, after you add New and Open menu items to the File menu, those menu items would belong to the DropDownItems collection of the File menu.

Clicking the ellipsis (. . .) next to DropDownItems will open the Items Collection Editor for that menu item. Figure 11-8 shows the Items Collection Editor for the Edit menu after menu items have been added to that menu item.

Figure 11-5
Properties window showing
the Items collection of
MenuStrip.

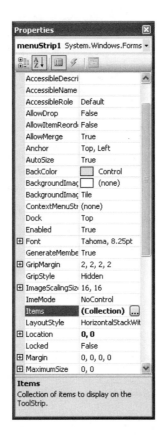

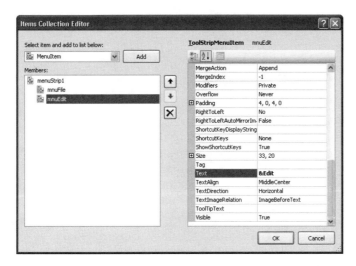

Figure 11-6 Items Collection Editor for MenuStrip.

Figure 11-7
Properties window showing
DropDownItems collection
of the File menu item.

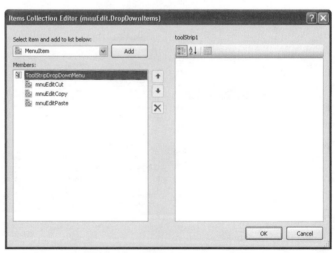

Figure 11-8   Items Collection Editor for the Edit menu item.

The procedure for adding subsidiary menu items to a menu item is essentially the same as adding ToolStripMenuItems to the MenuStrip; you choose MenuItem from the drop-down box and then click the Add button. You then may select the added subitem and in the right pane change its Name, Text, and other properties.

Enhancing the Menu Items

You can enhance menu items in several ways. You can add access or shortcut keys to facilitate keyboard access to menu items. You also can add separator bars to group together related menu items.

Access Keys

Although menu items usually are accessed by a mouse click, you also should enable the user to access menu items via the keyboard. Being able to access menu items via the keyboard instead of a mouse is an important convenience, as I have discovered on an airplane flight trying to use my laptop while wedged between two sumo-sized passengers. Indeed, for users with certain disabilities, the ability to access menu items via the keyboard instead of a mouse can be a necessity.

An access key is one way of enabling the user to access menu items via the keyboard. An access key is the keyboard combination of the ALT key plus a letter in the menu item that is underlined. For example, the keyboard combination for the File menu item is ALT-F, with the letter *F* in File being underlined.

To add an access key, in the menu item's Text property, simply type an ampersand (&) before the letter to be underlined. Figure 11-4 earlier in this chapter shows the result of typing **&File** as the Text property for the File menu item (the letter *F* in File is underlined).

The access shortcut may not appear when you run the application until you press the ALT key. This is standard behavior in Windows applications. As shown in Figure 11-9, in the Effects dialog box (shown by choosing the Display applet from the Control Panel | Appearance tab | Effects button), the option "Hide keyboard navigation indicators until I use the ALT key" is checked by default. If you want to change that behavior, simply uncheck that box.

Shortcut Keys

Shortcut keys are another method of enabling the user to access menu items via the keyboard. In Microsoft Word, the New menu item under the File menu can be accessed with the shortcut key CTRL-N.

Figure 11-9
Setting whether the
access shortcut is
hidden until the ALT
key is pressed.

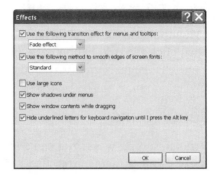

You can add a shortcut key at design time by selecting the menu item within the
Menu Designer, selecting the ShortcutKeys property from the Properties window,
and clicking the drop-down arrow. As Figure 11-10 shows, you can choose one or
more of CTRL, SHIFT, or ALT by checking a box and then choosing one of the values
offered in the drop-down list:

Figure 11-10
Shortcut key options
displayed in the Properties
window.

NOTE *You normally would not assign a shortcut key to a top-level menu item such as File or Edit because an access key already can be used to open that menu.*

Separator Bars

Separator bars are used to group related commands within a menu and make menus easier to read. In Microsoft Word, under the File menu, a separator bar separates the New, Open, and Close menu items from the menu items that follow them.

You may add a separator bar by setting the Text property of a menu item to a dash. Alternatively, in the Menu Designer, right-click the location where you want a separator bar and choose Insert | Separator.

Adding Functionality to the Menu Items

The purpose of a menu item is to do something when it is clicked. Therefore, you use the Click event procedure of the menu item to provide functionality for a menu item.

The Click event, of course, occurs when the user clicks the menu item. However, the Click event also occurs if the user selects the menu item using the keyboard and presses the ENTER key, or if the user presses an access key or shortcut key that is associated with the menu item.

The Click event is not raised for all menu items. It only is raised for menu items that do not have subsidiary menu items. The reason is when a menu item with subsidiary items is clicked, the behavior is to display the subsidiary menu items. Therefore, the Click event is not raised for parent menu items such as File and Edit. Instead, the behavior when a parent menu item is clicked is to display its subitems, such as, in the case of the File menu, New, Open, and Close.

You write code for the Click event procedure for a menu item by, in code view, choosing the menu item by name from the left drop-down list and Click from the right drop-down list. You then write within the created event procedure stub the code you wish to run when the menu item is clicked. For example, the following code outputs "New" to the Output window when a menu item named mnuFileNew is clicked:

```
private void mnuFileNew_Click
    (object sender, EventArgs e)
{
    Debug.WriteLine("New");
}
```

Disabling Menu Items

Although menu items should be functional, there are times when you may not want them to be functional. For example, in Microsoft Word, the menu items Cut and Copy under the Edit menu initially are grayed out, or disabled. They are grayed out because no text is selected; therefore, there is nothing to cut or copy. However, once you select text, Cut and Copy are no longer grayed out—in other words, they are enabled.

A menu item should not be enabled when the command it represents is not available. It would be frustrating for the application user to click Cut or Copy and see nothing happen. The application user might be misled into thinking there is something wrong with your application. When you gray out, or disable, a menu item, the application user is given a visual cue that the menu item is not available.

Disabling a menu item that should not be available has an additional advantage—error prevention. The code for cutting text may understandably assume there is selected text. If there is no selected text, executing the code for cutting text may cause an error. By disabling the menu item when no text is selected, the code for cutting text cannot be executed when no text is selected, thus avoiding the error.

Menu items are enabled by default when they are created. However, you can disable a menu item by setting its Enabled property to False. You can do this at design time, when the menu item is selected in the Menu Designer, through the Properties window. You also can disable a menu item via code:

```
mnuFileNew.Enabled = false;
```

If you want a menu item to be disabled when the application starts up, you could put this code in the Load event of the form.

Disabling the first or top-level menu item in a menu, such as the File menu item in a traditional File menu, disables all the menu items contained within the menu. Similarly, disabling a menu item that has submenu items disables the submenu items.

TIP *If all the commands on a given menu are unavailable to the user, you should hide as well as disable the entire menu. You hide the menu by setting the Visible property of the top-most menu item to False. This presents a cleaner user interface by not cluttering up your menu structure with disabled items. However, one caution: hiding the menu alone is not sufficient to disable it. You must also disable the menu, because hiding alone does not prevent access to a menu command via a shortcut key.*

Creating a Context Menu

Many Windows applications have context menus, which are displayed when the user clicks the right mouse button over an area of the form or over a control on the form. Figure 11-11 shows a context menu in Microsoft Word.

The word "context" in context menu derives from the fact that the particular menu items displayed often depend on the context, such as the application state, or where on the form or control the right mouse button was clicked. Indeed, in the .NET Framework, the ContextMenuStrip class represents shortcut or context menus.

Context menus typically are used to make available different menu items from a MenuStrip of a form that are useful for the user given the context of the application. For example, you can use a context menu assigned to a TextBox control to provide immediate access to menu items also found in the MenuStrip to cut, copy, and paste text, find text, change the text font, and so on.

The ability of a context menu to immediately access menu items of the main menu that might take several mouse clicks to access may be why a context menu also is called a *shortcut menu*, because the menu items on the context menu are a shortcut to menu items on the main menu. However, a context menu also may contain menu items not found in the form's MenuStrip.

Adding a ContextMenuStrip to a Form

The process of adding a context menu to a Windows form at design time and then adding menu items to it is similar to the corresponding process discussed already in this chapter in connection with the MenuStrip. You first add a ContextMenuStrip object to your form, and then you append to it ToolStripMenuItems objects.

Figure 11-11
Context menu.

You add a context menu to a form by following these steps, which are similar to how you add a MenuStrip to the form:

1. View the form in designer view.

2. Double-click the ContextMenuStrip component in the Toolbox. As shown in Figure 11-12, this adds a ContextMenuStrip component to the component tray.

3. In the Properties window for that form or control, choose the ContextMenuStrip object (the default name may be contextMenuStrip1) from the drop-down list for the form or control's ContextMenuStrip property. This associates the context menu with the form or a control on the form. You also can change this value dynamically through code when the program is running if the form has more than one context menu.

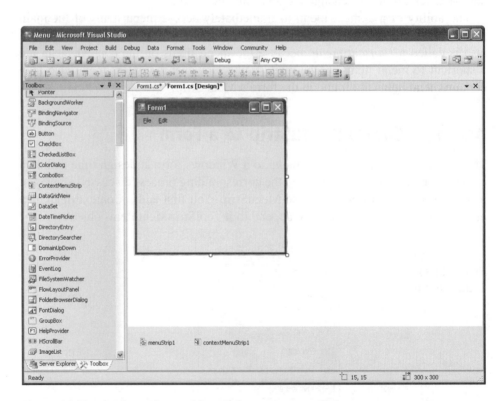

Figure 11-12 Adding a ContextMenuStrip component to a form.

Unlike with the main menu, you often will be adding a context menu to a control on the form, rather than the form itself. For example, in the Text Editor project later in this chapter, the context menu will belong to a TextBox control rather than the form.

Adding Menu Items to the ContextMenuStrip

Once you have added a ContextMenuStrip component to your Windows form, the next step is to add menu items to it. You can do so by typing in the menu items, by using the Items Collection Editor, or by copying menu items from existing items on the main menu and pasting them onto the context menu.

Typing in the Menu Items

You can add menu items to a context menu using the same method you used to add menu items to a main menu. You click the text "Type Here" and type the name of the desired menu item to add it. If the text "Type Here" is not displayed, you may display it by clicking the ContextMenuStrip component on the Windows form. To add another menu item, click another "Type Here" area within the Menu Designer. You click the area below the current menu item to add another menu item, or you can click the area to the right of the current menu item to add submenu items.

You then should name these menu items. If the context menu item parallels one on the main menu, one naming convention is to give the context menu item the same name, other than the prefix, for which you may use "cmnu" (instead of mnu), the letter *c* standing for "context." For example, if a context menu item parallels the main menu item Open under the File menu (named mnuFileOpen), you could name the corresponding context menu item cmnuFileOpen.

NOTE *One difference between a context menu and a main menu is that a context menu usually does not have a top-level item, such as File in the main menu.*

Items Collection Editor

You also can use the Items Collection Editor to add items to a context menu as well as to the main menu.

Figure 11-13 shows the Properties window for the ContextMenuStrip.

You also can add items to the ContextMenuStrip. As Figure 11-13 shows, the ContextMenuStrip has an Items collection property.

Figure 11-13
Properties window for the
ContextMenuStrip.

Clicking the ellipsis (. . .) next to Items will open the Items Collection Editor for the ContextMenuStrip, which is shown in Figure 11-14 after menu items have been added to the ContextMenuStrip.

You add ToolStripMenuItems to the ContextMenuStrip by choosing MenuItem from the drop-down box and then clicking the Add button. You then may select the added ToolStripMenuItem and in the right pane change its Name, Text, and other properties. Figure 11-14 shows the properties for the first menu item on the context menu.

Copying and Pasting

You may want the context menu to duplicate commands in the main menu. For example, the Cut, Copy, and Paste menu commands in Microsoft Word's Edit menu are often duplicated in a menu when you click on the document.

You do not need to re-create the entire menu structure when you want to duplicate a given menu's functionality. You may use the Menu Designer to copy menus by following these steps:

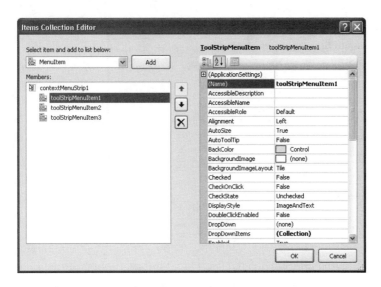

Figure 11-14   Items Collection Editor for ContextMenuStrip.

1. Within the Menu Designer, choose the MenuStrip component, select the menu item or items (using the SHIFT key for multiple items) you would like to duplicate, right-click them, and choose Copy, as shown in Figure 11-15.

2. Choose the ContextMenuStrip component, select the "Type Here" area where you would like the first menu item to appear, and then right-click and choose Paste, as shown in Figure 11-16.

3. Figure 11-17 shows the end result.

Figure 11-15
Copying items from the MenuStrip.

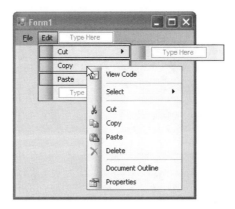

Figure 11-16
Pasting items into the
ContextMenuStrip.

Adding Functionality to Context Menu Items

You add functionality to menu items in a ContextMenuStrip the same way you add functionality to menu items in a MenuStrip—by using the Click event procedure of the menu item.

Often a context menu item corresponds to a menu item on the main menu. For example, on the main menu, you may have an Edit | Select All menu item named mnuEditSelectAll, and on a context menu, you may have a Select All context menu choice named cmnuEditSelectAll. If the user chooses Select All from the context menu, rather than writing a duplicate event procedure, you want the Click event procedure of the Edit | Select All menu item to run. You have two alternatives for having the Click event procedure for the main menu item also handle the Click event for the corresponding context menu item.

Figure 11-17
Context menu now
populated.

EventHandler Class

When you create a Click event procedure for a menu item named mnuEditSelect-All, the following code is created in the Form1.Designer.cs file (assuming the class name is Form1):

```
this.mnuEditSelectAll +=
    new EventHandler(this.mnuEditSelectAll_Click);
```

The object to which we are assigning an event handler is to the left of the combined addition and assignment operator (+=). That operator is followed by the new keyword, because a new event handler is being created. The new keyword is followed by the EventHandler class constructor, whose argument is the name of the method that will be handling the event (here, mnuEditSelectAll_Click).

You can have this event also handle the Click event of the context menu item via the following code, which you could put in the Load event procedure of the form:

```
cmnuEditSelectAll +=
    new EventHandler(mnuEditSelectAll_Click);
```

Other than the omission of the this keyword, which is unnecessary in this code context, the only difference between this code and the previous code snippet is that the object to which we are assigning an event handler is cmnuEditSelectAll, not mnuEditSelectAll. However, the argument for the EventHandler class constructor, the name of the method that will be handling the Click event of cmnuEditSelectAll, is the same, mnuEditSelectAll_Click.

Calling Another Event Procedure

The other alternative is to call the Click event procedure of the main menu item from the Click event procedure of the context menu item:

```
private void cmnuEditSelectAll_Click
    (object sender, EventArgs e)
{
    mnuEditSelectAll_Click(sender, e);
}
```

NOTE *You must pass the arguments sender and e to the mnuEditSelectAll_Click call because the Click event procedure of that main menu item expects those arguments.*

Text Editor Project

This project is a text editor. The application user can type and use the main menu or the context menu to cut, copy, and paste. Figure 11-18 shows the Text Editor project at run time with the context menu displayed.

Creating the Project

You can create the Text Editor project with the following steps:

1. Create a new Windows application.
2. Add a TextBox control to the form from the Toolbox. Name it txtEdit, set its Multiline property to True, and delete any text in its Text property. You also should resize the control so it is large enough to show multiple lines of text.
3. Add a MenuStrip component to the form from the Toolbox.
4. Using the Menu Designer, add a menu where the top-level menu is Edit and its menu items are Cut, Copy, and Paste. Name the Edit menu item mnuEdit, the Cut menu item mnuEditCut, the Copy menu item mnuEditCopy, and the Paste menu item mnuEditPaste.
5. Using the Properties window, set the MainMenuStrip property of the form to the name of your MenuStrip component.
6. Add a ContextMenuStrip component to the form from the Toolbox.

Figure 11-18
Text Editor project at run time.

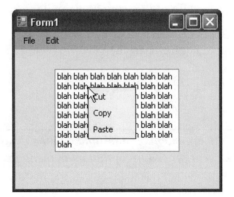

7. Using the Properties window, set the ContextMenuStrip property of the text box to the name of your ContextMenuStrip component. Also set the ShowImageMargin property of the ContextMenuStrip control to False so the context menu will not have a left-hand margin.

8. Copy the Cut, Copy, and Paste menu items from the MenuStrip to the ContextMenuStrip. Name these menu items in the context menu cmnuEditCut, cmnuEditCopy, and cmnuEditPaste, respectively.

9. In the Code editor, create a Click event procedure for the Edit | Cut menu item (mnuEditCut) and write the following code in it:

```
private void mnuEditCut_Click(object sender, EventArgs e)
{
    txtEdit.Cut();
}
```

10. In the Code editor, create a Load event procedure for the form and write the following code in it:

```
cmnuEditCut.Click += new EventHandler(mnuEditCut_Click);
```

11. In the Code editor, create a Click event procedure for the Edit | Copy menu item (mnuEditCopy) and write the following code in it:

```
private void mnuEditCopy_Click(object sender, EventArgs e)
{
    txtEdit.Copy();
}
```

12. In the Code editor, create a Click event procedure for the Edit | Copy context menu item (cmnuEditCopy) and write the following code in it:

```
private void cmnuEditCopy_Click
    (object sender, EventArgs e)
{
    mnuEditCopy_Click(sender, e);
}
```

13. In the Code editor, create a Click event procedure for the Edit | Paste menu item (mnuEditPaste) and write the following code in it:

```
private void mnuEditPaste_Click
    (object sender, EventArgs e)
{
    txtEdit.Paste()
}
```

14. In the Code editor, create a Click event procedure for the Edit | Paste context menu item (cmnuEditPaste) and write the following code in it:

```
private void cmnuEditPaste_Click
   (object sender, EventArgs e)
{
   mnuEditPaste_Click(sender, e);
}
```

Explanation of the Code

The TextBox class has Cut, Copy, and Paste methods. These methods work the same as the Cut, Copy, and Paste menu items of the Edit menu item in Microsoft Word and other Windows applications. The Cut method copies the selected text to the clipboard, but removes the selected text from the text box. The Copy method also copies the selected text to the clipboard, but does not remove the selected text from the text box. The Paste method copies the text in the clipboard to the text box, beginning with the cursor location in the text box.

The Cut, Copy, and Paste methods of the TextBox class are called in the Click event procedures of the corresponding Edit menu items: Edit | Cut (mnuEditCut), Edit | Copy (mnuEditCopy), and Edit | Paste (mnuEditPaste).

The Cut, Copy, and Paste methods of the TextBox class also could be called in the Click event procedures of the corresponding context menu items: Cut (cmnuEdit-Cut), Copy (cmnuEditCopy), and Paste (cmnuEditPaste). However, this would be a duplication of code. Here, the duplication is short, but in other circumstances it may not be. Therefore, it is useful instead to have each context menu item's functionality handled by the corresponding Edit main menu item.

The preceding section "Adding Functionality to ContextMenuStrip Menu Items" discussed two different alternatives of having a context menu item's functionality handled by the corresponding main menu item. To illustrate the use of both alternatives, the EventHandler class alternative is used for the Cut context menu item, and the calling of another event procedure alternative is used for the Copy and Paste context menu items.

Run the application. Type some text in the text editor, select some text, and then cut, copy, and paste, using the main menu and the context menu.

This text editor certainly is not ready for the commercial market. The Cut, Copy, and Paste items need to be disabled at the appropriate times. Additionally, further commands are needed, such as Undo, Select All, and so on. Nevertheless, the Text Editor project is useful in demonstrating how to link corresponding items on a main menu and a context menu, as well as showing some methods of the TextBox control.

Conclusion

Application users need to give commands to the application, such as to open, save, or close a file, to print a document, to cut, copy, or paste text, and so on. Application users give such commands through the GUI of the application. Two of the most common GUI elements through which application users give commands to an application are the main menu and the context or shortcut menu. In this chapter, you learned how to create them and to handle and link their events.

There is another common GUI element through which application users also give commands to an application—toolbars. In the next chapter, you will learn how to create toolbars and coordinate them with your menus.

Quiz

1. What class represents a main menu?

2. What class represents each item on a main menu?

3. What is an access key?

4. Is the Click event raised for all menu items?

5. How do you gray out a menu item so it is not available when it should not be?

6. What does the Items collection of the MenuStrip component contain?

7. What class represents the shortcut or context menu?

8. What class represents each item on a context menu?

9. What does the Items collection of the ContextMenuStrip component contain?

10. What are different alternatives of having a context menu item's functionality handled by the corresponding main menu item?

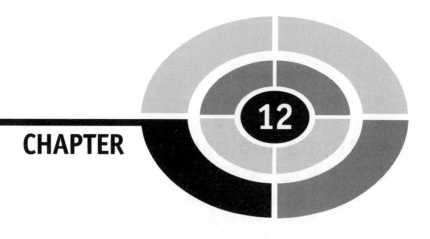

CHAPTER

Toolbars

This lesson is all about bars, but not the kind that inspired the song "Looking for Love in All the Wrong Places." In this chapter, we'll explore a kind of bar that will enable you to enhance your application both visually and functionally.

The toolbar is a part of every Windows programmer's life. You would be hard-pressed to find a Windows application that doesn't have a toolbar. Indeed, most Windows applications have several of them.

The functionality of a toolbar button generally duplicates the functionality of a menu item. For example, the toolbar button with the printer icon duplicates the functionality of the File | Print menu item.

There are two good reasons for using a toolbar even though it may duplicate the functionality of a menu. First, the buttons on the toolbar are immediately accessible. By contrast, the items on the menus may be nested several levels deep and can be accessed only by multiple mouse clicks or keystrokes. Second, a toolbar button usually has an image, whereas a menu item usually is text. Quite simply, visual items are more attractive and apparent to the application's user than text items. This is *Visual* C#, after all!

This chapter will show you, through enhancing the Text Editor project you created in Chapter 11, how to create toolbars for your forms, add buttons to them, and add images to the buttons. You also will learn how to associate the clicking of a particular toolbar button with the clicking of a corresponding menu item.

Creating a Toolbar

Just as the main menu is represented by the MenuStrip class, the toolbar is represented by the ToolStrip class. A ToolStrip object contains a collection of buttons or other types of controls.

Creating a toolbar is a two-step process: First, you add a ToolStrip object to your form. Second, you add buttons or other controls to the toolbar.

Adding a Toolbar to a Form

You add a ToolStrip object to a form using the following steps, similar to adding a MenuStrip object to a form. Try the following steps to add a ToolStrip to the Text Editor project you created in Chapter 11:

1. Open the Text Editor project.

2. Open the form in designer view.

3. Double-click the ToolStrip component in the Toolbox to add it to the form. Figure 12-1 shows the ToolStrip component after it has been added to the form.

As Figure 12-1 shows, the ToolStrip control, like the MenuStrip and Context-MenuStrip components, appears in the component tray. The ToolStrip control also appears as a large gray area under the menu area. This is where the toolbar will be located.

Figure 12-2 shows that, when the ToolStrip control has focus, or you click the four vertical dots on the left side of the ToolStrip control, a drop-down box appears on the left side of the ToolStrip control, and what is called a *smart task arrow* appears on the right side of the ToolStrip control.

The ToolStrip control is automatically associated with the form. This is unlike the ContextMenuStrip component, which is not associated with the form without you first setting the ContextMenuStrip property of the form.

NOTE *The toolbar we just added has the default name of toolBar1. You don't need to change this name because this project uses only one toolbar. However, if your application uses more than one toolbar, as many applications do, then you should choose logical names to differentiate among the different toolbars.*

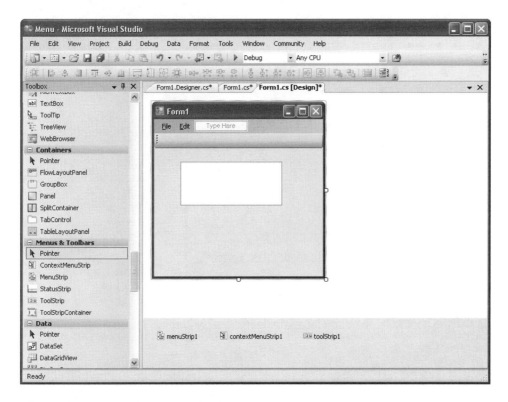

Figure 12-1   ToolStrip added to the form.

Adding Buttons to the Toolbar

The button, represented by the ToolStripButton class, is the most common type of control on a toolbar, and therefore it's the control covered in this section. However, toolbars may contain other types of controls. For example, in Microsoft Word, the formatting toolbar contains drop-down boxes for the type and size of fonts.

There are several different alternative methods by which you can add buttons or other controls to the toolbar. One alternative is the Items Collection Editor, which we used in Chapter 11 to add items to the main menu. Figure 12-3 shows the Items Collection Editor for the toolbar.

You can display the Items Collection Editor by displaying the Properties window for the toolbar and then clicking the ellipsis (…) next to the Items collection property shown in Figure 12-4.

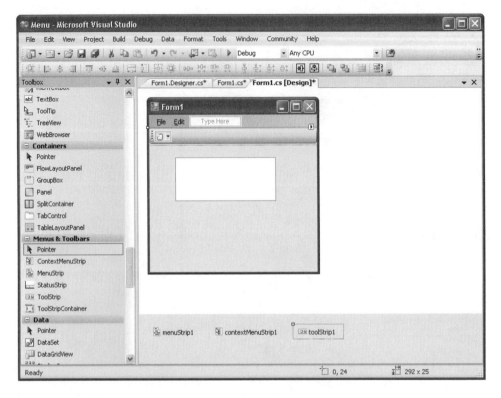

Figure 12-2   ToolStrip with drop-down box and smart task arrow.

You also can display the Items Collection Editor by first clicking the smart task arrow at the rightmost edge of the toolbar. This displays the ToolStrip Tasks pane shown in Figure 12-5. Clicking Edit Items… at the bottom of this pane displays the Items Collection Editor.

Once you display the Items Collection Editor, you first select the type of item to be added. The item usually is a button, but also may be another control, as shown in Figure 12-6.

Once you have chosen the control, you then click the Add button to add the control to the toolbar. Figure 12-7 shows the Items Collection Editor after three buttons have been added to the toolbar.

As Figure 12-7 also shows, choosing one of the buttons in the left pane shows the button's properties in the right pane. You should change each button's Name property. Later in this chapter, we will be using these buttons to parallel the functionality of the Edit | Cut, Edit | Copy, and Edit | Paste menu items. Accordingly,

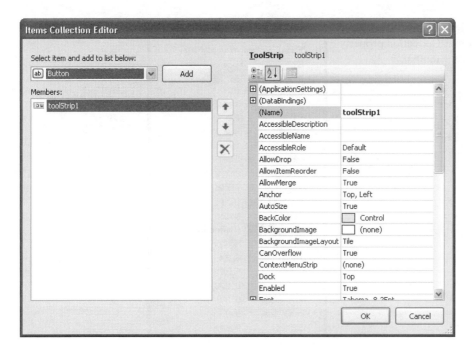

Figure 12-3   Items Collection Editor for the toolbar.

I have named the three buttons tbtnEditCut, tbtnEditCopy, and tbtnEditPaste. The "tbtn" prefix indicates a toolbar button, and the suffix (EditCut, EditCopy, or Edit-Paste) indicates the functionality of the toolbar button.

Additionally, delete the value of the Text property of each button, because these buttons will be displaying images, not text.

Click OK to close the Items Collection Editor and create the buttons you speci-fied. Figure 12-8 shows the toolbar area after several buttons have been added.

Associating Images with Toolbar Buttons

So far our toolbar is not very impressive. All the buttons look the same, with a ge-neric image that, as near as I can tell, looks like a sun over a mountain.

The most common visual cue for a toolbar button is an image. Figure 12-9 shows a toolbar in Microsoft Word. The images show each toolbar button's purpose, such as New, Open, and Save.

We are now going to add images to the toolbar buttons.

Figure 12-4
Items Collection property
of the toolbar.

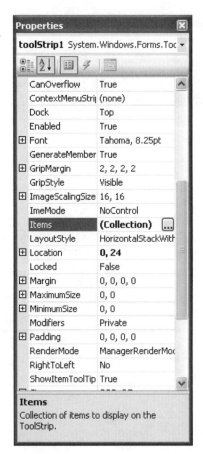

The first step concerns the DisplayStyle property of the ToolStripItem class. This property, which is an enumeration, determines whether an image or text may be displayed on a button. Table 12-1 lists the possible values for this property.

Using the Items Collection Editor, set each button's DisplayStyle property to Image (if necessary, given that it is the default) because we intend each button to

Figure 12-5
ToolStrip Tasks pane.

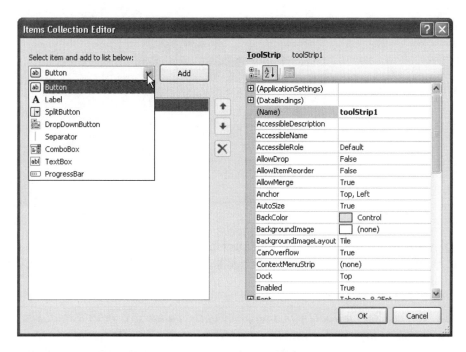

Figure 12-6   Drop-down box in Items Collection Editor.

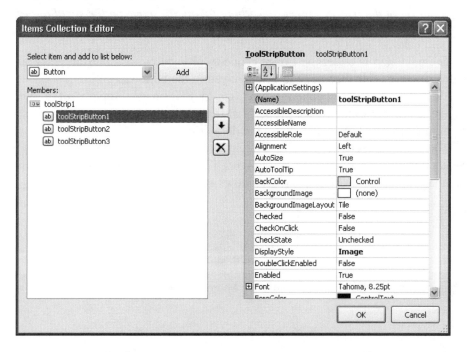

Figure 12-7   Items Collection Editor after three buttons have been added to the toolbar.

Figure 12-8
Toolbar with added
buttons.

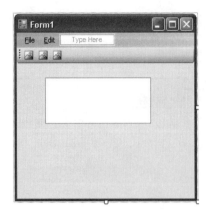

display an image but no text. Text is helpful to identify the purpose of a toolbar button. However, the small area of the button would be crowded by including text as well as an image.

NOTE *You can set the ToolTipText property of the button to a short textual hint of the button's purpose. For example, you could set the ToolTipText property of tbnEditCut to "Cut." Then, when the user hovers the mouse cursor over the button, a ToolTip of "Cut" will appear. A ToolTip has the advantage of a textual explanation of the button's purpose without taking up space on the small area of the button.*

The next step is to set the Image property of each button. This property, as its name suggests, sets the image to be displayed in the button.

Using the Items Collection Editor, go to the Image property of a button. Figure 12-10 shows the Image property of the Cut button, which currently is set to System.Drawing.Bitmap and shows the default image.

Click the ellipsis (...) next to System.Drawing.Bitmap. This will display the Select Resource dialog box shown in Figure 12-11. You use this dialog box to assign an image to a form or control in a Windows application.

Figure 12-9   Images on toolbar buttons in Microsoft Word.

Value	Description
Image	The ToolStripItem may display only an image. This is the default.
ImageAndText	The ToolStripItem may display both an image and text.
None	The ToolStripItem may not display either an image or text.
Text	The ToolStripItem may display only text.

Table 12-1   DisplayStyle Enumeration Values

Choose the Local Resource radio button and then click the Import button associated with it. This displays the Open dialog box shown in Figure 12-12, which you use to browse to and select an image file to be displayed on the button.

Visual Studio 2005 includes bitmap files you can use as toolbar images. These files are located by default within the directory C:\Program Files\Microsoft Visual Studio 8 \Common7\VS2005ImageLibrary. From there I went to the folder bitmaps\commands\highcolor, shown in Figure 12-13. As this figure shows, there are bitmap files (.bmp extension) for Cut, Copy, and (if you scroll further in the dialog box depicted in the figure) Paste.

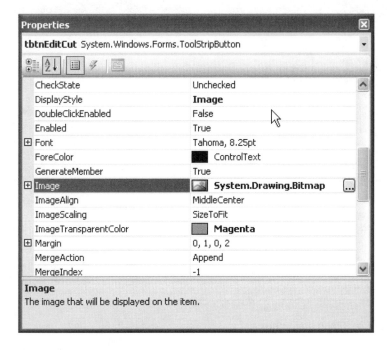

Figure 12-10   Image property of ToolStripButton.

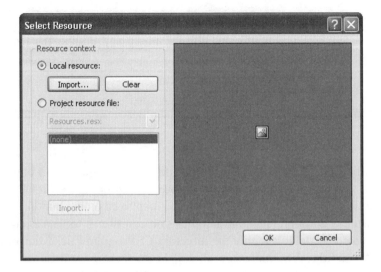

Figure 12-11   Select Resource dialog box.

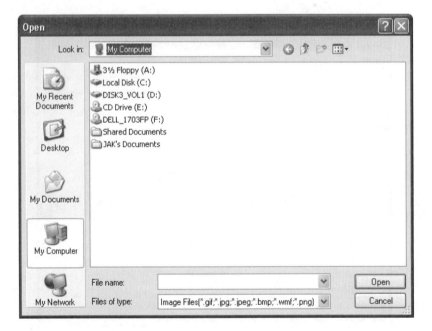

Figure 12-12   Open dialog box.

Figure 12-13   Bitmap Files for Cut, Copy, and Paste.

NOTE *You may not have these bitmap files installed, or they may be installed at a different location, depending on the particular edition you purchased or your installation options.*

Choose the Cut bitmap file for the Cut toolbar button and then click the Open button. As Figure 12-14 shows, the Select Resource dialog box now contains the image for Cut.

Click OK in the Select Resource dialog box. As Figure 12-15 shows, the Items Collection Editor now shows an image for the Image property of the Cut button.

Repeat the same process for the Copy and Paste buttons, except of course choose Copy.bmp for the Copy button and Paste.bmp for the Paste button. When done, click OK to close the Items Collection Editor. Figure 12-16 shows the toolbar, with images for Cut, Copy, and Paste.

NOTE *The size of the bitmap and the size of the toolbar button may be different. You can set the ImageScaling property to SizeToFit so the image will size to fit on the toolbar button.*

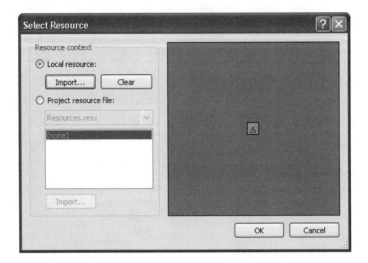

Figure 12-14 Select Resource dialog box containing the image for Cut.

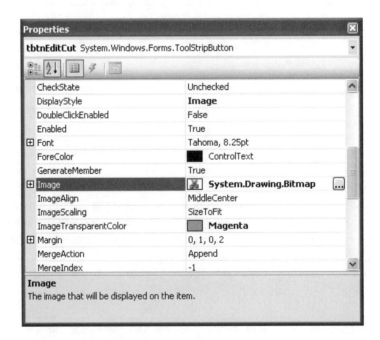

Figure 12-15 Items Collection Editor showing the image for the Cut button.

Figure 1-16
Toolbar buttons with
images for Cut, Copy,
and Paste.

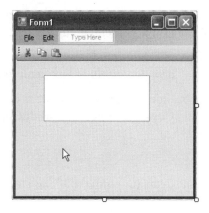

Associating Code with Clicks of Toolbar Buttons

The toolbar buttons look prettier now that each has an image on it, but they still don't do anything when they're clicked.

In this section, we'll write code so the Cut toolbar button provides the same cut action as the Cut menu item and context menu item we worked on in Chapter 11. Similarly, when you're finished with this section, the Copy toolbar button will provide the same copy action as the Copy menu item and context menu item, and the Paste toolbar button will provide the same paste action as the Paste menu item and context menu item.

The Cut, Copy, and Paste methods of the TextBox class also could be called in the Click event procedures of the corresponding toolbar buttons. However, as discussed in Chapter 11 in connection with context menu items, this would be a duplication of code. Here, the duplication is short, but in other circumstances it may not be. Therefore, it is useful instead to have each toolbar button's functionality handled by the corresponding Edit main menu item.

Chapter 11, in the section "Adding Functionality to ContextMenuStrip Menu Items," discussed two different alternatives of having a context menu item's functionality handled by the corresponding main menu item. The same discussion applies here to having a toolbar button's functionality handled by the corresponding main menu item. To illustrate the use of both alternatives, the EventHandler class alternative is used for the Cut context menu item, and the calling of another event procedure alternative is used for the Copy and Paste context menu items.

Add the following line of code to the Load event procedure of the form so the Click event procedure of the Edit |Cut menu item handles the Click event of the Cut toolbar button:

```
tbtnEditCut.Click += new EventHandler(mnuEditCut_Click);
```

Create a Click event procedure for the Copy toolbar button so it calls the Click event procedure of the Edit | Copy menu item (mnuEditCopy):

```
private void tbtnEditCopy_Click
    (object sender, EventArgs e)
{
    mnuEditCopy_Click(sender, e);
}
```

Finally, create a Click event procedure for the Paste toolbar button so it calls the Click event procedure of the Edit | Paste menu item (mnuEditPaste):

```
private void tbtnEditPaste_Click
    (object sender, EventArgs e)
{
    mnuEditPaste_Click(sender, e);
}
```

Conclusion

Application users use toolbars as well as menu items to give commands to an application. The functionality of a toolbar button generally duplicates the functionality of a menu item. However, the purpose of this duplication is that toolbar buttons have two advantages over menu items. First, toolbar buttons are immediately accessible, whereas menu items may be nested several levels deep and can be accessed only by multiple mouse clicks or keystrokes. Second, a toolbar button uses an image, which gives a more visual interface than the text of a menu item.

This chapter showed you how to create toolbars for your forms, add buttons to them, and add images to the buttons. Transitioning from the graphical user interface to code, you also learned how to associate the clicking of a particular toolbar button with the clicking of a corresponding menu item.

So far our Text Editor is not able to read from or write to any file from the hard drive. This functionality will be added in the next chapter.

Quiz

1. What class represents a toolbar?

2. What class represents each item on a toolbar?

3. What does the Items collection of the ToolStrip component contain?

4. Is a toolbar item limited to a button?

5. What are advantages of a toolbar over a corresponding menu?

6. What are different alternatives of having a toolbar item's functionality handled by the corresponding main or context menu item?

7. What does the DisplayStyle property of the ToolStripItem class determine?

8. What does the Image property of the ToolStripItem class determine?

9. What editor is useful in adding controls to a toolbar?

10. What is a good prefix for naming a toolbar button?

13

Accessing Text Files

Perhaps the most common purpose of Visual C# applications is to access, view, and modify data. The data is stored on the computer's hard drive as a file or files so it will be available even after the application exits.

Text files long have been used to store data. Text files preceded databases, but they often are not thought of as advanced as databases such as Oracle, SQL Server, and Access. Indeed, databases do have advantages over text files. However, unlike databases, with each one having a different format and therefore often can be understood only by applications that have the software for that particular database format, text files generally are universally understood by applications. For this reason, text files are used as a common language between applications that otherwise have incompatible software for data transfer between them.

I will show you in this chapter how to read from and write to a text file. First, however, I will show you how to add to your program Open and Save dialog boxes, such as those used in sophisticated programs like Microsoft Word, so you can open a text file to read from it, and save to a text file to write to it.

Open and Save File Dialog Boxes

In Microsoft Word and many other Windows programs, the application user may open a file located with the Open dialog box, which they display with the File | Open menu command or the Open toolbar button. Similarly, the application user may save information to a file with the Save dialog box, which they display with the File | Save menu command or the Save toolbar button.

The Open dialog box is a control of the OpenFileDialog class, and the Save dialog box is a control of the SaveFileDialog class. In this section, I will show you how to add Open and Save dialog boxes to your application.

Adding an OpenFileDialog Control to Your Form

Figure 13-1 shows an Open dialog box in Notepad.

You add an OpenFileDialog control to a form using the following steps, similar to adding a MenuStrip or ToolStrip object to a form. Try the following steps to add an OpenFileDialog control to the Text Editor project you created in Chapter 11 and enhanced in Chapter 12:

1. Open the Text Editor project.

2. Open the form in designer view.

3. Double-click the OpenFileDialog control in the Toolbox (it is in the Dialogs section) to add it to the form.

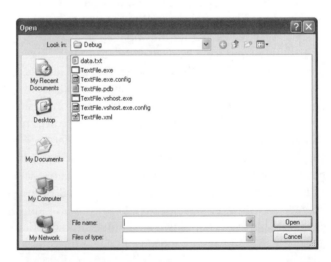

Figure 13-1   Open dialog box in Notepad.

Figure 13-2 shows the OpenFileDialog control after it has been added to the form. The OpenFileDialog won't appear directly on your form, but instead in the component tray below the form, as shown in Figure 13-2.

The default name of this control likely is OpenFileDialog1. Give this control a more logical name, such as dlgOpen. The "dlg" prefix indicates the control is a dialog box and the "Open" suffix indicates that the purpose of the dialog box is to open a file. You should also change the FileName property so that it doesn't display the control's name in the dialog box. You don't need to change any of the other default properties of this control.

Showing the OpenFileDialog Control

The MenuStrip, ContextMenuStrip, and ToolStrip controls also appear in the component tray. However, unlike these controls, the OpenFileDialog control won't appear on your form when you run your program. Instead, you need to write code to display the OpenFileDialog control.

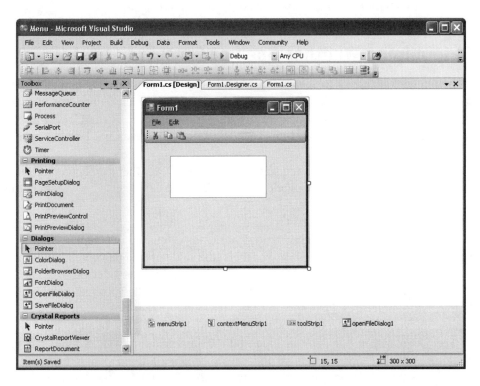

Figure 13-2   OpenFileDialog in component tray.

One of the methods of the OpenFileDialog class is ShowDialog. As the name suggests, its purpose is to show the Open dialog box. You can call the ShowDialog method via the following code, which starts with the name of the object (dlgOpen), followed by a period separating the object name from the method name (ShowDialog), followed by empty parentheses (because this method has no parameters):

```
dlgOpen.ShowDialog();
```

Let's test this code in the Text Editor project. Add a button to the form named btnRead with the Text property Read. Create the following Click event procedure for this button:

```
private void btnRead_Click(object sender, EventArgs e)
{
    dlgOpen.ShowDialog();
}
```

When you run the project and click the Read button, the OpenFileDialog control will appear, similar to Figure 13-1. The OpenFileDialog control is modal, meaning your application cannot continue until you close the Open dialog box by clicking one of its two buttons—Open (after selecting a file) or Cancel.

Determining Whether Open or Cancel Is Chosen

Although clicking either the Open or Cancel button will close the Open dialog box, it is important to know which button was chosen. If the Open button was chosen, we would want our code to open the selected file. However, if the Cancel button was chosen, we would not want our code to attempt to open a file because no file was selected.

From the code we have written so far, you can't tell whether the Open or Cancel button was chosen. Now we will add to the code so we can determine which button was chosen.

In addition to displaying the OpenFileDialog control, the ShowDialog method also returns a DialogResult. The DialogResult was discussed in Chapter 10 in connection with dialog forms. As discussed there, the value of the DialogResult returned by the ShowDialog method corresponds to the button the user selected to close the dialog box. For example, if the user chose the OK button, the value returned by the ShowDialog method is DialogResult.OK. However, if the user chose the Cancel button, the value returned by the ShowDialog method is DialogResult.Cancel.

The Open dialog box has an Open button instead of an OK button, but the DialogResult that corresponds to the user's choice of the Open button still is DialogResult.OK. Not surprisingly, the DialogResult is DialogResult.Cancel if the user instead chose the Cancel button to close the Open dialog box.

Here is the syntax for using the return value of the ShowDialog method to determine whether the user chose the Open or Cancel button:

```
DialogResult dr;
dr = dlgOpen.ShowDialog();
if (dr == DialogResult.OK)

    //Open button was clicked
else
    //Cancel button was clicked
```

This first statement creates a DialogResult variable because that is the data type returned by the ShowDialog method. The second statement calls the ShowDialog method and assigns its return value to the DialogResult variable we created in the first statement. The following if . . . else statement checks to see if the value of the DialogResult variable is DialogResult.OK. If it is, the Open button was clicked. Otherwise, the Cancel button was clicked.

Accordingly, modify the code in the Click event procedure of the Read button so it reads as follows:

```
private void btnRead_Click(object sender, EventArgs e)
{
    DialogResult dr;
    dr = dlgOpen.ShowDialog();
    if (dr == DialogResult.OK)
        MessageBox.Show("Open button was clicked");
}
```

Run the project. Click the Read button to display the Open dialog box. Select a file and click the Open button. The message box will display that the Open button was clicked. Close the message box. Click the Read button again to redisplay the Open dialog box. This time click the Cancel button. No message box will display, indicating that the Cancel button was clicked.

Identifying the File to Open

We have made progress! We can now determine through code whether the user chose the Open or Cancel button. The next step is to determine the name of the file the user chose if they selected the Open button, because we need that name to know which file to open.

The OpenFileDialog class has a FileName property whose value is a string containing the path to and the name of the file selected in the file dialog box. For example, if we chose the file data.txt in the C:\temp directory, the FileName property would be C:\temp\data.txt.

Usually you are interested in the FileName property only if the user chose the Open button. If the user chose the Cancel button instead, the FileName property is an empty string.

Modify the code in the Click event procedure of the Read button so it reads as follows:

```
private void btnRead_Click(object sender, EventArgs e)
{
   DialogResult dr;
   dr = dlgOpen.ShowDialog();
   if (dr == DialogResult.OK)
      MessageBox.Show(dlgOpen.FileName);
}
```

Run the project. Click the Read button to display the Open dialog box. Select a file and click the Open button. The message box will display the path to and the name of the file. You can now close the message box and then close the form.

SaveFileDialog Class

You use a SaveFileDialog control to add to your application the ability to save files using the built-in Save dialog box, which is shown in Figure 13-3.

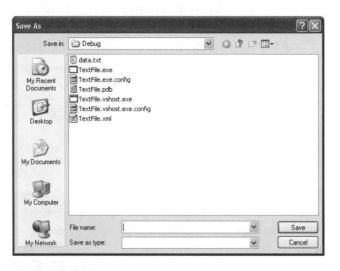

Figure 13-3 Save dialog box.

Note *The Save dialog box often is titled "Save As" rather than "Save," as in Figure 13-3. The title depends on, among other factors, if the contents are being saved to a different file than the one opened, or whether the file is being saved for the first time. The discussion in this chapter about the Save dialog box applies equally to the Save As dialog box.*

Add a SaveFileDialog control to your form, as you did the OpenFileDialog control earlier in this chapter. Name the SaveFileDialog control dlgSave. You don't need to change any of this control's other default properties.

The SaveFileDialog control, like the OpenFileDialog control, is modal, meaning your application cannot continue until you close the Save dialog box by clicking one of its two buttons—Save or Cancel.

Once you have learned how to use an OpenFileDialog control, using the SaveFileDialog control is easy. The reason is the ShowDialog method, DialogResult return value, and FileName property work the same way with a SaveFileDialog control as they do with an OpenFileDialog control. The DialogResult returned by clicking the Save button is DialogResult.OK, just as is the case with clicking the Open button in the OpenFileDialog control

Let's test this by adding to the Text Editor project another button to the form, named btnWrite with the Text property Write. Create the following Click event procedure for this button:

```
private void btnWrite_Click(object sender, EventArgs e)
{
    DialogResult dr;
    dr = dlgSave.ShowDialog();
    if (dr == DialogResult.OK)
        MessageBox.Show(dlgSave.FileName);
}
```

Run the project. Click the Write button to display the Save dialog box. Select a file and click the Save button. A message box will display the path to and the name of the file. Another message box always will advise you that the file already exists and ask you if you want to replace it. Answer yes to close the warning message box (don't worry, the file will not be replaced). The Save dialog box will close. Next, click the Write button to display the Save dialog box again. This time click the Cancel button. No message box will display, indicating that the Cancel button was clicked. Finally, close the form to end the application.

Reading from a Text File

I am always telling my students that the best way to learn computer programming is to write programs. Therefore, you will learn in this section how to display in the text box in the Text Editor project the contents of a text file selected in an Open dialog box. When we are finished writing code, clicking the Read button will display in the TextBox control the contents of a text file. Figure 13-4 shows how the application will appear after the Read button is clicked and the contents of a text file are displayed in the TextBox control.

Conversely, in the next section you will further enhance the project so that when you click the Write button, the application will write to the text file the contents of the TextBox control. Thus, if I make any changes to the text of the TextBox control and click the Write button, the text file will be updated with those changes.

StreamReader Class

We will use the StreamReader class to read from the text file. The word "stream" refers to a stream of data, moving from one place to another, in this case from a text file to your application. The word "reader" means the file is being read. As you might now guess, when we want to write to the file, we will use the StreamWriter class.

To use the StreamReader class, we first will declare a variable of that data type:

```
IO.StreamReader readerVar;
```

The term "IO" must precede "StreamReader" or else the compiler will complain that the term StreamReader is not defined. The reason is that the StreamReader class is part of the System.IO namespace.

Figure 13-4
Application displaying
the contents of a text file.

Importing the System.IO Namespace

The compiler will not look in the System.IO namespace unless we tell it to. One way to tell the compiler to look in the System.IO namespace is to precede Stream-Reader with System.IO.

There is an easier way to tell the compiler to look in the System.IO namespace. At the top of the code module, type the following:

```
using System.IO;
```

Including this one using statement means that you don't have to precede Stream-Reader (or StreamWriter) with System.IO each time you use that term in your code. Now you can declare the StreamReader variable readerVar in the Click event procedure of the Read button without preceding StreamReader with IO:

```
StreamReader readerVar;
```

Revise the code in your Read button Click event procedure to appear as follows:

```
private void btnRead_Click(object sender, EventArgs e)
{
    StreamReader readerVar;
    DialogResult dr;
    dr = dlgOpen.ShowDialog();
    if (dr == DialogResult.OK)
        MessageBox.Show(dlgOpen.FileName);
}
```

Instantiating a StreamReader Variable

Although we have created the StreamReader variable readerVar, right now that variable does not relate to any text file. Therefore, the next step is to connect the StreamReader variable readerVar to the text file we want to read. This process is known as *instantiating* the variable.

We will instantiate the StreamReader variable with the following statement:

```
readerVar = new StreamReader(dlgOpen.FileName);
```

This line of code will replace the code that showed the message box, MessageBox. Show(dlgOpen.FileName), because the message box was for illustration purposes, and we are now actually about to open the selected file for reading rather than just display its path and name.

Therefore, so far your Read button Click event procedure should read as follows:

```
private void btnRead_Click(object sender, EventArgs e)
{
    StreamReader readerVar;
    DialogResult dr;
    dr = dlgOpen.ShowDialog();
    if (dr == DialogResult.OK)
        readerVar = new StreamReader(dlgOpen.FileName);
}
```

Now let's take a careful look at the statement we've just added, starting from the right side of the assignment statement.

The New keyword is used to create a new StreamReader instance that points to the text file to be read. The term "StreamReader" in the statement New StreamReader(dlgOpen.FileName) indicates the type of instance being created. When the name of the function (here, StreamReader) is the same as the name of a class (also StreamReader), as it is here, it is called a *constructor*. The constructor is used to "construct" the new instance.

The constructor in this code example takes one argument—the name of the file to be read. That file name is obtained from the FileName property of the Open dialog box.

The right side of the assignment operator returns the new instance, which then is assigned to the StreamReader variable readerVar on the left side of the assignment operator. Now the StreamReader variable readerVar is connected to the text file we want to read.

Reading the Text File into the TextBox

The StreamReader class has a ReadToEnd method that returns a string representing the entire text of the text file. We then assign that string to the Text property of txtEdit so that the text of the TextBox control will display the entire text of the text file. Accordingly, add the following statement to your Read button's Click event procedure:

```
txtEdit.Text = readerVar.ReadToEnd();
```

Your Read button's Click event procedure now should read as follows (note that because there are now two statements conditional on the if control structure, they are enclosed in brackets):

```
private void btnRead_Click(object sender, EventArgs e)
{
    StreamReader readerVar;
    DialogResult dr;
    dr = dlgOpen.ShowDialog();
```

```
   if (dr == DialogResult.OK)
   {
      readerVar = new StreamReader(dlgOpen.FileName);
      txtEdit.Text = readerVar.ReadToEnd();
   }
}
```

The StreamReader class has other methods that are alternatives to ReadToEnd. The Read method reads a specified number of characters, and the ReadLine method reads a line. For example, if you want to load the data one line at a time into a row of a control, the ReadLine method might be a logical choice.

Closing the Text File

Once we have read the entire contents of the text file, there is no further need to read from it. Therefore, we should close the text file for reading. The StreamReader class has a Close method to accomplish this. Accordingly, add the following line of code to close the text file for reading:

```
readerVar.Close();
```

This completes the Read button Click event procedure, which now should read as follows:

```
private void btnRead_Click(object sender, EventArgs e)
{
   StreamReader readerVar;
   DialogResult dr;
   dr = dlgOpen.ShowDialog();
   if (dr == DialogResult.OK)
   {
      readerVar = new StreamReader(dlgOpen.FileName);
      txtEdit.Text = readerVar.ReadToEnd();
      readerVar.Close();
   }
}
```

Closing the text file for reading frees system resources, specifically memory. This is important. Memory is required to keep a file open for reading (or writing). When you don't need to keep the file open anymore, you should give the memory back to the operating system.

By analogy, a library would run out of books if patrons checked out books but never returned them when they were finished reading the books. Similarly, your computer only has so much available memory for applications (some memory is needed by the operating system itself). If applications don't return memory after checking it out, the operating system eventually will run out of memory. The consequence of the operating system running out of available memory for applications often is a general protection fault or illegal exception, bringing the user's work to a crashing halt.

Additionally, later in this chapter you may be writing to the same text file that you read. Trying to open a file for writing that already is open for reading may cause problems, which can be avoided by closing the file first before reopening it for another purpose.

Run the project. Click the Read button. Use the resulting Open dialog box to select and open a text file. The contents of that text file should be displayed in the text box. You can then close the application.

Writing to a Text File

The next step in enhancing the Text Editor project will be to write to the text file by copying the contents of the text box to the text file. The code to do this will be in the Click event procedure of the Write button.

StreamWriter Class

We will now change the code used previously in this chapter for the Click event procedure for the Write button by replacing the code displaying the message box with the following code:

```
StreamWriter writerVar;
writerVar = new StreamWriter(dlgSave.FileName, false);
```

The code for the Click event procedure of the Write button should now look like this:

```
private void btnWrite_Click(object sender, EventArgs e)
{
    DialogResult dr;
    dr = dlgSave.ShowDialog();
    if (dr == DialogResult.OK)
    {
        StreamWriter writerVar;
        writerVar = new StreamWriter
            (dlgSave.FileName, false);
    }
}
```

The two lines of code we just added may look familiar from the code we wrote earlier in this chapter for the StreamReader. There, we declared a StreamReader variable and then instantiated that variable using the StreamReader constructor to read a text file. Here, we are declaring a StreamWriter variable and then instantiating that variable using the StreamWriter constructor to write to a text file. As the name suggests, the StreamWriter class is used when writing to a text file.

The first argument of the StreamWriter constructor is the name of the text file. This is the same as the first argument of the StreamReader constructor. However, the StreamWriter constructor has an additional, second argument.

NOTE *The StreamWriter constructor, like the Show method of the MessageBox class, is overloaded, which means that it may be called with a different number of arguments.*

The data type of the second argument of the StreamWriter constructor is Boolean. The value of this second argument is true if you want to add to the existing contents of the text file, and false if instead you want to overwrite the existing contents of the text file.

In this project, we want to overwrite rather than add to the existing contents of the text file. Accordingly, the value of the second argument is false.

If you instead wanted to add to the existing contents of the file, you would use true instead of false as the second argument of the StreamWriter constructor. One example would be a log file, which logs events or problems. Normally you would want to add a new event or problem to the prior list, not erase the prior list in the process.

Writing from the TextBox to the Text File

The StreamWriter class has a Write method that writes the contents of its argument to the text file at which the StreamReader instance is targeted. In this application, we want to write the contents of the text box to the text file. Therefore, the argument is the Text property of the TextBox control. Accordingly, add the following code to the Click event of the Write button:

```
writerVar.Write(txtEdit.Text);
```

The code for the Click event procedure of the Write button should now look like this:

```
private void btnWrite_Click(object sender, EventArgs e)
{
   DialogResult dr;
   dr = dlgSave.ShowDialog();
```

```
if (dr == DialogResult.OK)
{
    StreamWriter writerVar;
    writerVar = new StreamWriter
        (dlgSave.FileName, false);
    writerVar.Write(txtEdit.Text);
}
}
```

Closing the Text File

We are now finished writing to the text file. Accordingly, we should close the text file for writing, as we closed the text file for reading earlier in this chapter. Accordingly, add the following statement to the Click event of the Write button:

```
writerVar.Close();
```

The completed code for the Click event procedure of the Write button should now look like this:

```
private void btnWrite_Click(object sender, EventArgs e)
{
    DialogResult dr;
    dr = dlgSave.ShowDialog();
    if (dr == DialogResult.OK)
    {
        StreamWriter writerVar;
        writerVar = new StreamWriter
            (dlgSave.FileName, false);
        writerVar.Write(txtEdit.Text);
        writerVar.Close();
    }
}
```

WARNING *Your program may make changes to your text file, and you don't want those changes to cause any problems on your computer. Accordingly, before you test this project, create a text file using Notepad or another plain text editor and then type in whatever contents you would like. However, don't use Microsoft Word or a comparable word processing program to create the text file because these programs include formatting characters as well as text.*

Run the project. Click the Read button. Use the resulting Open dialog box to select and open the text file you created. The contents of that text file should be displayed in the text box. Then, make changes in the text box. When you're done making changes in the text box, click the Write button. When the Save dialog box displays, find and choose the text file you created and then click the Save button. You may see a message box that informs you that the file you are saving to already exists and asking you if you want to replace it. Click the Yes button.

Run your application again and display the text file. The text should show the changes you made when you first ran the application.

This application is not yet ready for prime time. For example, we should disable the Write button until a file is opened with the Read button. We also should create File | Open and File | Save menu items and link their Click events to the Click events of the Read and Write buttons. You may wish to try to implement these enhancements. Nevertheless, this project is useful in demonstrating how to read from and write to a text file.

Conclusion

In this chapter, you learned how to add to your program Open and Save dialog boxes that sophisticated programs like Microsoft Word have. The Open dialog box is a control of the OpenFileDialog class. Similarly, the Save dialog box is a control of the SaveFileDialog class. You use the ShowDialog method to display each dialog box, and you use the DialogResult property to determine if the user chose the dialog box's Open or Save button, or instead the Cancel button. If the user chose the Open (or Save) button, you use the FileName property to retrieve the file name chosen by the user from the dialog box.

You also learned how to read from a text file using the StreamReader class and to write to a text file using the StreamWriter class. Although text files may not seem as advanced as databases, one advantage text files have over databases is that text files are universally understood by applications, whereas databases require specialized software.

However, databases also have their advantages, so the next chapter will be about them.

Quiz

1. The Open dialog box is a control of which class?

2. What method do you use to show an Open dialog box?

3. What is the return value of showing an Open dialog box?

4. What is the property of the OpenFileDialog class whose value is the file chosen by the user in an Open dialog box?

5. The Save dialog box is a control of which class?

6. What method do you use to show a Save dialog box?

7. What is the return value of showing a Save dialog box?

8. What is the property of the SaveFileDialog class whose value is the name of the file to be saved?

9. What class may you use to read from a text file?

10. What class may you use to write to a text file?

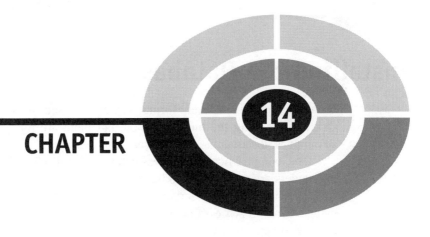

Databases

Up until now, we have saved data in a text file. But text files have their limitations. One limitation is that it is difficult to quickly retrieve specific data in a text file. There's usually no alternative to searching the text file from beginning to end, which can take a long time if the text file contains a lot of data.

Another limitation of a text file is its inability to link different but related data. For example, a store may have both a list of customers and a list of orders. Because the orders come from customers, the two different lists are related. But with a text file, there's no easy way to link an order in one list with a customer in another list.

A database does not have these limitations—you can quickly retrieve specific data using keys and indexes, and you can easily link different data.

Although there are many types of databases, fundamentally these different database types share a number of common characteristics. Accordingly, you will be able to apply what you learn here to different types of databases.

This chapter will get you started with databases. However, I'm not going to start with a dry theoretical discussion of what a database is because that information can be a little abstract if you haven't first spent some time working with one. So let's roll up our sleeves (figuratively, of course) and get started working with a database.

Installing the Database

Databases come in different formats. Microsoft Access, Microsoft SQL Server, and Oracle are among the most common, but there are many others, each with their advantages, disadvantages, followers, and detractors.

I'll be using a Microsoft Access database in this chapter solely because I believe my readers are more likely to have Microsoft Access than other database products such as Microsoft SQL Server and Oracle. Additionally, it is easier to get started using Microsoft Access than with most other database products. However, you will be able to apply what you learn here to other database formats such as Microsoft SQL Server and Oracle.

Obtaining the Northwind Traders Database

We will be working with the Northwind Traders database. It is a Microsoft Access database and is on the installation CD for Microsoft Access.

However, you can use the Northwind Traders database with Visual C# 2005 without having Microsoft Access. Microsoft permits you to download, free of charge, a version of this sample database for Access 2000. This version also will work if you have Access XP or 2003.

The download link at the time of this book is http://www.microsoft.com/downloads/details.aspx?FamilyID=c6661372-8dbe-422b-8676-c632d66c529c&displaylang=en. This link may change, particularly when Microsoft periodically reorganizes its website. In case you need to do a search, the title of the article is "Access 2000 Tutorial: Northwind Traders Sample Database."

Installing the Northwind Traders Database

The name of the installation file is Nwind.exe. Once you download this file onto your hard drive, double-click on it to start the installation process. The installation program will ask you to agree to a license to use the database and then ask where you want to save the database. Save it wherever you wish on the hard drive; just remember where you saved it.

The saved database may have the name Nwind.mdb or Northwind.mdb. The ".mdb" extension is an abbreviation of "Microsoft database" and is used for Access databases.

Connecting to the Database

If you have Access, you can view the Northwind Traders database from that application.

You can also view the Northwind Traders database via Visual C# 2005. You don't need to open or create a Windows application. However, you first need to connect Visual C# 2005 to the database.

To start the process of connecting Visual C# 2005 to the Northwind Traders database, choose the Tools | Connect to Database menu command. This will display the Choose Data Source dialog box similar to that shown in Figure 14-1 (yours may have a different number of choices).

As Figure 14-1 shows, the upper pane of the Choose Data Source dialog box lists different database formats, such as Access, SQL Server, and Oracle. Because Northwind Traders is an Access database, choose Microsoft Access Database File. Figure 14-2 shows the Choose Data Source dialog box after you choose Microsoft Access Database File.

As Figure 14-2 shows, the drop-down box below the upper pane, blank in Figure 14-1, now lists the one available data provider, .NET Framework Data Provider for OLE DB. A data provider is a code component that is used by your application to connect to a specific database format. There are many database formats, so there are many providers, at least one for each database format supported by the .NET Framework. The .NET Framework may have several alternative data providers for some database formats, but just has one, the .NET Framework Data Provider for OLE DB, for the Microsoft Access database format.

Figure 14-1   Choose Data Source dialog box.

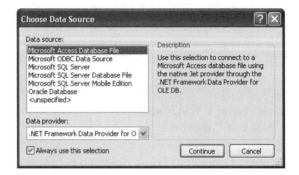

Figure 14-2 Data Source dialog box after the data source is selected.

As Figure 14-2 also shows, the Description area to the right of the upper pane, blank in Figure 14-1, now contains the following text: "Use this selection to connect to a Microsoft Access database file using the native Jet provider through the NET Framework Data Provider for OLE DB." The reason for the term "Jet" is that Microsoft Access uses the Jet database engine.

Finally, Figure 14-2 shows that once you have selected a data source and a data provider, the Continue button, disabled in Figure 14-1, now is enabled.

Click the Continue button. This will display the Add Connection dialog box shown in Figure 14-3.

Figure 14-3 Add Connection dialog box.

Figure 14-4 Add Connection dialog box after the database is selected.

Use the Browse button to find and choose the nwind.mdb (or Northwind.mdb) file you saved on your hard drive when you installed the Northwind Traders database. Once you have done this, as shown in Figure 14-4, the path to and the name of the database should appear in the Database File Name text box.

Note You don't need to worry about the user name and password in the Add Connection dialog box, unless you assigned a name and password to the database (which you don't need to do). This may be an issue with other database formats, but it's not an issue with Microsoft Access.

The next step is to test the connection. Click the Test Connection button. A message box stating "Test Connection Succeeded" should display, as in Figure 14-5.

Click the OK button. This saves the changes you made and closes the Add Connection dialog box.

Figure 14-5
Test connection succeeded.

Using Server Explorer

If you have Microsoft Access, you can use it to view the Northwind Traders database. If you don't, Visual C# 2005 has a tool called Server Explorer that permits you to view and make changes to databases on your computer or on any other computer to which you have network access and permissions.

Indeed, you should learn how to use Server Explorer even if you have Microsoft Access on your computer. First, you may find yourself working at another computer that doesn't have Microsoft Access. Second, and perhaps more important, when you're working with other database formats such as SQL Server and Oracle, you won't be able to use Microsoft Access.

You can display Server Explorer using the View | Server Explorer menu command. You don't need to first open or create a Windows application. Figure 14-6 shows Server Explorer after the Data Connections node was expanded by clicking the + sign to its left.

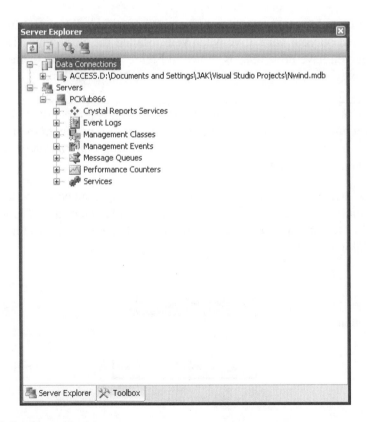

Figure 14-6 Server Explorer.

NOTE *Server Explorer on your machine will likely have different content than what's shown in Figure 14-6. For example, PCKlub866 is listed under the Servers node because that happens to be the name of the computer I used.*

The node underneath the Data Connections node should list the path and file name of the Microsoft Access database to which we just created a connection in the previous section "Connecting to the Database."

Exploring the Database

Click the + sign next to the Microsoft Access database under the Data Connections node. As Figure 14-7 shows, four nodes appear: Tables, Views, Stored Procedures, and Functions.

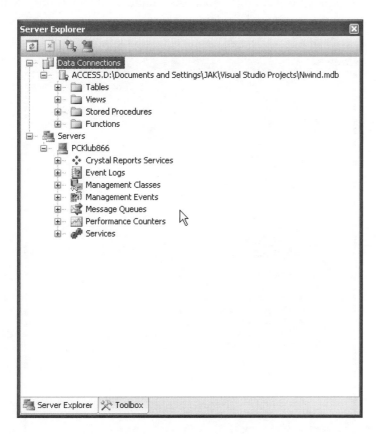

Figure 14-7   Server Explorer listing the Tables, Views, Stored Procedures, and Functions nodes.

A table is a collection of data on a particular subject. In this chapter, we'll be discussing a particular table, Customers. The Northwind Traders database has other tables, too, including those listing employees, products, orders, suppliers, and shippers.

A view is a collection of data, often obtained from more than one table. Examples of views in the Northwind Traders database include "Product Sales for 1995" and "Ten Most Expensive Products."

A stored procedure and a function each is generally a code component that generates a predefined subset of the data. Examples of stored procedures in the Northwind Traders database include "Alphabetical List of Products" and "Summary of Sales by Year." An example of a function in the Northwind Traders database is "Sales by Year."

Exploring the Customers Table

Click the + sign next to the Tables node. As Figure 14-8 shows, this displays the various tables in the Northwind Traders database.

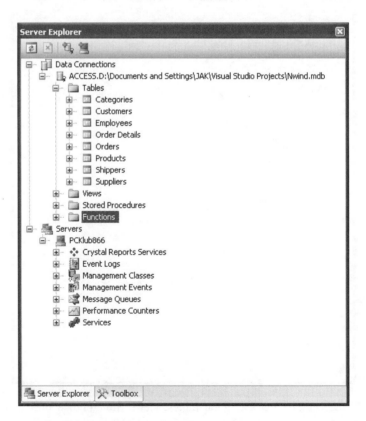

Figure 14-8 Server Explorer listing tables.

Click the + sign next to the Customers table. As Figure 14-9 shows, this displays the various fields of the Customers table.

Right-click the Customers table node and choose Show Table Data from the shortcut menu. As Figure 14-10 shows, the data in the Customers table then will be displayed.

As Figure 14-10 shows, the data in the Customers table is displayed in rows and columns. Each column, or field, represents a different piece of information, such as a name, title, or address. Each row, or record, concerns one customer. Together, the rows and columns provide information, such as the name, title, and address of each customer.

Different tables have different fields and a different number of records. Additionally, the fields are not always of a String data type, but instead may be of another data type, such as Integer or Boolean. The one thing tables have in common is that they're composed of fields (columns) and records (rows).

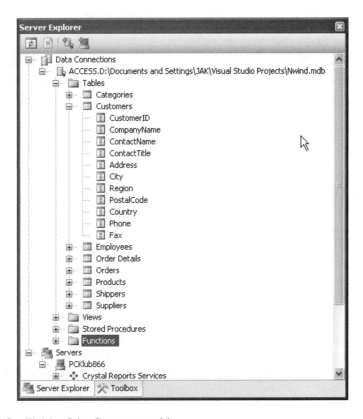

Figure 14-9   Fields of the Customers table.

Figure 14-10   Data in the Customers table.

Database Project

As you have heard me say several times already in this book, the best way to learn programming is to write programs. So let's put that saying into practice once again.

What the Project Does

This project, when finished, will, when the application starts up, fill a DataGrid-View control with data from four fields of the Customers table: CustomerID, ContactTitle, CompanyName, and ContactName. Figure 14-11 shows the project in action.

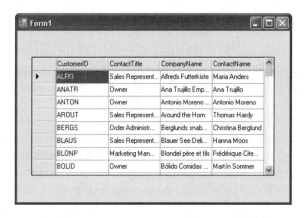

Figure 14-11   DataGridView control filled with data from the Customers table.

Creating the Form

Create a new Windows application. Add two controls to the default form.

The first control is an OpenFileDialog control. You learned about this control in Chapter 13. Name this control dlgOpen and delete any value in its FileName property. You do not need to change any of its other default properties.

The second control is a DataGridView control. This control displays data in a row and column format, much like the Customers table shown in Figure 14-10, or a spreadsheet.

When you add the DataGridView control, a DataGridView tasks pane displays, as shown in Figure 14-12.

You may accept the default values in this pane. However, center the DataGrid-View control in your form and rename it dgvData.

Figure 14-12
DataGridView Tasks
pane.

DataGridView Tasks
Auto Format...
Choose Data Source   (none)   ⌄
Edit Columns...
Add Column...
☑ Enable Adding
☑ Enable Editing
☑ Enable Deleting
☐ Enable Column Reordering
Dock in parent container

Importing Data Namespaces

The code components in the .NET class library used for database access are referred to by the name ADO.NET. You've probably already figured out the ".NET" portion of that name. ADO was an acronym for ActiveX Data Objects, a Microsoft data-access technology that preceded ADO.NET.

Several ADO.NET classes we will use in this chapter are part of the System. Data.OleDb namespace. As you may remember from previous chapters, the .NET library is organized in a hierarchal structure, each branch with its own namespace. System is a top-level namespace. Data is one of several namespaces belonging to System, and OleDb is one of several namespaces belonging to System.Data.

NOTE *There are other namespaces supporting other database types, such as OracleClient for Oracle databases and SqlClient for SQL Server databases.*

Thus, the OleDbConnection class we will be using in the next section technically is not just the OleDbConnection class but instead the System.Data.OleDb. OleDbConnection class. However, typing a System.Data.OleDb prefix before every reference to OleDbConnection or another ADO.NET class can quickly become a pain.

Fortunately, you can avoid having to prefix every reference to an ADO.NET class with System.Data.OleDb by inserting a using System.Data.OleDb statement before your class declaration. While you are at it, also import the System.Data namespace (if it has not already been imported by the IDE), because that namespace also will come in handy later:

```
using System.Data;
using System.Data.OleDb;
```

If the compiler does not recognize the root System.Data namespace, you may need to add a reference to the assembly that contains the namespace. Choose Add Reference from the Project menu to display the Add Reference dialog box shown in Figure 14-13.

Choose System.Data from the list and then click OK. The compiler will now recognize the root System.Data namespace.

Creating a Connection

Your application will be giving commands to the database to retrieve certain data. But before it can do so, your application needs to have a connection with the database.

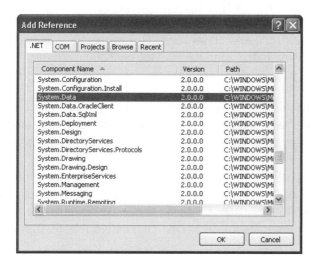

Figure 14-13   Add Reference dialog box.

Persistent Connection vs. Disconnected Application

Although an application needs to have a connection to a database to retrieve or change data, there is more than one way to design this connection. One alternative is to create a single connection that remains active until the application ends. This is called a *persistent connection.*

The other alternative is to create a connection only to retrieve data, end the connection, make changes to a local copy of the data while disconnected from the database, and connect back to the database only when necessary to synchronize these changes with the database. This is called a *disconnected application* because most of the time, the application is disconnected from the database.

As with most choices in life, there are tradeoffs between a persistent connection and a disconnected application. In general, Windows applications are more likely to use persistent connections, whereas web applications are more likely to be disconnected applications, but this is only a generalization, of course.

Because we are writing a Windows application, we will use a persistent connection.

OleDbConnection Class

The OleDbConnection class represents a connection to a data source. The following line of code not only declares an OleDbConnection variable, but also instantiates it:

```
OleDbConnection myConn = new OleDbConnection();
```

As explained in previous chapters, the term "instantiate" means to create a new instance—in this case, a new connection. This instantiation is performed by using the new keyword when declaring the OleDbConnection variable.

ConnectionString Property

The OleDbConnection class has a ConnectionString property. This property includes the provider being used and the path to and the name of the data source file.

The provider is "Microsoft.Jet.OLEDB.4.0." As mentioned in the previous section "Connecting to the Database," the reason for the term "Jet" is that Microsoft Access uses the Jet database engine. Additionally, as the Description area of the Choose Data Source dialog box shown earlier in Figure 14-2 reflects, the connection to a Microsoft Access database uses the native Jet provider through the NET Framework Data Provider for OLE DB. That native Jet provider is Microsoft.Jet. OLEDB.4.0.

We will obtain the path to and the name of the data source file through the Open-FileDialog control and its FileName property.

In this project, all the code will be written in the Load event of the form. Write the following code:

```csharp
private void Form1_Load (Object sender, EventArgs e)
{
    OleDbConnection myConn = new OleDbConnection();
    DialogResult dr;
    dr = dlgOpen.ShowDialog();
    if (dr == DialogResult.OK)
    {
        string strFile = dlgOpen.FileName;
        myConn.ConnectionString = "Provider=" +
            "Microsoft.Jet.OLEDB.4.0;Data Source="
            + strFile + ";";
    }
}
```

Opening the Connection

Once you've instantiated an OleDbConnection object and created its connection string, you may open the connection to your database using the OleDbConnection object's Open method:

```csharp
myConn.Open();
```

Accordingly, our code now reads as follows:

```
private void Form1_Load (Object sender, EventArgs e)
{
   OleDbConnection myConn = new OleDbConnection();
   DialogResult dr;
   dr = dlgOpen.ShowDialog();
   if (dr == DialogResult.OK)
   {
      string strFile = dlgOpen.FileName;
      myConn.ConnectionString = "Provider=" +
         "Microsoft.Jet.OLEDB.4.0;Data Source="
         + strFile + ";";
      myConn.Open();
   }
}
```

Creating a Command

Once you establish a connection, you'll next want to execute commands, such as to retrieve data that you want to view. You use an OleDbCommand object to execute commands to a database. The OleDbCommand class, like the OleDbConnection class, is part of the System.Data.OleDb namespace.

You instantiate an OleDbCommand object similar to how you instantiate an OleDbConnection object:

```
OleDbCommand myCMD = new OleDbCommand();
```

SQL Statement

Commands often are expressed in a SQL statement. SQL, alternatively pronounced as separate letters ("S-Q-L") or as "sequel," is an acronym for Structured Query Language. SQL is a standardized language for requesting information from a database.

The following SQL SELECT statement retrieves data from the CustomerID, ContactTitle, CompanyName, and ContactName fields in the Customers table:

```
SELECT CustomerID, ContactTitle, CompanyName,
   ContactName FROM Customers
```

SELECT is a keyword that indicates the SQL statement retrieves records. The SELECT statement does not change records. Other SQL statements, such as INSERT, UPDATE, and DELETE, do change records, by adding, editing, and deleting, respectively.

The names following the SELECT keyword are the names of table fields. Because there is more than one field, the field names are separated by commas.

FROM is also a keyword. The name following it, Customers, is the name of the table to which the fields belong.

CommandText Property

The OleDbCommand object has a CommandText property whose value may be a SQL statement. Accordingly, we will assign the SQL SELECT statement we discussed in the preceding section to the OleDbCommand object's CommandText property as follows:

```
myCMD.CommandText = "SELECT CustomerID, " +
    "ContactTitle, CompanyName, ContactName " +
    FROM Customers";
```

NOTE *The value of the CommandText property may also be a table name or the name of a stored procedure.*

Linking the Command to a Connection

The final step is to link the command to a connection to the database. The OleDbCommand object has a Connection property whose value is the database connection to be used by the command. Accordingly, the following code assigns the existing OleDbConnection variable myConn to the Connection property of the OleDbCommand object:

```
myCMD.Connection = myConn;
```

Therefore, our code now reads as follows:

```
private void Form1_Load (Object sender, EventArgs e)
{
    OleDbConnection myConn = new OleDbConnection();
    DialogResult dr;
    dr = dlgOpen.ShowDialog();
    if (dr == DialogResult.OK)
    {
        string strFile = dlgOpen.FileName;
```

```
    myConn.ConnectionString = "Provider=" +
        "Microsoft.Jet.OLEDB.4.0;Data Source="
        + strFile + ";";
    myConn.Open();
    OleDbCommand myCMD = new OleDbCommand();
    myCMD.CommandText = "SELECT CustomerID, " +
        "ContactTitle, CompanyName, ContactName " +
        FROM Customers";
    myCMD.Connection = myConn;
    }
}
```

Filling the DataGridView

We now have defined a database connection and command. Here are the remaining tasks:

1. Package the database connection and database command in an OleDbDataAdapter object.

2. Create a DataSet object.

3. Use the OleDbDataAdapter object to fill the DataSet.

4. Use the DataSet to fill the DataGridView.

Creating an OleDbDataAdapter

The OleDbDataAdapter class packages a database connection with a set of data commands.

The first step is to instantiate an OleDbDataAdapter variable, similar to how previously we instantiated the OleDbConnection and OleDbCommand variables:

```
OleDbDataAdapter myAdapter = new OleDbDataAdapter();
```

The OleDbDataAdapter class has a SelectCommand property whose value is a command that contains a SQL SELECT statement. Accordingly, the following code sets the OleDbDataAdapter variable's SelectCommand property to the OleDbCommand variable we instantiated and configured in the previous section:

```
myAdapter.SelectCommand = myCMD;
```

This statement not only connects the OleDbDataAdapter variable to the data command it will use, it also indirectly connects the OleDbDataAdapter variable to the database connection, because the OleDbCommand variable is connected through its Connection property to the OleDbConnection variable.

Accordingly, the code now reads like this:

```
private void Form1_Load (Object sender, EventArgs e)
{
    OleDbConnection myConn = new OleDbConnection();
    DialogResult dr;
    dr = dlgOpen.ShowDialog();
    if (dr == DialogResult.OK)
    {
        string strFile = dlgOpen.FileName;
        myConn.ConnectionString = "Provider=" +
            "Microsoft.Jet.OLEDB.4.0;Data Source="
            + strFile + ";";
        myConn.Open();
        OleDbCommand myCMD = new OleDbCommand();
        myCMD.CommandText = "SELECT CustomerID, " +
            "ContactTitle, CompanyName, ContactName " +
            FROM Customers";
        myCMD.Connection = myConn;
        OleDbDataAdapter myAdapter = new OleDbDataAdapter();
        myAdapter.SelectCommand = myCMD;
    }
}
```

Creating a DataSet

The data used to fill the DataGridView cannot come directly from the hard drive where the database is stored. Instead, an intermediate step is required. The data from the hard drive first must be loaded into memory, or RAM. Then, the data in RAM is loaded into the DataGridView.

NOTE *This approach has advantages. For example, it frees the application from having to exactly replicate the physical data and instead work with subsets, supersets, calculated fields, and so forth.*

A DataSet is a representation of the data (in this case, from several fields of the Customers table) that is stored in RAM.

The DataSet class is part of the System.Data namespace, so you should add a using System.Data statement if you (or the IDE) did not do so already earlier in this chapter in the section "Importing Data Namespaces":

```
using System.Data;
using System.Data.OleDb;
```

You may also need to add a reference to the assembly that contains the namespace System.XML. You do so the same way you added a reference to the assembly that contains the namespace System.Data earlier in this chapter in the section "Importing Data Namespaces," using the Add Reference dialog box shown earlier in Figure 14-13.

You instantiate a DataSet variable via the following code, similar to how previously we instantiated the OleDbConnection, OleDbCommand, and OleDbDataAdapter variables:

```
DataSet ds = new DataSet();
```

The next steps are to clear and then fill the DataSet.

The DataSet object has a Clear method. This method, as its name suggests, clears the DataSet of any leftover contents. There would be no leftover contents here because the code is running on application startup, but often you will need to use the Clear method, so it is a good idea to get into the habit of using it.

```
ds.Clear();
```

The OleDbDataAdapter object has a Fill method. This method, as its name suggests, fills the DataSet with its contents, which, once the DataGridView is connected to the DataSet as discussed in the next section, are then displayed in the DataGridView that is bound to the DataSet. The first argument is the DataSet to be filled. The second argument is the name of the source table (here, Customers).

```
myAdapter.Fill(ds, "Customers");
```

Accordingly, the code now reads as follows:

```
private void Form1_Load (Object sender, EventArgs e)
{
    OleDbConnection myConn = new OleDbConnection();
    DialogResult dr;
    dr = dlgOpen.ShowDialog();
    if (dr == DialogResult.OK)
    {
        string strFile = dlgOpen.FileName;
        myConn.ConnectionString = "Provider=" +
            "Microsoft.Jet.OLEDB.4.0;Data Source="
            + strFile + ";";
        myConn.Open();
        OleDbCommand myCMD = new OleDbCommand();
        myCMD.CommandText = "SELECT CustomerID, " +
            "ContactTitle, CompanyName, ContactName " +
            "FROM Customers";
        myCMD.Connection = myConn;
```

```
        OleDbDataAdapter myAdapter = new OleDbDataAdapter();
        myAdapter.SelectCommand = myCMD;
        DataSet ds = new DataSet();
        ds.Clear();
        myAdapter.Fill(ds, "Customers");
    }
}
```

Connecting the DataGridView to the DataSet

The final step is to connect the DataGridView to the DataSet. This step involves two properties of the DataGridView object: DataSource and DataMember.

The DataSource property is the data source of the data that the DataGridView is displaying. That data source is represented by the DataSet variable ds:

```
dgvData.DataSource = ds;
```

The DataMember property is the name of the table (here, Customers) in the data source of the data that the DataGridView is displaying:

```
dgvData.DataMember = "Customers";
```

Accordingly, the completed code now reads like so:

```
private void Form1_Load (Object sender, EventArgs e)
{
    OleDbConnection myConn = new OleDbConnection();
    DialogResult dr;
    dr = dlgOpen.ShowDialog();
    if (dr == DialogResult.OK)
    {
        string strFile = dlgOpen.FileName;
        myConn.ConnectionString = "Provider=" +
            "Microsoft.Jet.OLEDB.4.0;Data Source="
            + strFile + ";";
        myConn.Open();
        OleDbCommand myCMD = new OleDbCommand();
        myCMD.CommandText = "SELECT CustomerID, " +
            "ContactTitle, CompanyName, ContactName " +
            "FROM Customers";
        myCMD.Connection = myConn;
        OleDbDataAdapter myAdapter = new OleDbDataAdapter();
        myAdapter.SelectCommand = myCMD;
        DataSet ds = new DataSet();
        ds.Clear();
```

```
      myAdapter.Fill(ds, "Customers");
      dgvData.DataSource = ds;
      dgvData.DataMember = "Customers";
   }
}
```

Run the project! The DataGridView control should fill with data as shown previously in Figure 14-11.

Conclusion

Text files, which we've used up until now to save data, have several limitations. One limitation is a text file's inability to quickly retrieve specific data. There's usually no alternative to searching the text file from beginning to end, which can take a long time if the text file contains a lot of data.

Another limitation is the inability to store relations between different data. For example, a store may have both a list of customers and a list of orders—the orders come from customers. With a text file, there's no easy way to link an order in one list with a customer in another list.

A database does not have these limitations. Specific data may be quickly retrieved through keys and indexes, and different data may be easily linked.

This chapter used the Northwind Traders database. First, you learned how to obtain and install this database. After creating a new Windows application, you then created a connection between Visual C# 2005 and the database. In doing so, you selected the database format, a provider suitable for that format, and the path to and the name of the database.

Next, you learned how to use Server Explorer, a tool provided by Visual Studio 2005 that enables you to view databases on your computer without having to open or create an application.

The code components used for database-access code are organized in the .NET library under the name ADO.NET. ADO was an acronym for ActiveX Data Objects, a Microsoft data-access technology that was the predecessor to ADO.NET.

As you learned in this chapter, accessing the Northwind Traders database involves the following steps:

1. Establish a connection to the database.

2. Define the commands you want to make to the database.

3. Define a data adapter that packages the database connection and commands.

4. Create a DataSet and then fill it using the data adapter.

5. Fill a control (in this chapter, a DataGridView) from the DataSet.

You created an application that implemented these steps and filled a DataGrid-View control with data from four fields of the Customers table of the Northwind Traders database.

The project you created in this chapter is a Windows application. In the next chapter, you will learn to create a similar project that is a web application.

Quiz

1. What is a data provider?

2. What does Server Explorer enable you to do?

3. What is a table?

4. What may each column in a table also be called?

5. What may each row in a table also be called?

6. What is ADO.NET?

7. What class represents a connection to a data source?

8. What class would you use to execute commands to a database?

9. What class would you use to package a database connection with a set of data commands?

10. What is a DataSet?

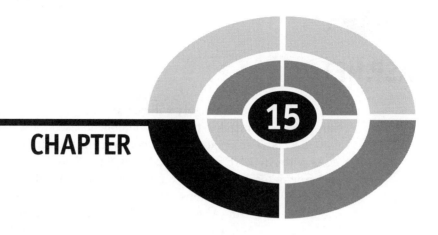

Web Applications

Throughout this book we have been writing Windows applications. Indeed, many of the applications with which you interact are Windows applications. For me, it is a rare day that I don't work with Microsoft Word and Outlook, for example.

However, I, and perhaps you as well, am interacting ever more frequently with web applications. One common type of web application is e-commerce, the *e* standing for electronic. For example, if you go to the website of Amazon or another online bookseller, you select a book (hint: this one) or another product, put the selected product in a virtual shopping cart, when finished go to a virtual check-out line, enter your credit card information (which better not be virtual), and make a purchase. You then can go to the website of the overnight delivery service and track the shipment as it wends its way across the country (or world) to you.

In this chapter, you will learn how to create a web application that displays information from a database, similar to the Windows application you created in Chapter 14.

ASP.NET

ASP.NET is a term you likely will hear of soon after you start creating web applications. ASP.NET refers to the code components used for web applications, similar to how ADO.NET refers to the code components used for database access.

As with ADO.NET, you already know the ".NET" portion of ASP.NET. ASP is an acronym for Active Service Pages, a Microsoft web application technology that preceded ASP.NET. For those of you who are familiar with ASP, ASP.NET is much easier to work with. ASP intermixed HTML with script code. By contrast, ASP.NET enables you to develop web applications in almost the same manner as Windows applications.

ASP.NET started with Visual Studio 2005's predecessor, Visual Studio.NET. The version number of ASP.NET then was 1.x—first 1.0, then 1.1. With Visual Studio 2005, the version number is 2.x, starting with 2.0.

There are other, competing technologies for the creation of web applications. ASP.NET is Microsoft's, and consequently the one heavily supported in Visual Studio 2005.

Internet Information Services

Visual Studio 2005 requires one of the following operating systems: Windows 2000 Professional, Windows XP Home or Professional, Windows 2000 Server, or Windows 2003 Server. On all but Windows XP Home Edition, Internet Information Services (IIS) is an optional component that may be installed with the operating system. IIS may not actually be installed on your computer because it may not be part of the default installation of your operating system. However, if IIS is not installed, you can add it as described in this section.

NOTE *You cannot install IIS on Windows XP Home Edition unless you make some Registry changes that are not supported by Microsoft and therefore probably are not a good idea to try.*

Unlike ASP.NET 1.x and Visual Studio.NET, ASP.NET 2.x and Visual Studio 2005 do not require you to install IIS to create web applications that run locally (that is, on your computer). Nevertheless, unless you have Windows XP Home Edition, installing IIS does give you more options, such as making your web pages accessible from more than your local computer, and costs you nothing.

Determining If IIS Is Already Installed

To determine if IIS is already installed on your computer, open Add/Remove programs from the Control Panel. From the left menu bar, choose Add/Remove Windows Components. This will display the Windows Components Wizard shown in Figure 15-1.

In Figure 15-1, Internet Information Services (IIS) is checked, but with a dark background. This indicates some but not all of the components of IIS are installed. If IIS is checked but with a white background, as is Internet Explorer in Figure 15-1, then all of the components of IIS are installed. If IIS is unchecked, as is the Indexing Service in Figure 15-1, then IIS is not installed.

If IIS is checked, but with a dark background as in Figure 15-1, then you need to check which of its components are installed. To do so, in the Windows Components Wizard, highlight Internet Information Services (IIS) and click the Details button. This will display, as shown in Figure 15-2, a dialog box showing the individual components of Internet Information Services (IIS).

In Figure 15-2, almost all of the check boxes are checked because those components happen to be installed on my computer. This may not be the case on your computer, depending on which components of IIS you previously may have installed.

You don't need the FTP (File Transfer Protocol) and SMTP (Simple Mail Transfer Protocol) services, but I recommend you install the other components.

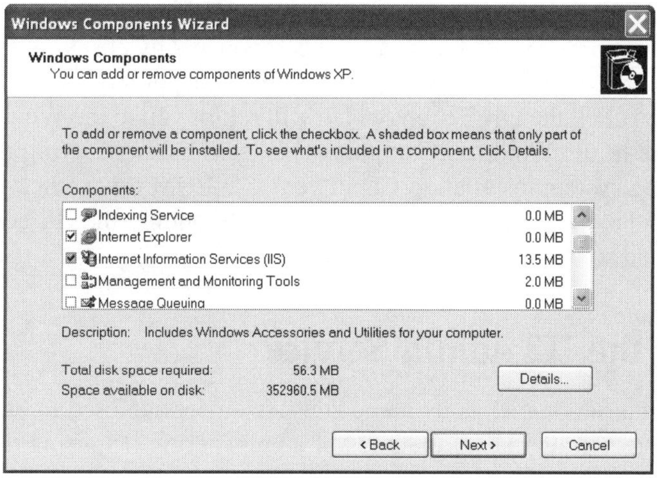

Figure 15-1   Windows Components Wizard.

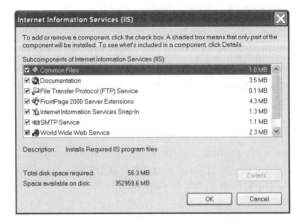

Figure 15-2   IIS components.

Installing IIS

If you do need to install IIS or components of it, first locate the installation CD of your operating system, because you may need it. If IIS is unchecked in the Windows Component Wizard (refer to Figure 15-1), first check it and then click the Next Button. If IIS is checked in the Windows Component Wizard but the check box has a dark background, just click the Next button.

Clicking the Next button displays the Internet Information Services (IIS) dialog box shown in Figure 15-2. Choose all the components by checking the boxes that are not already checked, again with the possible exception of the FTP and SMTP services. Then click the OK button, which will return you to the Windows Components Wizard. In the Windows Components Wizard, after verifying that you have your operating system installation CD in your CD-ROM drive, click the Next button and continue to proceed until you are finished adding the IIS components. If prompted to do so, restart your computer.

Starting the IIS Admin Service

The IIS Admin Service is, as its name suggests, a service used to administer IIS. Although there are alternative methods of administering IIS, using the IIS Admin Service may be the easiest.

Open the Administrative Tools folder in Control Panel. This folder is shown in Figure 15-3.

Next, choose the Services shortcut to open the Services folder. Click the Extended tab and highlight IIS Admin. As Figure 15-4 shows, to the left is

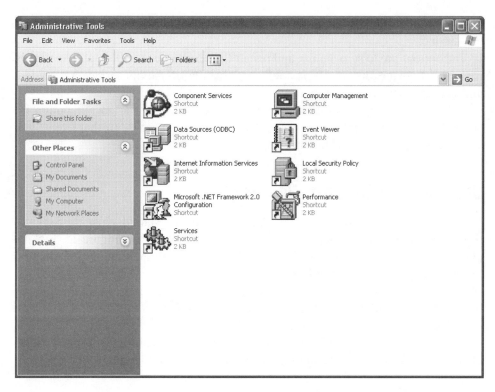

Figure 15-3   Administrative Tools folder in Control Panel.

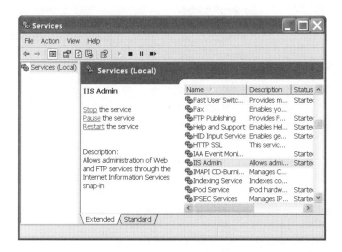

Figure 15-4   Services folder with the IIS Admin Service selected.

a description of the IIS Admin service as well as options to stop, pause, and restart the service.

The options are to stop, pause, and restart the service because the service already is started. In that event, you have confirmed that the IIS Admin service has started, and you are done with this step.

However, if the IIS Admin service has stopped or never started, the option instead would be to start the service, as shown in Figure 15-5. In that event, you would choose Start to start the service.

Starting the Default Website

Once you have confirmed that the IIS Admin service has started, close the Services folder and go back to the Administrative Tools folder shown in Figure 15-3. Next, choose the Internet Information Services shortcut to open the Internet Information Services dialog box shown in Figure 15-6.

Click the + sign next to the local computer name (mine is JAKXP; yours is likely different) and the click the + sign next to the Web Sites folder below it. Figure 15-7 shows a subfolder named Default Web Site.

If Default Web Site is followed by a parenthetical indicating it is stopped, right-click Default Web Site and choose Start from the shortcut menu.

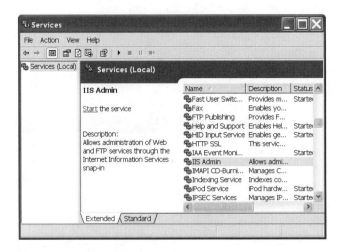

Figure 15-5   Option to start the IIS Admin Service.

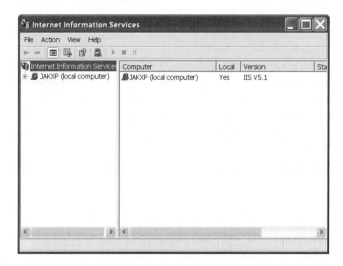

Figure 15-6   Internet Information Services dialog box.

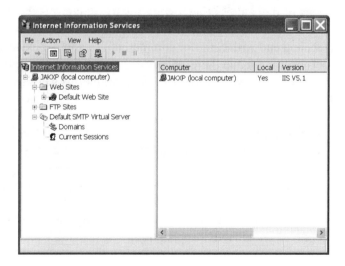

Figure 15-7   Default Web Site in the Internet Information Services dialog box.

URL

Your home or apartment has an address by which it may be located. A web page similarly has an address by which you may locate it through your web browser.

The address of your home or apartment usually is in the form of a number followed by a street name, such as 1313 Mockingbird Lane. The address of a web page, referred to as a URL, an acronym for Uniform Resource Locator, similarly has a certain form.

The following explanation will use as an example the URL for Microsoft's home page, http://www.microsoft.com/default.aspx.

The first part of the address (here, http) indicates what protocol to use. HTTP is an acronym for Hypertext Transfer Protocol. HTTP defines how messages are formatted and transmitted, and what actions web servers and browsers should take in response to various commands. For example, when you enter a URL in your browser, this actually sends an HTTP command to the web server directing it to fetch and transmit the requested web page.

There are protocols other than HTTP. One is similarly named HTTPS, a secure form of HTTP often used for credit-card transactions on the Internet. Another is FTP, the File Transfer Protocol, used for transferring files.

The second part of the address (here, www.microsoft.com) is the domain name where the resource is located. Domain names commonly start with www, short for World Wide Web, and end with com (for commercial) or another extension, such as net or org. In between is a name (here, Microsoft) that often corresponds to the organization or individual who owns the website. For example, my website is http://www.genghiskhent.com, based on my students' fond (?) nickname for me, Genghis Khent.

The third part of the address is the specific web page being accessed (here, default.aspx). Web pages are named in a similar fashion to other files, a descriptive name followed by a dot and an extension.

In Windows applications, the extension indicates the application used to open the file, such as .doc for Microsoft Word, .xls for Microsoft Excel, and so forth. Web pages may have extensions such as .htm or .html. The .aspx extension indicates that the web page is part of an ASP.NET application.

Your Computer as the Web Server

A web server is a computer that delivers (serves up) web pages. For example, if you visit Microsoft's home page, http://www.microsoft.com/default.aspx, by entering that address in your web browser (such as Internet Explorer, Netscape, or Mozilla), a computer somewhere on the Internet fetches a page on the Microsoft website and sends its content to your browser, where that content then is displayed in your computer's web browser.

In this chapter, however, your computer will act as the web server for the web applications you will be creating.

Type the URL **http://localhost/** in your web browser (this won't work if you have Windows XP Home, as already mentioned). Figure 15-8 shows the web page that then displays on the Windows XP operating system.

You may legitimately wonder, what is localhost? You have heard of microsoft.com and other .com and .net URLs, but localhost may be a new one for you. The answer is, localhost is your computer, which now is acting as a web server.

Virtual and Physical Paths

When you type http://www.microsoft.com in your web browser, you are accessing a page stored on the hard drive of a computer Microsoft is using as a web server.

Similarly, when you typed http://localhost and the web page shown in Figure 15-8 was displayed, that web page also was stored on your computer's hard drive.

By default, http://localhost maps to the C:\Inetpub\Wwwroot folder on your hard drive. You can confirm this by right-clicking Default Web Site (refer to Figure 15-7) and choosing Properties from the shortcut menu to display the Default Web Site

Figure 15-8   Default web page.

Figure 15-9   Default Web Site Properties dialog box.

Properties dialog box, which is shown in Figure 15-9 with the Home Directory tab chosen. The local path is c:\inetpub\wwwroot.

The address bar in Figure 15-8 shows that the URL of the web page is http:// localhost/localstart.asp. Therefore, the URL http://localhost/localstart.asp maps to the file C:\Inetpub\Wwwroot\localstart.asp on your hard drive.

The web URL http://localhost/localstart.asp is known as the *virtual* path to the web page. The file path C:\Inetpub\Wwwroot\localstart.asp is known as the *physical* path to the web page. However, they both point to the same place.

Creating a Web Application

Creating a web application is different from creating a Windows application. You use the File | New | Website menu command instead of the File | New | Project menu command.

The File | New | Website menu command displays the New Web Site dialog box shown in Figure 15-10.

The top pane shows available templates. Choose ASP.NET Web Site. This is the proper choice for creating a website with ASP.NET support, which is what we want to do here.

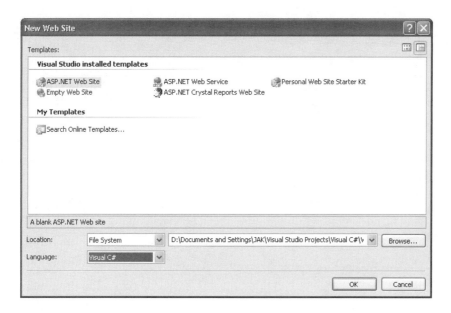

Figure 15-10   New Web Site dialog box.

In the Location drop-down box, choose File System. The other choices, FTP and HTTP, both protocols discussed earlier in this chapter, are for creating ASP.NET websites on other computers. In this chapter, you will be creating the website on your computer.

In the Language drop-down box, choose Visual C#. The other choices, Visual Basic and Visual J#, are other languages in Visual Studio 2005 you may use to create an ASP.NET application.

Click the Browse button to select where on your hard drive you wish to create the files for the ASP.NET web application. I chose a Visual C# folder I previously had created in the Visual Studio Projects folder under My Documents. I typed after the path to the Visual C# folder (for example, D:\Documents and Settings\JAK\My Documents\Visual Studio Projects\Visual C#\) **WebSite** for the name of the project. Of course, you could choose a different location or name for your project.

When finished, click the OK button, and Visual Studio 2005 will create a bare-bones but working ASP.NET application.

ASP.NET Development Server

When Visual Studio 2005 is finished creating the ASP.NET application, run the application by choosing Start or Start Without Debugging from the Debug menu. The result will be a blank web page, as shown in Figure 15-11.

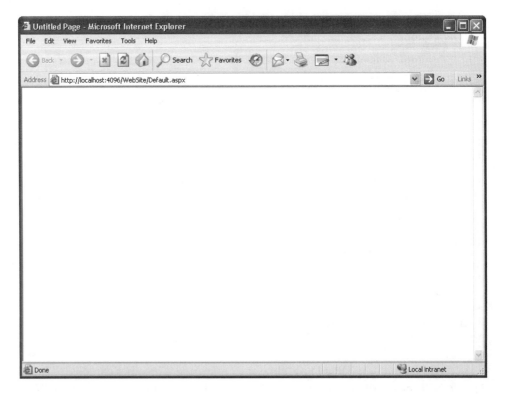

Figure 15-11 ASP.NET web page.

The URL shown in the address bar of the web browser in Figure 15-11 is http://localhost:4096/Website/Default.aspx. The http://localhost part of the URL is explained in the previous section "Your Computer as the Web Server." Website is the name of the web application, and default.aspx the name of the web page (or web form) that Visual Studio 2005 creates by default, much like a Windows form is created by default when you create a Windows application.

What is new, and its meaning may not be immediately clear, is the ":4096" following localhost. The colon (:) means that the number following is a port number (here, 4096).

NOTE *The particular port number assigned by Visual Studio 2005 may be different than 4096.*

A port is a logical (as opposed to physical) connection in a computer. For example, when you access a web page with your web browser, your request, and the web server's response, goes through port 80.

As mentioned in the previous section "Internet Information Services," ASP.NET 2.x and Visual Studio 2005 do not require you to install IIS to create web applications that run locally (that is, on your computer as opposed to a computer elsewhere on the Internet). Instead, local web applications are handled through the ASP.NET Development Server, which uses various port numbers (here, 4096).

You may have an icon for the ASP.NET Development Server in your system tray. If so, double-click it. The ASP.NET Development Server dialog box will appear, as shown in Figure 15-12.

The ASP.NET Development Server dialog box shows the following information (though not in this order from top to down):

- **Physical Path**   The location you chose in the New Web Site dialog box shown in Figure 15-10

- **Port**   The port chosen by the ASP.NET Development Server for access to local web applications (here, 4096)

- **Root URL**   The root or base for web applications, http://localhost:4096, followed by the name of this web application (here, WebSite)

- **Virtual Path**   The path from the root URL of http:/localhost:4096 to your web application

That is about all we can do for now with this blank web application. Close the ASP.NET Development Server dialog box shown in Figure 15-12 and the blank web page shown in Figure 15-11.

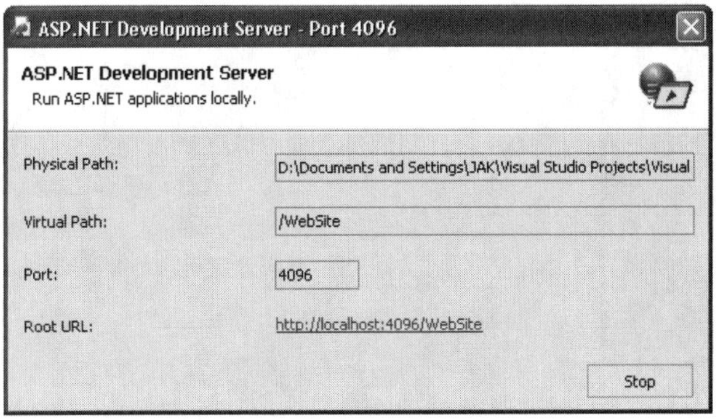

Figure 15-12   ASP.NET Development Server dialog box.

ASP.NET Application IDE

Figure 15-13 shows the Integrated Development Environment (IDE) for the ASP. NET application we created by clicking OK in the New Web Site dialog box shown in Figure 15-10.

As with Windows applications, the form in web applications, often called a *web form*, also has both a design view (shown in Figure 15-13), complete with a Toolbox and Solution Explorer, and a code view, shown in Figure 15-14.

This similarity between the IDEs for Windows applications and web applications makes it easier for you to learn to develop web applications.

Although the respective IDEs of Windows and web applications are similar, they are not the same. For example, the web form has, in addition to a design and code view, an HTML view, shown in Figure 15-15 and accessed by clicking the Source tab, in which you can view the HTML code of the form, which after all is a web page.

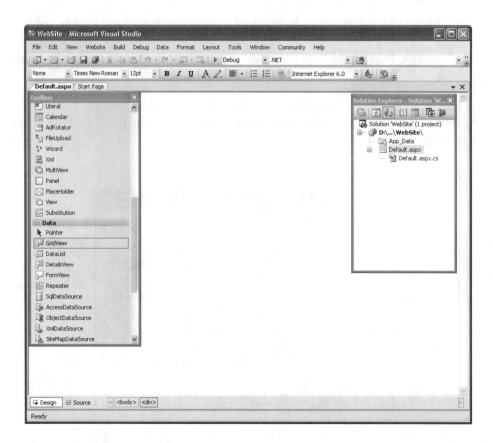

Figure 15-13 ASP.NET application IDE.

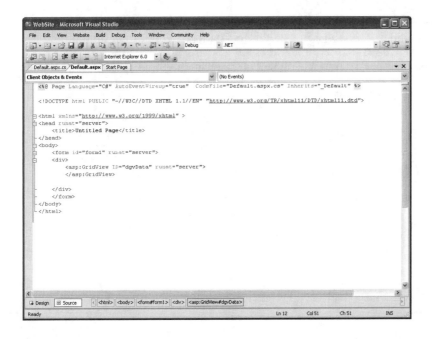

Figure 15-14   Code view.

Figure 15-15   HTML view of the form.

Creating a Database Web Application

We will now create a web application that parallels the Windows application we created in Chapter 14. That Windows application displayed in a DataGridView control the contents of four fields of the Customers table of the Northwind Traders database. The web application you will create similarly will display the contents of the same four fields of the Customers table of the Northwind Traders database, but in a web browser, as shown in Figure 15-16.

Adding a GridView Control

The Windows application we created in Chapter 14 has a DataGridView control through which we viewed the database information. For whatever reason, the web application equivalent of the Windows DataGridView control does not have the same name, but a slightly different one, GridView.

Figure 15-16 Web application in action.

Start with the web application you created in the previous section. View the web form in designer view and click the Design tab. Then look in the Toolbox for a GridView in the Data group, as shown in Figure 15-17.

Figure 15-17   GridView in Toolbox.

If you don't see the GridView in the Toolbox, you need to add it. Right-click the Toolbox and choose "Choose Items..." from the shortcut menu. This will display the Choose Toolbox Items dialog box shown in Figure 15-18.

Select the check box for the GridView for which the namespace is System.Web. UI.Controls. Next, click the OK button to close the Choose Toolbox Items dialog box. GridView should now be added to the Toolbox, as in Figure 15-17.

Once the GridView is in the Toolbox, you add it to the web form by dragging and dropping or double-clicking, just as you would add a control to a Windows form.

When you add the GridView control, a GridView Tasks pane displays, as shown in Figure 15-19. You may accept the default values in this pane. However, using the Properties window, rename the GridView control (using its ID property) dgvData to keep its name consistent with the DataGridView control in the Windows application, because we are attempting to port the code from the Windows application to this web application.

Locating the Database on the Web Server

The GridView is the only control we will be adding to the web form. There is no web application equivalent of the OpenFileDialog, which we used in the Windows application in Chapter 14.

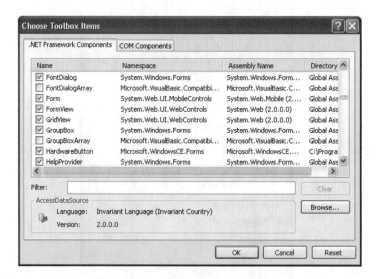

Figure 15-18   Choose Toolbox Items dialog box.

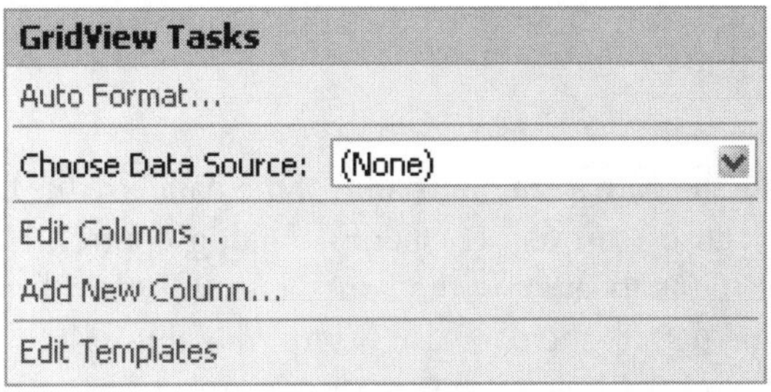

Figure 15-19 GridView Tasks pane.

Additionally, we would not want the user to select the location of the database. In a Windows application, the database often may be on the user's computer. Therefore, it is logical to have the user locate and select the database file using the OpenFileDialog control. By contrast, in a web application, the database will not be on the user's computer, but rather a web server elsewhere on the Internet. For security reasons, the user should not be permitted to browse the files on the web server as the user would for the files on their own computer. Instead, the web application should specify where the database file is.

Often the database is located in a subfolder of the web application to ease the task of locating it through code, as next will be discussed. By default, the ASP.NET application created by Visual Studio 2005 has a subfolder named App_Data, likely short for "application data." Copy the nwind.mdb (or Northwind.mdb) file into the App_Data folder from wherever you saved nwind.mdb in when creating the Windows database application in Chapter 14.

Now that you have located the database on your hard drive within the web application files, the remaining task is how to locate the database in code.

As discussed in Chapter 14, the ConnectionString property of the OleDbConnection object requires the path to and the name of the database file. In the Windows database application in Chapter 14, you obtained the path to and the name of the database file (represented by the String variable strFile) by using the FileName property of the OpenFileDialog control:

```
OleDbConnection myConn = new OleDbConnection();
DialogResult dr;
dr = dlgOpen.ShowDialog();
if (dr == DialogResult.OK)
{
    string strFile = dlgOpen.FileName;
    myConn.ConnectionString = "Provider=" +
```

```
    "Microsoft.Jet.OLEDB.4.0;Data Source="
    + strFile + ";";
}
```

You cannot obtain the path to and the name of the database file the same way in this web application because there is no OpenFileDialog control. However, you know where the database file is located, in the app_data subfolder of the web application. Therefore, the virtual path to the database is http://localhost:4096/Website/app_data/nwind.mdb.

However, the ConnectionString property requires the physical path, not the virtual path. In this case, you know the physical path because the database file is on your computer. However, when you are working with remote web servers, you may not always know the physical path, or even if you did, the administrator of that web server may change it. Therefore, you need to be able to translate the virtual path into a physical path.

The HttpServerUtility class, which also can be referred to as the Server class, has a MapPath method that returns the physical file path that corresponds to (is mapped to) the specified virtual path on the web server. The following statement assigns to the String variable strFile the physical path to the database file:

```
string strFile = Server.MapPath("app_data\\nwind.mdb");
```

NOTE *The double backslash (\\) is necessary because the backslash is an escape character in the C# language. You may need to change the reference to nwind.mdb to Northwind.mdb if the latter is the file name on your computer.*

The way this works is that the MapPath method starts by mapping the physical path that corresponds with the virtual path to the web application, http://localhost:4096/Website. The argument then is appended to that physical path. The method then returns the physical path that corresponds the full virtual path to the database file, http://localhost:4096/Website/app_data/nwind.mdb.

Accordingly, the preceding code from Chapter 14 would be replaced with the following:

```
OleDbConnection myConn = new OleDbConnection();
string strFile = Server.MapPath("app_data\\nwind.mdb");
myConn.ConnectionString = "Provider=" +
    "Microsoft.Jet.OLEDB.4.0;Data Source="
    + strFile + ";";
```

Adding Code

The next step is to write code. To do so, go to the code view of the web form.

First, we will import the System.Data namespace (if not already imported by the IDE) and the System.Data.OleDb namespace for the same reason as we did in Chapter 14:

```
using System.Data;
using System.Data.OleDb;
```

Second, as in Chapter 14, all the code will go in the Load event, this time of the web page. This event procedure belongs to the Page object, which represents the web form.

To create an event procedure, similar to with Windows forms, you choose (Page Events) from the left drop-down box and then the event (here, Load) from the right drop-down box. This creates an event procedure stub. Then write code so your Page_Load event procedure reads as follows:

```
private void Page_Load (Object sender, EventArgs e)
{
    OleDbConnection myConn = new OleDbConnection();
    string strFile = Server.MapPath("app_data\\nwind.mdb");
    myConn.ConnectionString = "Provider=" +
        "Microsoft.Jet.OLEDB.4.0;Data Source="
        + strFile + ";";
    myConn.Open();
    OleDbCommand myCMD = new OleDbCommand();
    myCMD.CommandText = "SELECT CustomerID, " +
            "ContactTitle, CompanyName, ContactName " +
            FROM Customers";
    myCMD.Connection = myConn;
    OleDbDataAdapter myAdapter = new OleDbDataAdapter();
    myAdapter.SelectCommand = myCMD;
    DataSet ds = new DataSet();
    ds.Clear();
    myAdapter.Fill(ds, "Customers");
    dgvData.DataSource = ds;
    dgvData.DataMember = "Customers";
    dgvData.DataBind();
}
```

This code differs in only two substantive respects from the corresponding code in the Form Load event procedure in Chapter 14. First is the use of the MapPath method as discussed in the previous section "Locating the Database on the Web Server." The second is the last statement, the call to the DataBind method of the GridView. This method is commonly used in web applications to bind data from a source (here, a DataSet) to a control (here, a GridView).

WARNING *If you don't call the DataBind method, the web application will run without error, but the GridView will be blank, because it was not bound to the data source.*

Run your web application from the Debug menu, again just as you would a Windows application. The web page should display, with the GridView filled with information, as shown earlier in Figure 15-16. When you are done, close the web page using its close button to close the application.

Conclusion

Of course, there is much more than this to web applications. Entire courses and books are devoted to web applications. However, this chapter should give you an overview of how to create a working web application that displays information from a database.

This is the last chapter in this book. However, it should not be the last chapter in your learning Visual C# 2005. Rather, this book hopefully has given you a good foundation for learning more.

Quiz

1. What is ASP.NET?
2. What is a URL?
3. What is HTTP?
4. What does the .aspx extension indicate?
5. What is the difference between a virtual path and a physical path to a web page?
6. What project template could you use to create a web application?
7. What is the web control that corresponds to the DataGridView control used in Windows applications?
8. What is the method of the HttpServerUtility class that returns the physical file path that corresponds to (is mapped to) the specified virtual path on a web server?
9. What is the name of the class that is the web application equivalent of the Form class in a Windows application?
10. What is the method of the GridView that needs to be called in a web application so the GridView will not be blank?

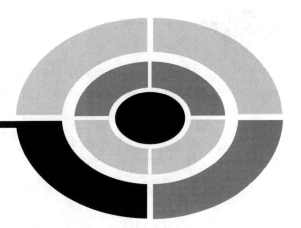

Final Exam

Questions

1. What is an IDE?
2. What is a computer program?
3. What is a programming language?
4. What is machine language?
5. What does "higher level" mean in the context of a programming language?
6. What does "lower level" mean in the context of a programming language?
7. What is the purpose of a compiler?
8. What is a class in a programming language?
9. What is an object of a class?
10. What are namespaces used for?

11. What is a property of a class?

12. What are characteristics of a Windows application?

13. What is an event of a class?

14. What is an event procedure?

15. What is the purpose of the assignment operator?

16. What is the purpose of the Toolbox?

17. How do you add a control from the Toolbox onto your form?

18. What is the purpose of the Name property of a control?

19. What is a naming convention?

20. What are purposes of the text displayed by a Label control?

21. What is a parameter of an event procedure?

22. What does a data type signify?

23. What is the purpose of a variable?

24. Does C# require you to declare a variable before you refer to it in code?

25. What is a local variable?

26. Do you have to assign a value to a variable when you declare it?

27. What is a difference between a constant and a variable?

28. Do you have to assign a value to a constant when you declare it?

29. What is the significance of operator precedence?

30. Which operator provides only the remainder resulting from division?

31. Which operator has precedence, an arithmetic operator or the assignment operator?

32. What is the purpose of the Parse method of the Int32 class?

33. What is the purpose of the ToString method of the Int32 class?

34. What is a method of a class?

35. What does the WriteLine method of the Debug class do?

36. What is the data type of the result of a comparison performed by a comparison operator?

37. Which operators have precedence, comparison or arithmetic?

38. What is the purpose of a logical operator?

39. Which logical operator operates on only one operand rather than two?

40. Which operators have precedence, comparison or logical?

41. What does modal mean?

42. What is a conditional statement?

43. Which namespace should you import to use the Debug class?

44. What is an exception?

45. What does the TryParse method of the Int32 class do?

46. Which two controls are commonly used with the if control structure?

47. What is the primary difference between the if . . . else if statement and the switch control structure?

48. What is a loop?

49. What is a difference between the do . . . while statement and the for and while statements?

50. What is a difference between the foreach statement and the for loop?

51. What is an array?

52. What is the difference between declaring an array variable and a scalar variable?

53. What is the lowest index of an array?

54. What is the relationship between the number of elements in an array and the highest index in that array?

55. What is a method?

56. What is the significance of the void return type?

57. What does the private access specifier do when applied to a method?

58. What does calling a method do?

59. What is the significance of an array being a reference type?

60. What are some reasons for writing your own methods?

61. Is a message box modal or modeless?

62. What value is returned by the Show method of the MessageBox class?

63. Do buttons in a message box automatically have a DialogResult value?

64. What is the data type of a variable you may use to store the return value of the Show method of the MessageBox class?

65. What method do you use to display a modal form?

66. What is the return value from showing a dialog form?

67. Do buttons in a dialog form you create automatically have a DialogResult value?

68. What method do you use to display a form as modeless rather than modal?

69. What class represents a main menu?

70. Is the Click event raised for all menu items?

71. How do you gray out a menu item so it is not available when it should not be?

72. What does the Items collection of the MenuStrip component contain?

73. What class represents the shortcut or context menu?

74. What does the Items collection of the ContextMenuStrip component contain?

75. What are different alternatives of having a context menu item's functionality handled by the corresponding main menu item?

76. What class represents a toolbar?

77. What class represents each item on a toolbar?

78. What does the Items collection of the ToolStrip component contain?

79. What are advantages of a toolbar over a corresponding menu?

80. What are different alternatives of having a toolbar item's functionality handled by the corresponding main or context menu item?

81. What method do you use to show an Open dialog box?

82. What is the return value of showing an Open dialog box?

83. What is the property of the OpenFileDialog class whose value is the file chosen by the user in an Open dialog box?

84. What method of the SaveFileDialog class do you use to show a Save dialog box?

85. What is the return value of showing a Save dialog box?

86. What is the property of the SaveFileDialog class whose value is the name of the file to be saved?

87. What class may you use to read from a text file?

88. What class may you use to write to a text file?

89. What is a data provider?

90. What is a table?

91. What may each column in a table also be called?

92. What may each row in a table also be called?

93. What is ADO.NET?

94. What is a DataSet?

95. What is ASP.NET?

96. What is a URL?

97. What is HTTP?

98. What is the difference between a virtual and a physical path to a web page?

99. What is the method of the HttpServerUtility class that returns the physical file path that corresponds to (is mapped to) the specified virtual path on a web server?

100. What is the name of the class that is the web application equivalent of the Form class in a Windows application?

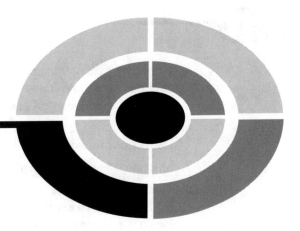

Answers

Chapter 1

1. Visual Studio 2005 includes, in addition to Visual C#, support for other programming languages such as C++ and Visual Basic.

2. You need either the Windows 2003, XP, or 2000 operating system to install and run Visual C# 2005.

3. You should use the Windows Application project template to start creating a Windows application.

4. IDE is an acronym for Integrated Development Environment. The term "development environment" refers to Visual C# 2005's role as an application to assist you in developing applications. The term "integrated" means the tools to design your application and write, test, and run your code are all together in one application.

5. A computer cannot do anything without step-by-step instructions from us telling it what to do. These instructions, written by a computer programmer, are called a computer program.

6. A programming language is used by computer programmers to write instructions for computers.

7. Machine language is a programming language that is understood by computers.

8. The term "higher level" means that a programming language such as Visual C# 2005 is far closer to the structure and syntax of human language than to the ones and zeroes understood by a computer.

9. The term "lower level" means that a programming language such as machine language is far closer to the ones and zeroes understood by a computer than it is to the structure and syntax of human language.

10. In general, a compiler translates the code you write into corresponding machine language instructions. The compiler in Visual C# 2005 translates the code into an intermediate language that then is translated into machine language.

Chapter 2

1. Designer view is the view of your form you would choose when you want to design your form, such as resizing the form or adding controls to it.

2. Code view is the view of your form you would choose when you want to view or write the code of your application.

3. Programming languages, including Visual C#, use classes to represent a person, place, thing, or concept.

4. An object of a class is a single instance of a class, just like each of us could be said to be an object or instance of a Person class.

5. Namespaces are used to organize code in a logical manner.

6. A property is a characteristic or attribute of a class.

7. A Windows application has a graphical user interface (GUI) and is event-driven.

8. An event is something that happens to an object of a class, such as a result of user interaction.

9. An event procedure contains code that executes when a specific event happens to a specific object.

10. The purpose of the assignment operator is to assign the expression to its right to the variable or property to its left.

Chapter 3

1. TextBox, Label, ListBox, and Button are all controls.

2. The purpose of the Toolbox is to display controls that you can add to your form.

3. You may add a control from the Toolbox onto your form either by double-clicking the control in the Toolbox or by dragging the control from the Toolbox and then dropping it onto the form,

4. The Name property of a control is used to identify that control in code.

5. A naming convention is a consistent method of naming, such as when naming controls.

6. The value of the Text property of a Label control determines the text that will be displayed by the label.

7. The text displayed by a label may identify another, adjacent control, or it may display data.

8. A single statement in C# may take up two or more lines in the code editor.

9. A parameter represents information that is available to an event procedure.

10. A delegate is used to specify which procedure handles an event that happens to a particular object.

Chapter 4

1. A data type signifies whether the data is numeric, text, yes/no, and so forth.

2. A floating-point number is a number that may have a value to the right of the decimal point.

3. No, you cannot change the data type of a built-in property of a form.

4. The purpose of a variable is to store data of your choosing.

5. Yes, C# requires you to declare a variable before you refer to it in code.

6. A local variable is a variable declared inside of a procedure.

7. A class member–level variable is declared as a member of a class.

8. No, you do not have to assign a value to a variable when you declare it.

9. A constant's value cannot change during the life of the program, whereas a variable's value may change during the life of the program.

10. Yes, you have to assign a value to a constant when you declare it.

Chapter 5

1. The addition operator works with string as well as numeric variables.

2. Operator precedence determines, when there are two or more arithmetic operators, which arithmetic operation is done first.

3. You can override default operator precedence with parentheses.

4. The increment (++) operator increases the value of a numeric variable by one.

5. Integer division is when both operands of division are a whole number data type when only the quotient is reported and any remainder is dropped.

6. The % (modulus) operator provides only the remainder resulting from division.

7. All arithmetic operators have precedence over the assignment operator.

8. The Parse method of the Int32 class converts the string representation of an integer into actual integer values.

9. The ToString method of the Int32 class converts an integer into its string representation.

10. A method is something an object of a class does.

Chapter 6

1. The WriteLine method of the Debug class outputs a line to the Output window.

2. The data type of the result of a comparison performed by a comparison operator is Boolean, either true or false.

3. No, the == operator, not the = operator, is used for equality comparison.

4. Yes, you can use the equality and inequality (== and !=) comparison operators with strings as well as with numeric data types.

5. The ANSI or ASCII value of a character is a corresponding integer value.

6. With the & operator, if the first expression is false, the second expression still is evaluated. By contrast, with the && operator, if the first expression is false, the second expression is not evaluated.

7. Arithmetic operators have higher precedence than comparison operators.

8. A logical operator is used to combine multiple comparisons.

9. ! is the logical operator that operates on only one operand rather than two.

10. Comparison operators have higher precedence than logical operators.

Chapter 7

1. Modal means a form must be closed before the application user can return to any other form in the application.

2. Modeless.

3. The statement is conditional if the statement executes only if the value of the relational expression following the if or else if keyword is true.

4. You should import the System.Diagnostics namespace to use the Debug class.

5. The three varieties of an if control structure are if, if . . . else, and if . . . else if.

6. An exception is a problem that occurs while the program is executing that must be dealt with before the program can proceed.

7. The TryParse method of the Int32 class converts the string representation of an integer into an actual integer value, but also returns a Boolean value (true or false) indicating whether the conversion was successful.

8. The CheckBox and RadioButton controls.

9. The primary difference in the if . . . else if statement and the switch control structure is that the if and else if clauses both may evaluate completely different expressions, whereas a switch control structure may evaluate only one expression, which then must be used for every comparison.

10. The case default part of a switch control structure performs the same purpose as an else clause in an if control structure.

Chapter 8

1. A loop is a structure that repeats the execution of code until a condition becomes false.

2. A difference between a while statement and a for statement is that a for statement generally is intended to run a fixed number of times, whereas a while statement may run an indefinite number of times.

3. A difference between the do . . . while statement and the for and while statements is that a do . . . while statement tests a condition at the bottom of the statement, whereas the for and while statements test a condition at the top of the statement.

4. The foreach statement executes the statement block for each element in a collection, instead of a specified number of times, as is the case with the for statement.

5. Examples of nesting are a loop within a loop, and an if control structure within a loop.

6. An array permits you to use a single variable to store multiple values.

7. The difference between declaring an array variable and declaring a scalar variable is that with an array variable, unlike with a scalar variable, the array name is followed by a pair of square brackets, and within the square brackets you indicate the highest index of the array.

8. The lowest index of an array is zero.

9. The number of elements in an array is one greater than the highest index in that array because the index of the first element is zero.

10. Yes, if you declare an array without assigning a value to its elements, its elements have a default value, the value depending on the data type of the array.

Chapter 9

1. A method is a block of one or more code statements that execute when called upon to do so.

2. The void return type indicates that a method does not return a value.

3. The usual return type of an event procedure is void.

4. The private access specifier limits access to the class in which the procedure was declared.

5. There optionally may be a return statement in a function whose return type is void.

6. Calling a method causes it to execute.

7. When a parameter is passed by value, any change to the value of the parameter in the called method does not affect the value of the corresponding argument in the calling method. By contrast, when a parameter is passed by reference, any change to the value of the parameter in the called procedure does affect the value of the corresponding argument in the calling procedure.

8. The ref parameter attribute performs a similar but not exactly the same purpose as the out keyword.

9. The significance of an array being a reference type is when an array name is an argument, the value of that argument is the array's address in memory.

10. Writing your own methods enables you to organize your code in smaller, easier-to-read code blocks. Additionally, if you are performing essentially the same task from several places in the program, you can avoid duplication of code by putting the code that performs that task in one method, as opposed to repeating that code in each place in the program that may call for the performance of that task. Further, if you later have to fix a bug in how you perform that task, or simply find a better way to perform the task, you only have to change the code in one place rather than many.

Chapter 10

1. A message box is modal.

2. The Show method of the MessageBox class returns a member of the DialogResult enumeration corresponding to the button the user clicked.

3. No, you may call the Show method of the MessageBox class with a different number of arguments because that method is overloaded.

4. Yes, buttons in a message box automatically have a DialogResult value.

5. You would use the DialogResult data type for a variable you use to store the return value of the Show method of the MessageBox class.

6. An enumeration is a list of related choices.

7. You use the ShowDialog method of the Form object to display a modal form.

8. The return value of showing a dialog form is the DialogResult property of that form.

9. No, buttons in a dialog form you create do not automatically have a DialogResult value; you have to assign a value to the DialogResult property of each button.

10. You use the Show method of the Form object to display a modal form.

Chapter 11

1. A main menu is represented by the MenuStrip class.

2. Each item on a main menu is represented by the ToolStripMenuItem class.

3. An access key is the keyboard combination of the ALT key plus a letter in the menu item that is underlined.

4. No, the Click event is raised only for menu items that do not have subsidiary menu items, because when a menu item with subsidiary items is clicked, the behavior is to display the subsidiary menu items.

5. You gray out a menu item so it is not available when it should not be by setting its Enabled property to False.

6. The Items collection of the MenuStrip component contains a collection of the ToolStripMenuItems belonging to the MenuStrip.

7. The shortcut or context menu is represented by the ContextMenuStrip class.

8. Each item on a context menu is represented by the ToolStripMenuItem class.

9. The Items collection of the ContextMenuStrip component contains the ToolStripMenuItems belonging to the ContextMenuStrip.

10. Different alternatives of having a context menu item's functionality handled by the corresponding main menu item include using the EventHandler class and calling another event procedure.

Chapter 12

1. The toolbar is represented by the ToolStrip class.

2. Each item on the main menu is represented by the ToolStripItem class.

3. The Items collection of the ToolStrip component contains a collection of the ToolStripItems belonging to the ToolStrip.

4. No, a toolbar item is not limited to a button, but instead may be one of several other types of controls.

5. Toolbar buttons are immediately accessible, whereas menu items may be nested several levels deep and can be accessed only by multiple mouse clicks or keystrokes. Additionally, a toolbar button uses a graphic, which gives a more visual interface than the text of a menu item.

6. Different alternatives of having a toolbar item's functionality handled by the corresponding main or context menu item include using the EventHandler class and calling another event procedure.

7. The DisplayStyle property of the ToolStripItem class determines whether an image or text may be displayed on a button.

8. The Image property of the ToolStripItem class determines the image displayed on a button.

9. The Items Collection Editor is useful in adding controls to a toolbar.

10. One good prefix for naming a toolbar button is tbtn, with "t" standing for toolbar and "btn" standing for button.

Chapter 13

1. The Open dialog box is a control of the OpenFileDialog class.

2. You use the ShowDialog method of the OpenFileDialog class to show an Open dialog box.

3. The return value of showing an Open dialog box is either DialogResult.OK, if the user chose the Open button, or DialogResult.Cancel, if the user chose the Cancel button.

4. The OpenFileDialog class has a FileName property whose value is a string containing the path to and the name of the file selected in the Open dialog box.

5. The Save dialog box is a control of the SaveFileDialog class.

6. You use the ShowDialog method of the SaveFileDialog class to show a Save dialog box.

7. The return value of showing a Save dialog box is either DialogResult.OK, if the user chose the Save button, or DialogResult.Cancel, if the user chose the Cancel button.

8. The SaveFileDialog class has a FileName property whose value is a string containing the path to and the name of the file to be saved.

9. You may use the StreamReader class to read from a text file.

10. You may use the StreamWriter class to write to a text file.

Chapter 14

1. A data provider is a code component that is used by your application to connect to a specific database format.

2. Server Explorer enables you to view and make changes to databases on your computer or on any other computer to which you have network access and permissions.

3. A table is a collection of data, usually on a particular subject such as customers, employees, and so on.

4. Each column in a table also may be called a field.

5. Each row in a table also may be called a record.

6. The code components used for database access in the .NET class library are referred to by the name ADO.NET.

7. The OleDbConnection class represents a connection to a data source.

8. You use the OleDbCommand class to execute commands to a database.

9. You use the OleDbDataAdapter class to package a database connection with a set of data commands.

10. A DataSet is a representation of the data stored in RAM.

Chapter 15

1. The code components used for web applications in the .NET class library are referred to by the name ASP.NET.

2. A URL, an acronym for Uniform Resource Locator, represents an address of a web page.

3. HTTP is an acronym for Hypertext Transfer Protocol. HTTP defines how messages are formatted and transmitted, and what actions web servers and browsers should take in response to various commands.

4. The .aspx extension indicates that the web page is part of an ASP.NET application.

5. A URL such as http://localhost/localstart.asp would be the virtual path to a web page, whereas a file path such as C:\Inetpub\Wwwroot\localstart.asp would be the physical path to a web page.

6. You may use the ASP.NET Web Site project template to create a web application.

7. GridView is the web control that corresponds to the DataGridView control used in Windows applications.

8. MapPath is the method of the HttpServerUtility class that returns the physical file path that corresponds to (is mapped to) the specified virtual path on a web server.

9. Page is the name of the class that is the web application equivalent of the Form class in a Windows application.

10. DataBind is the method of the GridView that needs to be called in a web application so the GridView will not be blank.

Final Exam

1. IDE is an acronym for Integrated Development Environment. The term "development environment" refers to Visual C# 2005's role as an application to assist you in developing applications. The term "integrated" means the tools to design your application and write, test, and run your code are all together in one application.

2. A computer cannot do anything without step-by-step instructions from us telling it what to do. These instructions, written by a computer programmer, are called a computer program.

3. A programming language is used by computer programmers to write instructions for computers.

4. Machine language is a programming language that is understood by computers.

5. The term "higher level" means that a programming language such as Visual C# 2005 is far closer to the structure and syntax of human language than to the ones and zeroes understood by a computer.

6. The term "lower level" means that a programming language such as machine language is far closer to the ones and zeroes understood by a computer than it is to the structure and syntax of human language.

7. In general, a compiler translates the code you write into corresponding machine language instructions. The compiler in Visual C# 2005 translates the code into an intermediate language that then is translated into machine language.

8. Programming languages, including Visual C#, use classes to represent a person, place, thing, or concept.

9. An object of a class is a single instance of a class, just like each of us could be said to be an object or instance of a Person class.

10. Namespaces are used to organize code in a logical manner.

11. A property is a characteristic or attribute of a class.

12. A Windows application has a graphical user interface (GUI) and is event-driven.

13. An event is something that happens to an object of a class, such as a result of user interaction.

14. An event procedure contains code that executes when a specific event happens to a specific object.

15. The purpose of the assignment operator is to assign the expression to its right to the variable or property to its left.

16. The purpose of the Toolbox is to display controls that you can add to your form.

17. You may add a control from the Toolbox onto your form either by double-clicking the control in the Toolbox or by dragging the control from the Toolbox and then dropping it onto the form.

18. The Name property of a control is used to identify that control in code.

19. A naming convention is a consistent method of naming, such as naming controls.

20. The text displayed by a label may identify another, adjacent control, or it may display data.

21. A parameter represents information that is available to an event procedure.

22. A data type signifies whether the data is numeric, text, yes/no, and so forth.

23. The purpose of a variable is to store data of your choosing.

24. Yes, C# requires you to declare a variable before you refer to it in code.

25. A local variable is a variable declared inside of a procedure.

26. No, you do not have to assign a value to a variable when you declare it.

27. A constant's value cannot change during the life of the program, whereas a variable's value may change during the life of the program.

28. Yes, you have to assign a value to a constant when you declare it.

29. Operator precedence determines, when there are two or more arithmetic operators, which arithmetic operation is done first.

30. The % (modulus) operator provides only the remainder resulting from division.

Answers

31. All arithmetic operators have precedence over the assignment operator.

32. The Parse method of the Int32 class converts the string representation of an integer into an actual integer value.

33. The ToString method of the Int32 class converts an integer into its string representation.

34. A method is something an object of a class does.

35. The WriteLine method of the Debug class outputs a line to the Output window.

36. The data type of the result of a comparison performed by a comparison operator is Boolean (true or false).

37. Arithmetic operators have higher precedence than comparison operators.

38. A logical operator is used to combine multiple comparisons.

39. ! (Not) is the logical operator that operates on only one operand rather than two.

40. Comparison operators have higher precedence than logical operators.

41. Modal means a form must be closed before the application user can return to any other form in the application.

42. The statement is conditional if the statement executes only if the value of the relational expression following the if or else if keyword is true.

43. You should import the System.Diagnostics namespace to use the Debug class.

44. An exception is a problem that occurs while the program is executing that must be dealt with before the program can proceed.

45. The TryParse method of the Int32 class converts the string representation of an integer into an actual integer value, but also returns a Boolean value (true or false) indicating whether the conversion was successful.

46. The CheckBox and RadioButton controls.

47. The primary difference in the if . . . else if statement and the switch control structure is that the if and else if clauses both may evaluate completely different expressions, whereas a switch control structure may evaluate only one expression, which then must be used for every comparison.

48. A loop is a structure that repeats the execution of code until a condition becomes false.

49. A difference between the do statement and the for and while statements is that a do . . . while statement tests a condition at the bottom of the statement, whereas the for and while statements test a condition at the top of the statement.

50. The foreach executes the statement block for each element in a collection, instead of a specified number of times.

51. An array permits you to use a single variable to store multiple values.

52. The difference between declaring an array variable and declaring a scalar variable is that with an array variable, unlike with a scalar variable, the array name is followed by a pair of square brackets, and within the square brackets you indicate the highest index of the array.

53. The lowest index of an array is zero.

54. The number of elements in an array is one greater than the highest index in that array because the index of the first element is zero.

55. A method is a block of one or more code statements that execute when called upon to do so.

56. The void return type indicates that a method does not return a value.

57. The private access specifier limits access to the class in which the procedure was declared.

58. Calling a method causes it to execute.

59. The significance of an array being a reference type is when an array name is an argument, the value of that argument is the array's address in memory.

60. Writing your own methods enables you to organize your code in smaller, easier-to-read code blocks. Additionally, if you are performing essentially the same task from several places in the program, you can avoid duplication of code by putting the code that performs that task in one method, as opposed to repeating that code in each place in the program that may call for the performance of that task. Further, if you later have to fix a bug in how you perform that task, or simply find a better way to perform the task, you only have to change the code in one place rather than many.

61. A message box is modal.

62. The Show method of the MessageBox class returns a member of the DialogResult enumeration corresponding to the button the user clicked.

63. Yes, buttons in a message box automatically have a DialogResult value.

64. You would use the DialogResult data type for a variable used to store the return value of the Show method of the MessageBox class.

65. You use the ShowDialog method of the Form object to display a modal form.

66. The return value of showing a dialog form is the DialogResult property of that form.

67. No, buttons in a dialog form you create do not automatically have a DialogResult value; you have to assign a value to the DialogResult property of each button.

68. You use the Show method of the Form object to display a modal form.

69. A main menu is represented by the MenuStrip class.

70. No, the Click event is raised only for menu items that do not have subsidiary menu items, because when a menu item with subsidiary items is clicked, the behavior is to display the subsidiary menu items.

71. You gray out a menu item so it is not available when it should not be by setting its Enabled property to False.

72. The Items collection of the MenuStrip component contains a collection of the ToolStripMenuItems belonging to the MenuStrip.

73. The shortcut or context menu is represented by the ContextMenuStrip class.

74. The Items collection of the ContextMenuStrip component contains a collection of the ToolStripMenuItems belonging to the ContextMenuStrip.

75. Different alternatives of having a context menu item's functionality handled by the corresponding main menu item are using the EventHandler class and calling another event procedure.

76. The toolbar is represented by the ToolStrip class.

77. Each item on the main menu is represented by the ToolStripItem class.

78. The Items collection of the ToolStrip component contains a collection of the ToolStripItems belonging to the ToolStrip.

79. Toolbar buttons are immediately accessible, whereas menu items may be nested several levels deep and can be accessed only by multiple mouse clicks or keystrokes. Additionally, a toolbar button uses a graphic, which gives a more visual interface than the text of a menu item.

80. Different alternatives of having a toolbar item's functionality handled by the corresponding main or context menu item are using the EventHandler class and calling another event procedure.

81. You use the ShowDialog method of the OpenFileDialog class to show an Open dialog box.

82. The return value of showing an Open dialog box is either DialogResult.OK if the user chose the Open button or DialogResult.Cancel if the user chose the Cancel button.

83. The OpenFileDialog class has a FileName property whose value is a string containing the path to and the name of the file selected in the Open dialog box.

84. You use the ShowDialog method of the SaveFileDialog class to show a Save dialog box.

85. The return value of showing a Save dialog box is either DialogResult.OK if the user chose the Save button or DialogResult.Cancel if the user chose the Cancel button.

86. The SaveFileDialog class has a FileName property whose value is a string containing the path to and the name of the file to be saved.

87. You may use the StreamReader class to read from a text file.

88. You may use the StreamWriter class to write to a text file.

89. A data provider is a code component that is used by your application to connect to a specific database format.

90. A table is a collection of data, usually on a particular subject such as customers, employees, and so on.

91. Each column in a table also may be called a field.

92. Each row in a table also may be called a record.

93. The code components used for database access in the .NET class library are referred to by the name ADO.NET.

94. A DataSet is a representation of the data stored in RAM.

95. The code components used for web applications in the .NET class library are referred to by the name ASP.NET.

96. A URL, an acronym for Uniform Resource Locator, represents an address of a web page.

97. HTTP is an acronym for Hypertext Transfer Protocol. HTTP defines how messages are formatted and transmitted, and what actions web servers and browsers should take in response to various commands.

98. A URL such as http://localhost/localstart.asp would be the virtual path to a web page, whereas a file path such as C:\Inetpub\Wwwroot\localstart.asp would be the physical path to a web page.

99. MapPath is the method of the HttpServerUtility class that returns the physical file path that corresponds to (is mapped to) the specified virtual path on the web server.

100. Page is the name of the class that is the web application equivalent of the Form class in a Windows application.

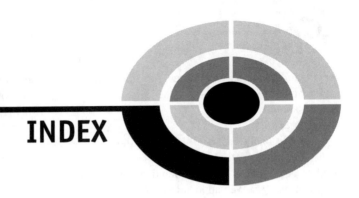

INDEX

Symbols

; (semicolon), 38–39, 109, 112, 114–117, 138, 139, 149, 150

+ (addition) operator, 80–82, 85

= (assignment) operator, 39, 83–84, 113

*/ (asterisk and forward slash), 40

%= (combined) operator, 83

*= (combined) operator, 83

+= (combined) operator, 60, 83, 84

−= (combined) operator, 83

/= (combined) operator, 83

&& (conditional And) operator, 100–101, 104, 144

|| (conditional Or) operator, 101–102, 104

{ } (curly braces), 36, 109, 111–113, 116, 117, 137–139, 148, 150, 157

-- (decrement) operator, 84–85

/ (division) operator, 80–82

\\ (double backslash), 290

// (double forward slash), 39–40

" (double quotation marks), 39, 65

== (equality) operator, 97–99

/* (forward slash and asterisk), 40

> (greater than) operator, 97, 99

>= (greater than or equal to) operator, 97, 99

++ (increment) operator, 84–85, 139, 149

!= (inequality) operator, 97–99, 146

< (less than) operator, 96, 99

<= (less than or equal to) operator, 97, 99

& (logical And) operator, 101, 104

! (logical Not) operator, 103–104, 145–146

| (logical Or) operator, 102, 104

% (modulus) operator, 80–82, 90

* (multiplication) operator, 80, 81

' (single quotation marks), 66

^ (Xor) operator, 102–104

A

About dialog box, 176

Access keys, 201, 202

Access specifiers:

    for class member variables, 73

    for constants, 75

    general rules for, 73

    in method header, 157

    of variables, 68–69

Action events, 35, 36

Active Server Pages (ASP), 272

Add Connection dialog box, 252–253

Add New Item dialog box, 185

Addition (+) operator, 80–82, 85

Address (Internet), 278 (*See also* Uniform Resource Locator)

ADO.NET, 260

Algorithms, 89–91

Aligning Label controls, 49

All Windows Forms category, 44, 45

ALT key, 201, 202

American National Standards Institute (ANSI), 98, 128